Contents

3 Editorial

OVERVIEW OF FACULTY DEVELOPMENT PROJECTS: WHAT HAPPENS, WHAT WORKS

16 Curriculum Transformation: A Brief Overview, *Elaine Hedges*

23 Faculty Development: A Consortial Model, *Myrna Goldenberg and Shirley C. Parry*

31 Writing Everybody In, *Myrna Goldenberg and Barbara Stout*

CONSCIOUSNESS, EXPERIENCE, PEDAGOGY, AND THE CURRICULUM

45 Feminist Pedagogy and Techniques for the Changing Classroom, *Shirley C. Parry*

55 Identity and Diversity: An Exploratory Assignment, *Anne M. Wiley*

69 Teaching in (Puerto Rican) Tongues: A Report from the Space In-Between, *Liza Fiol-Matta*

77 Rethinking the "Southern Lady," *Sara W. Smith*

81 Integrating Scholarship on Minority Women into Health, Physical Education, and Dance, *Carole M. Cascio*

84 Achieving Gender Equity in Science Education, *Wendy Eisner*

IN THE CLASSROOM: ENGLISH, SPEECH, DANCE

88 Transforming Required English Composition, *Suzanne S. Liggett*

94 Changing Style, Changing Subject: The Required Composition Course, *Dianne Ganz Scheper*

100 Writing the Self in a Changing World, *Liza Fiol-Matta*

113 Revising an Interpersonal Communication Course, *Catherine T. Motoyama*

118 Changing the Dance Curriculum, *Diana Evans Cushway*

IN THE CLASSROOM: SOCIAL SCIENCE AND HISTORY

123   Transforming a Criminal Justice Curriculum, *Marie Henry* and *Vicky E. Dorworth*

135   Revising Economic History: Self-Integration and Course Integration, *Barbara Bourne Murray*

139   Revisioning Business Ethics, *E. Michelle Rabouin*

IN THE CLASSROOM: MATHEMATICS, PHYSICS, AND COMPUTERS

146   Changing Introductory College Mathematics, *Chiu-Min Lai*

150   Integrating Scholarship on Women into Physics, *Lalitha Dorai*

160   A Note on Gender and Computer Literacy, *Ned M. Wilson*

RESOURCES: COURSE SYLLABI

163   Concepts of Physical Science, *Lalitha Dorai*

165   World Civilization, *David A. Berry*

170   Introduction to Microeconomics, *Kostis Papadantonakis*

181   Business Ethics: a Core Course, *E. Michelle Rabouin*

187   Women Writers: Multicultural Perspectives, *Diane Lebow*

RESOURCES: BIBLIOGRAPHIES

201   The Integration of Women's Studies and Feminist Pedagogy into the Core Curriculum: An Annotated Bibliography, *Barbara Bollmann, Judith McManus, E. Michelle Rabouin,* and *Peggy Valdez-Fergason*

215   National Center for Curriculum Transformation: Resources on Women, *Sara Coulter, Elaine Hedges, Beth Vanfossen*

222   Minority Women and the Dance Curriculum: An Annotated Bibliography, *Carole M. Cascio*

229   Selected Business Ethics Bibliography, *E. Michelle Rabouin*

233   Selected Annotated Bibliography for Economists and Other Social Scientists, *Kostis Papadantonakis*

239   Newsbriefs

Editorial

The Community College in the United States: A Profile of Innovation and Change

This issue of *Women's Studies Quarterly* spotlights educators' efforts to transform the curriculum in community colleges. In the hierarchy of higher education in the United States, the nation's 1,469 community colleges—defined as accredited post-secondary institutions, whose highest award is the associate's degree—have long been considered at the lowest rung on the ladder.[1] This status has been conferred as much by misconception of the task of the community colleges as by the elitism of the higher education system. For many years, the community college has been considered primarily the site of training for career programs and vocational education. Therefore liberal arts and sciences faculty at the community college, unlike their colleagues in the applied vocational fields, are often perceived as lesser scholars. They are considered to be representatives from the world of higher knowledge whose task is to provide a humanist, "well-rounded" education to students who are characteristically seen in terms of their value as employable workers.

While community colleges have always responded to the job market and employment needs of the region and the country, their history reflects the ambiguity in which they are still held. The junior college idea was proposed in the latter half of the nineteenth century, partially in response to the perceptions of educational leaders in the university and college systems that there was a kind of student who did not meet what they considered to be the requirements for attendance at the more elite institutions which they led. According to Arthur M. Cohen and Florence B. Brawer, much of the reasoning behind the development of the junior college had to do with creating the conditions for the Stanfords and Harvards of the United States to undertake their research and intellectual agendas without being pressed to educate the freshman and sophomore undergraduates. The notion that these students would be more properly served by a separate system drove the early proposals for the creation of the junior college, in effect adding a thirteenth and fourteenth grade to the high school.[2]

However, as a post-secondary educational institution which was not clearly provided for in the formulations of compulsory and public education in this country, the junior college was in the peculiar position of evolving an ethos out of its own practice. Where was it to fit within the scheme of the traditional educational system of the United States? Was it to exist merely to provide a finishing of the educational process initiated by the K–12 curricula—a kind of post-high-school high school? Was it to function as a pre-college education, alleviating college and university faculty of the need to teach the rudiments of academic thinking and comportment? Was the junior college, in fact, not pre-collegiate at all but the site in which to provide the first two years of a college education under the supervision of a teaching faculty well versed in their disciplines but who were without a required investment in research or publishing? Or, was it—in response to the growing needs of changing technologies, increased immigration, and post-Depression realities—primarily a place in which to retrain American workers in timely vocational and career education programs?

As we know, today's community colleges are all of these and more. Although the formal function of community colleges as finishing high schools has all but disappeared, the needs of students who seem less prepared and academically skilled than previous high school graduates have dictated that the colleges respond to filling in the gaps left by students' secondary school experiences. By and large, however, community colleges provide instruction and services within four overarching areas. The first area of instruction, vocational and career programs leading to either a certificate or an associate degree in applied science, is affected most often by occupational trends and retraining efforts. Programs in nursing, medical technology, dental hygiene, physical therapy, and x-ray technology are often the most competitive and selective in the colleges.

The second area of instruction includes transfer and liberal arts programs, from which students plan to continue baccalaureate studies. These programs lead to an associate degree in science or the arts and include programs in, for example, fields such as accounting and management, which enhance a student's immediate employability, as well as education and other traditional liberal arts fields of concentration.

Developmental or remedial programs—most often focused on mathematics, reading, and writing skills—constitute the third area of the community college mission. These programs, and the learning resource centers that complement them, are a vital part of the services and specialized knowledge provided by the colleges. However, their importance in the overall curriculum and mission of the colleges is often misunderstood and even scapegoated. For example, in times of scarcity of funding for education, the presence of these services leads some people to claim community colleges are non- or precollegiate in nature.

Finally, the variety of community and adult education programs demonstrates a provocative commitment to education in the broadest sense. While the courses they offer may not award academic credit, these programs often house important outreach educational endeavors to prisons, community centers, shelters, and other special populations.

This diversity of educational agendas makes the community college an exciting and challenging place in which to work. Still, it is important to underscore that traditionally the community college has suffered from too little understanding of its place as an innovative educational institution. Many of the areas of innovation are in the teaching and pedagogy that are responsive to the multiple needs of diverse student populations. Although elite and state universities and colleges receive more press and attention, today's community college is a major postsecondary educational site in the United States. According to the American Association of Community Colleges, "public community colleges enroll more students than any other sector of higher education . . . community college students made up over one-third of all postsecondary students and over 40 percent of all undergraduates [in fall 1992]."[3] Women represented approximately 58.4 percent of the community college population in 1994. Statistics reveal that ethnically 76 percent of community college students are non-Hispanic White, 11 percent are African-American, 8 percent are Hispanic, 4 percent are Asian/Pacific Islander, and 1 percent are Native American. Despite what may seem to be low overall percentages, the American Association of Community Colleges reports that more so-called minority students who go on to postsecondary schooling choose public community colleges over four-year institutions to begin their higher education. In fact, 43 percent of all black undergraduates, 55 percent of all Hispanic undergraduates, and 57 percent of all Native American undergraduates attend community colleges.[4] These numbers indicate how important the two-year college has become as students from groups disproportionately excluded from pursuing higher education find themselves welcomed at their community colleges.

Since its inception, the American community college has also been the institution of choice for older students and students returning to school for training in career programs. According to the National Center for Education Statistics, business is the most popular field of study among all age groups in the community colleges. Older students also lean toward occupational fields, such as computer and information technology, health, and education. Younger students are still more likely to enroll in life science, social and behavioral science, and liberal arts and humanities.[5]

According to the U.S. Department of Education, "the number of college students will climb from 14.1 million in 1991 to 16 million in 2002, with a greater growth in minority enrollments, the number of female students rising at twice the rate of male students, and with a growing proportion of students expected in the age-group 35 and older."[6] These population projections indicate that it behooves higher education institutions to pay special attention to the diversity of their students. As we respond to the need for preparing our students for the changing demands of workplace and careers, "community college programs and undergraduate certificates will be in as much, or perhaps even greater, demand than postbaccalaureate updating."[7] We must accept the reality that for most students, and particularly the community college student, higher education is less an intellectual encounter than it is the path towards a job and economic survival.

So, while it is a compelling argument, the call for reforming the curriculum to reflect the nation's overall diversity is not merely one of making the classroom experience more reflective of the students sitting in our classrooms. If this were so, curriculum would be dictated only by regional and community ethnic, socioeconomic, and racial demographics. But the diversity in student population varies from college to college, sometimes even from program to program within one institution. Community colleges run the gamut—from the inner-city multicultural classrooms, the historically black colleges, ethnically homogeneous tribal colleges, overwhelmingly white colleges in the heartland, and so on. No matter what the demographics, courses need to be balanced so as to include the complexity of the subject matter, including dissenting voices, critiques of the disciplinary approaches, and gaps in the traditional knowledge base. Only in this way can we strive to facilitate as truthful and complete a learning process as possible for all students. Because they will leave the community college classroom for the workplace in a world increasingly affected by global economic trends and transnational migrations, all students, including those from dominant groups, will benefit from challenging the assumptions derived from the experiences of privileged groups.

Teaching at a student-centered institution such as the community college resembles the secondary school system in methodology and work load. Like the high school, there is generally more emphasis placed on individualizing the learning experience for the student. For example, mass-enrolled, auditorium-sized introductory courses are usually not found at the two-year college. Pedagogy is emphasized and courses often structured with more built-in steps (such as quizzing, testing, oral presentations, time management skills, and critical thinking activities, to name a few) to assess and facilitate individual progress. Similarly, the teaching load resembles more closely that of the high school than of the four-year college and university. Full-time schedules average four or five classes a term, or thirteen to fifteen hours a week of classroom teaching, which is double the yearly load at most senior colleges.[8] Full-time faculty report spending an average of 46.6 hours weekly on teaching and administrative tasks.[9]

Unlike the secondary school system, though, the community college's structure is derived from the traditional higher education model. The professorate is designated similarly (assistant, associate, and full), and the positions of lecturer and instructor, traditionally nondoctorate appointments, round out the teaching faculty. In fact, over half of community college faculty (56 percent) are instructors.[10] With office hours, one-to-one conferencing with students, and class preparation taking up the rest of the week, the publish-or-perish syndrome found in other levels of higher education usually does not play a role in tenuring or promotion. Longevity of employment often hinges on proven commitment to the institution and department— an endeavor requiring additional hours of service. The lesser importance given to research and writing in one's disciplinary field at the community college notwithstanding, faculty often pursue scholarly work despite conditions that differ from those of their colleagues in four-year colleges. There are fewer opportunities for travel and conference funds, research stipends, teaching and/or graduate assistance, access to up-to-date technology, and course released time, and those opportunities that do exist must be divided up among many.

One area of inquiry, however, has become a hallmark of two-year colleges. Increasingly, faculty and administration join together to create laboratories of internal research, discovering new ways to help students learn. These collaborative efforts have led colleges to implement knowledge about learning styles and cognition. Experiments configuring different structures of learning communities have encouraged pairing and clustering of courses which bring faculty together across disciplinary boundaries. Faculty have also been instrumental in establishing programs and services for students with learning disabilities and in creating developmental courses that integrate college-level materials with basic skills instruction. Because community college faculty place teaching at the center of their professional commitment, research on how students learn is quickly translated into teaching practice.

Where faculty are situated within the institution also differs significantly between junior colleges and senior colleges. While strong disciplinary and departmental ties characterize many community colleges, divisions (such as humanities or social sciences), rather than departments, are frequently the key administrative units. This division structure—where, for example, sociologists, psychologists, economists, and political scientists work together in the same unit—encourages cross-disciplinary and multi-disciplinary discussions about course content and methodology. Instructors reevaluate their courses through newly acquired angles of vision and discuss these insights with colleagues both within and outside of their own disciplines. Thus, the divisional structure of the community college has the potential to facilitate rethinking one's own field and, therefore, one's courses.

One area of concern, in which community colleges differ significantly from both the secondary school and the senior college, is the growing trend toward relying on part-time faculty.[11] This is worrisome for several reasons. First, part-time instructors are disenfranchised from the governance of the institution or the divisions which hire them; they are unable for the most part to take part in faculty development projects, and largely are without voice in affecting the curriculum. Dependent on piecing together a living wage by holding several jobs, they are also unable to provide students with the follow-up that full-time faculty can facilitate during office hours and through personal contacts in the college. Most part-time faculty are skilled teaching professionals with qualifications similar to those of full-time faculty. But budget-conscious institutions often count on them as cheap labor: "Part-time instructors are to the community college as migrant workers are to the farms."[12]

One of the major achievements of curriculum transformation projects, such as the two projects discussed in this issue, is their effect on the required introductory and survey courses. The junior college courses such as English Composition, Introduction to Psychology, Microeconomics, World Civilization, and Women Writers presented here, of course, have their counterparts in the four-year college. This similarity—or perhaps more accurately stated, this overlap—stems both from the mission of the community college to provide a basic intellectual foundation for all its students as well as from its commitment to students who have chosen to begin their postsecondary education at the two-year college.

A substantial number of community college students attend college to prepare for the baccalaureate, particularly in states where community colleges are considered campuses of the state university system. Thus, courses are designed to coincide with university and senior college requirements; they follow university, not high school, models. Honors programs and linkages with four-year colleges (for example, enhanced transfer opportunity programs) further challenge potential transfer students to prepare for upper-level coursework. Since curriculum integration projects are being found in an increasing number of four-year colleges, students from community colleges who take transformed or integrated courses enhance their transfer status. Because they come to the senior college their third year with the same grounding in introductory courses as students who enter the four-year college directly, they are just as likely to be successful in completing their course of study.

The prebaccalaureate and career programs are only two of the areas covered by the community college curriculum. Though not discussed in this issue of *Women's Studies Quarterly,* other tasks of the community colleges in a reconceptualized educational system include the arrangements they have with high schools and elementary schools. While high schools are being created and housed on campus (sometimes known as "middle colleges"), partnerships with area high schools are also taking participating faculty off the campus and into the community.[13] Similarly, colleges have also forged cooperative education ventures with small businesses and large corporations; with public assistance and child welfare agencies; with prisons and homeless shelters; and with community service programs. These, and other reconfigurations of the learning environment, are also potential sites for innovative curriculum reform.

One trend which is currently influencing the nature of the community college, and specifically the curriculum of both introductory and elective courses, is the slowly changing perception towards teaching at the two-year college. One indicator of the collegiate nature of the community college as we enter the twenty-first century is the

increasingly more professionalized and credentialized faculty
employed there. While for many years the master's degree was an
acceptable terminal degree for teaching and tenuring at the community college, rightly or wrongly "Ph.D. preferred" standards are
becoming more commonplace in job searches and promotions.[14] As
jobs in higher education become more difficult to find, teaching in
the community college has begun to attain a credibility that draws
both specialized faculty and recent graduates from prestigious universities who often find that the only jobs available in their disciplines
or fields are to be found at the community college. In many areas of
the country—for example, the Ph.D.-saturated northeast—teaching
at a community college is becoming increasingly less stigmatizing.
This has impacted positively the climate for curriculum revision at
what previously may have been perceived by these same job seekers
as a less-than-college-level site of instruction. Many scholars coming
into the community college system today have benefited from feminist, queer, and critical race theory critiques of the disciplines and
disciplinary knowledge, and they infuse their courses with these
insights. Their contributions will become more visible as community
colleges integrate pluralism initiatives and a commitment to inclusive
education across class and social difference into their curricular and
extracurricular agendas.

Recognizing the role that community colleges play in the overall
educational schema of the United States is important for women's
studies professionals and others engaged in curriculum transformation. Not only do women make up the majority of community college
students, but women make up over half of community college faculty
as well. According to the American Association of Community
Colleges, female faculty are most often found in the areas of education, health sciences, and humanities while male faculty make up
the majority in engineering, natural sciences, and social sciences
programs. It is interesting to note that female faculty tend to avail
themselves more often of institutional incentives for professional
development than do men, and are "more likely to use funding allo-
cated for facilitating professional travel, upgrading training/teaching
skills, tuition remission, and dues for professional associations."[15]
This suggests that female faculty are engaged in keeping themselves
current in their fields and tend to participate more often in curriculum transformation and other faculty development projects that
impact faculty renewal.

The need for curriculum transformation projects, such as those
which produced the materials offered in this issue, is underscored

when one takes into account that women faculty report that the major portion of their time—68.5 percent—is devoted to teaching while only 4.2 percent of their time is spent in research.[16] With the general lack of institutional support for research, publications, presentations at national conferences, and other activities which enable faculty to be conversant in the ongoing debates in their fields, all faculty at the community college benefit tremendously from faculty development seminars and initiatives. These offer the chance to renew scholarship in reading and in discussion groups—often in dialogue with visiting scholars in the field. For faculty teaching in isolated colleges, this access to information as well as to outside scholars and facilitators is even more important.

Another disturbing statistic which underscores the importance of curriculum and other diversity initiatives is the fact that the faculty at the community college remains overwhelmingly non-Hispanic white (81.1 percent). Despite the gains in minority faculty hirings over the past two decades, only 8.4 percent are black; 5.2 percent are Hispanic; 3.6 percent are Asian; and 0.9 percent are Native American.[17] Given these numbers, it is clear that colleges cannot rely exclusively on their faculty of color to ensure inclusion of study about the languages, cultures, and contributions of people of color to the history and development of humankind.[18]

This issue of *Women's Studies Quarterly* draws on the results of two projects that brought the work of curriculum transformation developed in women's studies programs to the community college. The first, the FIPSE-funded Maryland Community College Project, was coordinated by the women's studies program at Towson State University in 1989, and was directed by Elaine Hedges, Myrna Golden-berg, and Sara Coulter. The five colleges that participated were Anne Arundel Community College, the Community College of Baltimore, Essex Community College, Montgomery College, and Prince George's Community College. Myrna Goldenberg and Shirley Parry give the background of this project in their essay, "Faculty Development: A Consortial Model."

In 1993, the Ford Foundation launched the Curriculum Mainstreaming and Teaching Initiative (CMTI), whose overall purpose was to encourage the development of curriculum mainstreaming of women's studies scholarship in selected community and tribal colleges. The Ford initiative, directed by Liza Fiol-Matta and Myrna Goldenberg, included twelve community colleges and/or districts, and two tribal colleges: Camden County College (NJ); the Community College of Denver; Essex Community College (MD); Essex Community College

(NJ); Greenfield Community College (MA); LaGuardia Community College (NY); the Los Angeles Community College District (CA); Nassau Community College (NY); Navajo Community College (Navajo Nation); Parkland College (IL); the Peralta Community College District (CA); the San Mateo County Community College District (CA); Shelby State Community College (TN); and Turtle Mountain Community College (Turtle Mountain Chippewa Nation). Approximately 120 faculty participated in the syllabi and course revision activities sponsored by each college, while the larger college communities were beneficiaries of on-campus seminars, film series, library resource acquisitions, and mini-conferences.

The women's studies program at Towson State University has been the site of several transformation projects over the past twenty years. A new enterprise for them is the creation of a National Center for Curriculum Transformation, which serves as a clearinghouse and a repository of scores of materials from curriculum projects nationwide. Elaine Hedges, co-director of the Center, summarizes the history and experiences of curriculum integration initiatives in her article, "Curriculum Transformation: An Overview." Myrna Goldenberg and Barbara Stout enumerate changes which faculty in the Maryland-FIPSE Project reported and offer several recommendations for transforming the content of introductory courses in their article, "Writing Everybody In."

Changing course content and revising for inclusion is a process which goes beyond cutting and pasting together a syllabus from models, good intentions notwithstanding. Inevitably, change occasions shifts in consciousness and a reevaluation of both what we teach and what we were taught. Much of the work of curriculum transformation over the past decade has addressed the intersections of race, class, and ethnicity, as well as gender, and has called on faculty to explore these personal dynamics within themselves and their teaching. In the second section of this volume, "Consciousness, Experience, Pedagogy, and the Curriculum," we present several products which have resulted from this type of inquiry.

Shirley Parry's essay, "Feminist Pedagogy and Techniques for a Changing Classroom," offers several ways to link theoretical material with classroom praxis. Anne M. Wiley's article, "Identity and Diversity: An Exploratory Assignment," models an experiential activity addressing the connections between racism and sexism which can be adapted for a variety of purposes (counseling, pluralism initiatives, and so on). The two "personal is political" essays, by Sara W. Smith and Liza Fiol-Matta, illustrate what happens when we allow ourselves to question and to contextualize our own learning and historical realities. Finally, Carole M. Cascio's essay, "Integrating Scholarship on Minority Women in Health, Physical Education, and Dance," and Wendy Eisner's "Achieving Gender Equity in Science Education" demonstrate how it is possible to rectify the gaps in set curricula.

As in the four-year college and university, curriculum transformation at the community college addresses gender issues in science and technology, allied health, biology, economics, engineering, marketing, mathematics, nursing, and psychology, but more often from a practical application of the knowledge and experience than from research applications. The three sections titled "In the Classroom" offer several suggestions for discipline-specific revision. Teachers of English composition, literature, dance, speech, criminal justice, business, economic history, mathematics, computer science and physics offer their experiences of participating in curriculum transformation faculty development projects and rethinking their disciplines and approaches to addressing the gaps and deficiencies in the curriculum for both introductory and elective courses. These are complemented by the syllabi and discipline-specific bibliographic resources which end the volume.

The task of transforming the curriculum should involve all who are interested in educating for truth and justice. Projects like the ones whose results we present here strive to make the classroom a site of empowerment. All levels of the educational system—K–12, community colleges, senior colleges and universities, professional and technical schools, and graduate programs—will be strengthened if we can embrace as a common goal equitable treatment of all and critical inquiry into the nature of knowledge and learning. The experiences of the faculty who have contributed to this volume demonstrate exciting and important ways that individuals can effect change. We hope that these models provide a basis for continuing that task as we prepare to educate our students, and ourselves, to meet the challenges of work and self in the twenty-first century.

A note from the editor: This is my first issue as General Editor of *Women's Studies Quarterly.* It has been especially gratifying that it highlights curriculum at the community college, the scenario of most of my professional career. I must thank Myrna Goldenberg, co-editor of this issue and codirector of the Ford Program from which the majority of the materials presented here were culled, for the guidance she provided during the run of the projects and the many ways she contributed to this volume. I would also like to thank Sara Coulter and

Elaine Hedges, women's studies trailblazers, for their generous consent to include the materials from the FIPSE Project and from the Center for Curriculum Transformation at Towson State. Sara Cahill, my editor at the Feminist Press, made the learning curve just that much easier. Finally, I thank Florence Howe, publisher of the Feminist Press, and the true ghost editor of this issue. I am especially lucky to be benefiting from her many years of experience. In particular, I value her skillful editing, insightful reading, and welcome advice on setting priorities for producing a journal like the *Quarterly*. It is not often that one has the opportunity to learn from a pioneer, from a founding-mother, and I have been able to do just that.

—Liza Fiol-Matta

NOTES

1. There are 1,024 publicly supported community colleges and 445 private institutions in the United States. "Community Colleges: General Information and Resources," A Digest from the ERIC Clearinghouse for Community Colleges, http://www.gseis.ucla.edu/ERIC/eric.html.
2. Arthur M. Cohen and Florence B. Brawer, *The American Community College, Third Edition* (San Francisco: Jossey-Bass, 1996). Cohen and Brawer recount the establishment of what would become today's community college in their first chapter, "Background: Evolving Priorities and Expectations of the Community Colleges," pp. 1–38.
3. American Association of Community Colleges, Research Brief, "Community College Enrollment," http://www.aacc.nche.edu/research/brief10.htm.
4. National Center for Education Statistics, cited in American Association of Community Colleges, "Community College Enrollment."
5. Cited in American Association of Community Colleges, Research Brief, "Older Students in Community Colleges," http://www.aacc.nche.edu/research/brief7.htm.
6. Peggy Gordon Elliott, *The Urban Campus: Educating the New Majority for the New Century* (Washington, DC/Phoenix: American Council on Education/Oryx Press, 1996), p. 135.
7. Elliott, p. 136. The increasing importance of the community college for the economic well-being of the United States is evident in President William Jefferson Clinton's election promise to make "clear that 2 years of college should be as universal as high school." The "HOPE Scholarship Plan," would guarantee "2 Years of Tuition at the Average Community College for Any Student Who Earns a B Average." [sic] Despite the somewhat condescending wording of the proposal—students will be eligible for a "second year if they work hard, stay off drugs, and earn at least a B average in their first year"—it is clear that the proposal paves the way towards making 14 years of education if not compulsory at least highly desirable, or in the words of the White House news release, "the Standard

for All Americans." http://www.whitehouse.gov/WH/dispatch/060496. html.

8. Cohen and Brawer, p. 76.
9. American Association of Community Colleges, Research Brief, "Faculty in Community Colleges," http://www.aacc.nche.edu/research/brief9. htm.
10. "Faculty in Community Colleges."
11. Estimates of the number of part-time faculty vary. The AACC reports that approximately 44 percent of faculty are employed part time and 56 percent full time by their institutions ("Faculty in Community Colleges"). Cohen and Brawer point out that in 1992 part-time faculty accounted for 53 percent of the workforce and suggest that these changes in ratios reflect the way that the nation's economy affects enrollment in the community college. *The American Community College,* p. 85.
12. Cohen and Brawer, p. 85.
13. See J. E. Lieberman (ed.), *Collaborating with High Schools. New Directions for Community Colleges,* no. 63. (San Francisco: Jossey-Bass, 1968).
14. Overall, the number of faculty with the Ph.D. is still low, approximately 15.5 percent. The Master's degree remains the highest degree attained for 61 percent of the faculty. 17.5 percent report the Bachelor's as their highest degree. "Faculty in Community Colleges."
15. American Association of Community Colleges, Research Brief, "Female Faculty in Community Colleges," http://www.aacc.nche.edu/research/fema_fac.htm.
16. "Female Faculty in Community Colleges."
17. "Faculty in Community Colleges."
18. American Association of Community Colleges, monograph, *Making Good on Our Promises: Moving Beyond Rhetoric to Action,* 1995.

Liza Fiol-Matta is an assistant professor in the English department at LaGuardia Community College at the City University of New York. She was project coordinator of the Ford Foundation Mainstreaming Minority Women's Studies and codirector of the Ford Foundation Curriculum Mainstreaming Teaching Initiative. With Mariam K. Chamberlain, she coedited Women of Color and the Multicultural Curriculum: Transforming the College Classroom *(New York: The Feminist Press, 1994). She is also active in Puerto Rican Studies and Latina Feminist Studies. She is a poet and a fiction writer and is currently working on a manuscript titled* Ni de aquí, Ni de allá: A Meditation on Puerto Rican Identity.

Curriculum Transformation: A Brief Overview

Elaine Hedges

Curriculum transformation is a process whereby faculty in colleges, universities, and secondary schools study the new scholarship on women (with emphasis on the diversity of women) in order to incorporate the insights and information from that study into their courses. In format, such projects usually involve faculty from different disciplines who meet in seminars or workshops to discuss readings, revise courses, and often create new courses. Typical designs for such projects range from summer- or semester-long seminars to multi-year projects and multi-institutional consortia.

A Brief History of Curriculum Transformation

The seeds of curriculum transformation were planted in the late 1960s, when scholars and teachers in higher education began to respond to the growing recognition that coverage of women—specifically their experiences, perspectives, and diversity—was almost completely absent from the traditional curriculum. For example, surveys of academic disciplines revealed that history textbooks devoted less than one percent of their coverage to women; that syllabi in literature courses contained on average only eight percent women authors; that the most widely used textbook in art history courses included not a single woman artist; that studies of "human" behavior in psychology courses were based on research using only male samples; that in sociology the study of women was more often than not confined to special units on the family or on minority groups; and that even scientific procedures were often less objective than is commonly believed.[1] Such discoveries raised grave questions about the validity of the version of human experience offered by the liberal

Excerpted, with permission, from Elaine Hedges, *Getting Started: Planning and Organizing Curriculum Transformation* (Baltimore, MD: National Center for Curriculum Transformation Resources on Women, Towson State University, 1996). Copyright © 1996 by the National Center for Curriculum Transformation Resources on Women.

arts, and therefore about the essential claim that a liberal arts education provides students with models of human experience and behavior that best equip them for living.

The 1970s therefore saw the development of women's studies as a new area of scholarly inquiry. At this time, women's studies was frequently modeled on the courses and programs in Black studies, while being spurred by the extensive research by feminist scholars that such programs and courses generated and encouraged. Interest in women and in gender as a category of analysis subsequently began to develop in a large number of disciplines. The veritable explosion of new research findings, many of which challenged older ways of thinking about social reality, was soon responded to by scholars and researchers in the various academic disciplines and by graduate students. Large numbers of faculty, however, especially those trained in earlier decades, were often unaware of, indifferent or even hostile to new developments. In addition, faculty were often too busy with teaching and other responsibilities to engage in the study necessary to assimilate the new knowledge.

In the 1980s, to assist the integration of this new knowledge into the traditional curriculum and to alter traditional courses, a number of universities across the nation sponsored faculty development projects designed to bring to faculty the new scholarship on women.

By the late 1980s, feminists of color and their scholarship had achieved more visibility in the academy, and their work was significantly affecting curriculum transformation. As women of color pointed out, much of the early scholarship on women had either explicitly or implicitly addressed issues of concern primarily to white, middle-class women in the United States and Western Europe. It was now essential to examine race and class biases, and to address the issue of the diversity of women. Curriculum transformation projects of the 1990s thus have reflected the shift in emphasis from "women" as often undifferentiated to a more complex focus on women in their full range of diversity—a diversity naturally flowing from women's heterogeneity of race, ethnicity, religion, sexual orientation, and social class location. Many recent curriculum transformation projects have therefore focused on diversity among women in the United States, while others have adopted an international perspective.

The Effect of Projects on Faculty

For some of those who undertake curriculum transformation, the results can be profound. Consider these remarks made by the participants of a community college project:

The most important change that occurred for me is not in the syllabus, but in my viewing the entire field from a different perspective. The project stimulated me to learn more about many new areas, to learn more about my own course, to read more . . . to reach out to my students more successfully. It was a riveting and exciting experience. . . .

The project was an incredibly wonderful experience for me. . . . I found the readings, workshop meetings, and guest speakers extremely stimulating. . . . I grew intellectually and gained confidence I didn't know I lacked. This is without doubt the most exciting sustained intellectual work I've done since graduate school. . . .

I've not become a feminist. I've not abandoned the canon. But I have discovered some books by women to rotate through my courses —books I wouldn't have found without this project. . . . Gender issues have now become a regular part of my thinking when I plan any course. And not just including a book by a woman, but thinking about women throughout the course, in all the books.[2]

While evaluations of the effects of curriculum transformation projects on faculty suggest that about one-quarter of participants experience little or no change as a result of involvement in the project, about one-third experience great change, as illustrated in the first two quotations above. And the remainder, such as illustrated in the third quotation, experience moderate change, resulting in modifications of and additions to their courses, assignments, syllabi, and ways of teaching.[3] Moreover, such evaluations, done at the conclusion of projects, do not describe the ongoing changes that many faculty will continue to experience. The end of a project is often only the beginning of a process of continuous change.

Overall, the large majority of faculty report satisfaction and gratification with the results of curriculum transformation projects, despite the hard work involved. The following are the kinds of results most frequently reported.

1. Changes in Course Content, Organization, and Methodology

Change can range from minimal to maximal, from adding one new book or topic or concept to integrating new material and perspectives throughout the course, to completely reconceptualizing the structure and content of the course.[4] One study of eleven projects, funded by the Ford Foundation under its "Mainstreaming Minority Women's Studies Initiative," determined that the most common changes made in a course syllabus were the addition of a new text, changes in topics or concepts, and the integration of new material throughout the course.[5] Three-fourths of the faculty in the Ford projects made at least some changes in their syllabi. In addition, not only are courses revised, but new courses are often created as the result of curriculum transformation projects.

2. Changes in Pedagogy

Seeing students as active rather than passive learners, replacing the lecture approach with more interactive pedagogics, and emphasizing the development of critical thinking rather than retention of facts and "coverage" of material are changes frequently found in feminist teaching methods. For example, the major differences in teaching styles that faculty in the University of Washington project reported included adopting cooperative approaches and interactive pedagogy, placing greater emphasis on critical thinking, and becoming more willing to share or delegate authority to students.[6]

These changes in teaching methods often reflect faculty's altered views of student needs and experiences. Faculty members of the University of Washington project expressed greater respect for students and their capacity to learn, greater respect for student diversity, and a willingness to see conflict and disagreement as part of both their own and students' learning process.

A comparison of pre- and post-tests of faculty attitudes in a community college curriculum transformation project also revealed significant new leaning among faculty toward increasing the emphasis in their courses on social issues and problems. In addition, faculty developed a desire for course content to allow students to discover themselves as unique individuals and to clarify their beliefs and values; and increasingly encouraged students to examine diverse views about all issues covered.[7]

3. Professional Change

As one consequence of curriculum transformation projects, faculty have changed their research interests. The new knowledge and perspectives they acquire inspire many faculty to redirect their research or define new areas for investigation. For others, the project inspires a new or rekindled interest in doing research and in participating in professional conferences.

The larger changes involve reconceptualizations reported, for example, by the curriculum transformation project conducted at UCLA in 1989–1991: "[Faculty] began to learn how to reconceive history, periods, and borders; how to value experience differently; how to question the frames of reference or voices at work when we speak of a dominant culture as a tradition; and how to think in terms of heterogeneity even within seemingly homogeneous 'ethnic' and 'women's' studies."[8]

Effects on Students

Students are the ultimate recipients of curriculum transformation efforts, and many across the country have been and are being reached through the revised and new courses that emerge from curriculum transformation projects. Revised introductory courses in the disciplines and courses that count towards general education requirements especially affect large numbers of students. Montana State, for example, noted that over 1,300 students were enrolled in twenty-seven revised courses in 1980–1981. At Yale, one out of every five students was enrolled in courses affected by the curriculum transformation project there.

The specific effects on students of such revised courses—ranging from the acquisition of new knowledge to changes in perception, attitudes, and values—are of course difficult to measure, especially in the short term. And no long-range studies have been undertaken. However, those analyses and evaluations of the impact of women's studies courses on students that have been undertaken may be used to indicate the likely effects of courses emerging from curriculum transformation projects, since the goals of such courses are all similar to one another. In *The Courage to Question: Women's Studies and Student Learning,*[9] the evaluators of the reviewed women's studies programs concluded that the following were the most important effects that these programs had on students:

• Becoming aware of and familiar with new intellectual content, specifically a women's studies knowledge base that included recognition of the social construction of gender and of knowledge; the interlocking oppression of women; women's lived relations to patriarchy; and women's power and empowerment.
• Experiencing personalized learning that linked the intellectual and the experiential.
• Acquiring a sense of voice and empowerment.
• Developing critical perspectives.
• Recognizing difference and diversity.

While these are some of the most widely reported effects on students of curriculum transformation projects, it should be noted that such projects, given their time limits, attempt to lay the groundwork for continued, on-going change as well. In other words, the ultimate impact of curriculum transformation is intended to be long-term and is only partially indicated by the results achieved by the end of the project, as reported by project directors and surveys.

Today the need for information about developing and sustaining curriculum initiatives is greater than ever, as the goals of such projects have become more comprehensive, and as funding for them has become harder to find. The earliest projects, begun in the late 1970s and early 1980s, usually emerged out of women's studies programs, and their goal was to include the experiences and perspectives of women in the curriculum. That goal by now has been both more carefully defined and broadened. The development of ethnic studies programs and scholarship, as well as recent new directions in women's studies scholarship, have emphasized the differences and diversity among women. Hence, curriculum projects today focus increasingly on issues of diversity and on the interrelationships among gender, race, class, ethnicity and other forms of difference. Rethinking both what and how we teach has become more complex and more challenging, and the experience of successful projects is therefore all the more valuable.

For more information concerning resources for curriculum transformation, see "National Center for Curriculum Transformation: Resources on Women" in the "Resources: Bibliographies" section of this issue.

NOTES

1. Coulter, Sara, K. Edgington, and Elaine Hedges. *Resources for Curriculum Change. Integrating the Scholarship on Women.* Baltimore: Towson State University, 1986.
2. Towson State University Evaluation Report, 1992.
3. Vanfossen, Beth. "Towson State University Evaluation Report." Baltimore: Institute for Teaching and Research on Women, Towson State University, 1994. Unpublished paper.
4. Schmitz, Betty, et al. "Women's Studies and the Transformation of the Curriculum in Higher Education." In *Handbook of Research on Multicultural Education,* edited by James A. Banks and Cherry McGee Banks. Boston: Allyn and Bacon, 1995.
5. Ginorio, Angela B., Johnnella E. Butler, Candace Conte, Marsha Brown, and Betty Schmitz. "Incorporating American Ethnic Minority Women into the Curriculum: An Evaluation of Curriculum Change Projects, January 1989–December 1992." Final Report to the Ford Foundation.

Seattle, WA: Northwest Center for Research on Women, University of Washington, n.d.
6. University of Washington Curriculum Transformation Project, 1992–1993, 4, *Selected Materials*, n.d.
7. Vanfossen, Beth (1994).
8. Rowe, Karen. "Shifting Models, Creating Visions: Process and Pedagogy for Curriculum Transformation." In *Women of Color and the Multicultural Curriculum: Transforming the College Classroom*, edited by Liza Fiol-Matta and Mariam K. Chamberlain, 36. New York: The Feminist Press, 1994.
9. Musil, Caryn, ed. *The Courage to Question: Women's Studies and Student Learning*. Association of American Colleges, 1992.

Elaine Hedges *was codirector of a four-year FIPSE-funded curriculum transformation project at Towson State University, 1983–1987, and a two-year FIPSE community college project, 1988–1990, which involved five institutions from the Baltimore and Washington D.C. area. She is currently a codirector of the National Center for Curriculum Transformation Resources on Women at Towson State University.*

Faculty Development:
A Consortial Model

Myrna Goldenberg and Shirley C. Parry

In the autumn of 1988, forty-five faculty members from five Maryland community colleges (Montgomery College, Anne Arundel Community College, Prince George's Community College, Community College of Baltimore, and Essex Community College) began meeting regularly to study the recent scholarship on women and minorities and subsequently to modify their courses and their pedagogy and to test the changes in the classroom. Codirected by Sara Coulter and Elaine Hedges of Towson State University and Myrna Goldenberg of Montgomery College, these faculty belonged to a two-year project funded by the Fund for the Improvement of Post-Secondary Education (FIPSE). The project was collaborative, linking Towson State University with the five community colleges, and it was consortial, bringing together in a common and long-lasting enterprise five community colleges that usually do not work together.

Thirty-eight participants were women, two of whom were African American. Seven of the participants were men, one of whom was Hispanic. The faculty were almost entirely self-selected; most had been teaching for more than ten years when the project began. During each of the project's two years, the five participating colleges enrolled a total of almost 60,000 credit students, sixty percent of whom were women. Minority students, especially African Americans and Asian Americans, were and continue to be present in significant numbers in most of the colleges. In the one predominantly black college in the project, seventy-two percent of the students are women.

During the year of planning preceding the actual project, the Towson State University/Community College Advisory Committee on Curriculum Integration facilitated informal faculty discussion groups and other activities on feminist scholarship and pedagogy at each of the community colleges. These groups proved popular. At Anne Arundel Community College the participation of academic deans helped create administrative support for the project. At both Anne Arundel and Prince George's Community College, Advisory Committee members arranged lectures, readings, and film viewings as well as the publication of pertinent articles in campus newsletters and newspapers. The Advisory Committee also prepared its members for the project by encouraging them to raise issues of gender integration in both departmental and campus-wide curriculum committees. (Montgomery College had already initiated an extensive integration project in 1984, and had held college-based summer institutes in 1987 and 1988 to integrate the scholarship on women into the curriculum.)

The structure of the project was complex. Each faculty member participated in one of the five workshops that were at the heart of the project: biology/allied health; fine arts; history/philosophy; literature/composition; and social sciences (psychology, sociology, and business). The workshops were microcosms of the whole project because each included one faculty member from each of the five colleges. Five workshop sessions were scheduled each semester on Friday afternoons from 2:00 to 4:30 to avoid conflicts with evening teaching loads. These sessions moved from campus to campus, so that each workshop met at each campus at least once a semester. The coordinators of these discipline-based workshops, all of whom were community college faculty, met regularly with the project directors to discuss workshop procedures and progress. In consultation with the project directors, the workshop coordinators organized each session, selected the background readings, and established the format. The coordinators' focus on the new scholarship in their disciplines, along with their enthusiasm, encouraged the project participants to study the new materials and to consider their applications in the classroom. Aware of faculty participants' interests, the coordinators functioned as resource persons, tailoring materials and approaches to the needs of each workshop participant.

Each participating faculty member also belonged to a campus group, which was led by a campus coordinator. Several times each semester, project faculty and campus coordinators met, working to develop broad campus support. At campus meetings, participating faculty shared their progress and problems, and discussed ideas that emerged from readings or presentations on the new scholarship. They raised concerns, especially about local campus politics that affected the project. Ideally, these faculty members became and functioned as a community of scholars within their larger campus communities, sharing and receiving feedback on their developing ideas.

The two-year project was divided into two parts: planning and implementation. Planning formally began with an early fall weekend retreat. There the directors and the workshop and campus coordinators were able to meet one another, review materials from integration projects elsewhere in the nation, and focus on the objectives of their project and the means to meet them. At the retreat, the directors also acquainted campus coordinators with the variety of resources available through Towson State University. Betty Schmitz, then at the University of Maryland, and an expert on transformation projects, served as the first of several project consultants; she placed the project in national perspective and offered specific suggestions gleaned from other projects. Other retreat sessions focused on workshop models, facilitator training, curriculum transformation stage theory, feminist theory, and the application of theory to the classroom. The coordinating group examined sample syllabi and critiqued videotapes and other materials for use in the projects.

The planning retreat exceeded expectations. It was especially valuable in helping the coordinators develop an identity as a team. The momentum and understanding established at the retreat would be essential in weathering the strain of competing priorities and overcrowded schedules during the life of the project.

The following semester marked the beginning of the three-semester faculty involvement. Prior to the first meeting, faculty were sent introductory readings and were asked to complete a questionnaire on how they plan their courses, including how they determine course goals or objectives.[1] Participants then gathered for a half-day orientation which included a presentation by Elaine Hedges on the historical development and the conceptual bases of feminist approaches to scholarship. They met four additional times that semester in their assigned workshops, where they discussed readings on feminist theory, feminist scholarship from an interdisciplinary perspective, and the broad issues that arise when one begins to reconceptualize the structure and content of one's field. At general meetings of the project faculty, consultants Margaret Andersen of the University of Delaware and Johnnella Butler of the University of Washington addressed issues of race and ethnicity in the context of curriculum transformation. Toward the end of this first semester, the faculty were introduced to stage theory (see Goldenberg and Stout, "Writing Everybody In," this issue) and were asked to consider specific ways in which they might revise a course they expected to teach the following fall semester.

This assignment paved the way for summer research projects and a two-day Summer Institute on Feminist Pedagogy. Frances A. Maher of Wheaton College and Mary Kay Thompson Tetrault of California State University at Fullerton presented their research on feminist pedagogy, stimulating a discussion of women students' behavior in the classroom, and, especially, of women's silences: oppressive silences explored in the book *Women's Ways of Knowing;* ambiguous silences of many community college students and of some workshop participants; and empowering silences of teachers encouraging and making room for their students' voices. At individual workshop sessions, faculty shared the results of their summer research projects and the revisions they had made to a course module for the fall semester.

The second year of the project was extremely busy. Not only did faculty participants experiment with course transformation, but they also met with consultants in their disciplines, developed workshop reports and bibliographies, and presented their work at state and national conferences. During the fall semester, faculty reported on their course revisions in workshop meetings, taught their revised modules, and evaluated their students' responses. After discussing their experiences with workshop colleagues, they reshaped their courses, helped by this collaborative approach to course transformation. Moving into the spring semester, feedback from workshop colleagues helped shape course revisions, and faculty participants adapted one another's revisions to their own courses as participants taught more fully transformed courses and continued to share their experiences. During the year, Betty Schmitz and Elizabeth Woods (Barnard College) consulted with the fine arts workshop; Jo Ann Pilardi (Towson State University) with the history and philosophy workshop; Paula Rothenberg (William Paterson College) with the social science workshop; Lynn Z. Bloom (University of Connecticut) with the literature/composition workshop; and Sue Rosser (then at the University of South Carolina) with the biology/allied health workshop. Discussions with experts in individual disciplines were particularly valuable in working out specific classroom strategies and assignments. In addition, each college had the opportunity to schedule and thus help sponsor a consultant, and so several of the consultants gave campus-wide lectures and met with faculty who were not part of the project but who were interested in integrating the scholarship on women and minorities into their courses.

During the final semester of the project, the faculty participants continued implementing and evaluating their course revisions as they also prepared, individually and collectively, oral and written reports of their work. Faculty contributed individual essays that recounted their experiences as they reconceptualized their courses and experimented with transformed modules or syllabi. Several of the essays in this volume are based on these reports. At a meeting of the whole project, faculty identified the central issues of curriculum transformation in their disciplines and the results of their course revisions.

One feature of the project is particularly noteworthy. Faculty kept journals in which they recorded their reactions to their readings, to consultants' lectures, to the dynamics of their workshops, and to the process of reconceptualizing their courses. These journals revealed excitement, doubt, interest, anxiety, and satisfaction about the project, and recorded both personal and professional changes. In some cases, faculty thought the project through as they wrote about it. They also used the journal to recommend changes in the project. At first, the journals generated many complaints; some faculty were resistant to writing in them. But in the long run the journals proved to be effective stimuli for coming to terms with course revision, for approaching course revision systematically and analytically, and for evaluating the effect of revisions as they occurred.

Significant changes in course content and classroom dynamics continue to occur as a result of this faculty development initiative, in which a total of over 45 courses were revised. Several examples will suggest the project's range and diversity. A psychology professor introduced new units on sexuality and gender roles into her courses, while an English 101 teacher evaluated composition textbooks for gender, race, and class bias. Another participant introduced female slave narratives into her American literature course. An African-American teacher of history and economics worked at solving the problem of including more material on black women while dealing with the resistance of her black male colleagues and students. A philosophy professor now begins her course in the history of philosophy and religion with goddess worship rather than with the Greeks, to challenge the male construction of religious and philosophical systems. A required interdisciplinary course now includes art and music by women as well as discussions of the historical and social conditions that either facilitated or hindered their participation in the arts. Two professors in sociology and economics have reorganized their courses to focus on key questions that lead students to explore, through new readings and their own experience, the nature of inequality and the intersections of gender, race, and class.

As befits the emphasis on teaching in community colleges, all project faculty paid serious attention to pedagogy as well as to course content. The range of pedagogical approaches that they explored and implemented is evident in the essays written by faculty about their process of course revision.

Almost without exception, the faculty in the project expressed excitement about relearning the content of their fields. One participant wrote in her journal that "students have a right, even a need, to encounter not materials that I enjoy . . . [but] rather . . . materials that enrich their perspectives. Guess it is time for my mind to retrain." Another wrote, "My involvement in this project . . . has been energizing, bringing me back to a desire to do more scholarly research." Another said, "FIPSE has been the most important and interesting aspect of my teaching career since graduate school, and even graduate school was not as complete in scope as this project has been. I feel more intellectually stimulated and am participating in my own 'self-discovery' in ways I did not feel were possible."

These faculty responded quickly and enthusiastically when they were given even modest amounts of released time to revisit their disciplines, particularly in the company of their peers. Four of the five colleges supported at least five faculty participants in the project with a minimum of three hours of released time for three consecutive semesters. Montgomery College gave seventeen faculty three hours of released time each semester and four faculty, who functioned as coordinators, six hours released time for four semesters.

The project's twofold campus and discipline structure fostered both intra- and cross-campus collegiality and cooperation, which has, in fact, facilitated the dissemination and extension of curriculum transformation work since the project's conclusion. Moreover, the structure countered two types of isolation: that of a single college working alone, and that of a single faculty member working alone to generate change. We hoped, using this structure, to build networks of faculty within colleges as well as networks of faculty and colleges across the state.

While journal writing facilitated individual thinking and insight, among the features that contributed to the project's success on a group level was the multi-campus collaborative structure, embodied in the discipline workshops. Meeting with colleagues from other colleges is both stimulating and liberating. Hearing fresh and different points of view is often provocative, and the new setting provides an opportunity to leave parochial campus politics behind. Participants functioned on an equal footing, despite disparities in their familiarity with feminist scholarship. The group of participants was more diverse than could have been possible at any one of the colleges alone. As participants struggled to understand what their lives as members of gender, race, class, and ethnic groups mean, and to see how the biases of white androcentric scholarship have determined the content and the context of the material of their traditional courses, they often rejoiced to have experienced this collaboration.

Because curriculum integration projects are seldom found at community colleges, coordinators and participants also developed small- and large-scale dissemination activities. Each campus coordinator developed strategies to disseminate the project at her college. These activities ranged from initiating reading groups and faculty development summer seminars on gender and women's scholarship to creating new courses, which, at one of the colleges, helped support a newly launched women's studies program, and at another offered students an opportunity, through a travel-study course, to visit sites of significant events in women's history. Project members also disseminated the group's work at a statewide community college faculty conference. In addition, workshop participants spoke on behalf of the project at discipline-based conferences, such as the Modern Language Association, the Conference on College Composition and Communication, and the College Art Association, as well as at the Community College Humanities Association and at both regional and national meetings of the National Women's Studies Association. One participant published articles about the project in *Community College Week* and *Innovations Abstract*.

Genuine curriculum change is a long-term process. Curriculum transformation projects can establish the foundation and goals for change as faculty continue to explore new materials and methods in subsequent semesters. To be successful, the projects must respond to the needs of the institutions and faculty they are serving. The Towson State University/Maryland Community College Project provided an effective model of collaboration that colleges and universities can adapt to their campuses.

NOTE

1. "Course Planning Exploration," NCRIPTAL, Ann Arbor.

The recipient of the ACCT 1996 William H. Meardy Faculty Member Award, **Myrna Goldenberg** *teaches English and women's studies at Montgomery College in Maryland. She is codirector of several local, state, and national curriculum transformation projects, including the Ford Foundation Curriculum Mainstreaming Teaching Initiative and the FIPSE Towson*

State/Maryland Community Colleges Project. She has published numerous articles on curriculum transformation, American Jewish women, and Holocaust studies, and she lectures frequently, both nationally and internationally, on women in the Holocaust.

Shirley C. Parry *worked on the Towson State/Maryland Community Colleges Curriculum Integration Project. She is professor of English and director of women's studies at Anne Arundel Community College in Arnold, Maryland, and has done extensive work on the fiction of Paule Marshall.*

Writing Everybody In

Myrna Goldenberg and Barbara Stout

When Montgomery College and four other Maryland community colleges engaged in projects to bring recent scholarship on women and minorities into the curriculum, they were participating in the continuous pattern of change that has characterized American higher education for over three centuries. These projects are significant to community college teaching, especially the teaching of English, for three reasons: Their subject matter coincides with the community college student body; their principles acknowledge the community college teaching situation; and their results include expanded uses of writing and attention to language in many disciplines. Participating faculty were reminded of the power of language to shape thinking.

Since the early eighteenth century, college curriculum has been through constant change—though usually slowly and often contentiously—to accommodate new knowledge, new ways of conceiving and transmitting knowledge, and new student populations. The expansion of the curriculum has always paralleled and continues to parallel the democratization of both the student population and the system of higher education. The fundamental movement is well known: from the early clerical/classical schools with their small, selected numbers of young, male, nearly all white students to today's plenitude of all kinds and sizes of institutions, serving men and women in all adult age groups from the multiple cultures that comprise the nation.

Changes in curriculum eventually followed the expansion of the student population and the expansion of knowledge itself. In the late nineteenth century, the founding of women's colleges and the limited enrollment of women into major colleges and universities led to the development of new fields, such as home economics and social work. In the late 1940s, the phenomenon of mass education, largely attributed to the introduction of the G.I. Bill and the establishment of a national network of community colleges, markedly expanded the

A slightly different version of this essay appears in *Two-Year College English: Essays for a New Century*, edited by Mark Reynolds (Urbana, IL: NCTE, 1994). Copyright © 1994 by the National Council of Teachers of English. Reprinted with permission.

student population not only by numbers but, more importantly, by social demographics. Working-class and minority veterans, encouraged by the G.I. Bill, enrolled in colleges and universities and changed the curriculum through their experiences and insights. Their interests were honed by the war as well as by their often unprivileged backgrounds. They demanded a serious, practical course of study that prepared them for advanced study or good careers. Many were married men. Reluctant or unable to become typical undergraduates, they were probably the original nontraditional students. And many of them went to their local community colleges. Then, in the 1960s and 1970s, desegregation and gender equity regulations led to minority studies and women's studies programs. Most recently, the assertion that knowledge is socially constructed has expanded the curriculum by challenging the status quo and by questioning the claim of objectivity. This pattern of growth continues, with the interaction of scholarship, student populations, and curriculum reform ongoing—at times quietly, at times controversially.

About 85 colleges and universities have participated in serious efforts to transform higher education curriculum so that it reflects the experiences and contributions of women and minorities. Given the strong links between this effort and community college demographics, it seems that increasing numbers of community colleges will get involved. So far, these projects have included community colleges in California, colleges in the Rocky Mountain/Western States projects, colleges in New Jersey as part of that state's Transformation Project, and the Maryland colleges that are the focus of this essay. Montgomery College is fortunate to have had enough interest, support, and leadership from faculty and administrators for involvement in two projects—one of its own and then the larger collaborative effort between Maryland colleges and Towson State University.

The first curriculum transformation project at Montgomery College was the Balancing the Curriculum Institute, a six-week summer project in 1987 and again in 1988 during which twelve self-selected faculty agreed to study a set of readings gathered by the institute director, to revise a unit of a course, to critique one another's revisions, and to again revise the unit. Faculty from art history, biology, chemistry, computer science, English, history, psychology, and sociology were funded by the college, receiving a stipend and a book allowance. This project was repeated the following summer, attracting another twelve faculty.

The second project, called the Towson State University/Maryland Community Colleges Project, involved six institutions and took place over four semesters and one summer, therefore demanding a large amount of coordination and planning. (See "Faculty Development: A Consortial Model," by Myrna Goldenberg and Shirley Parry, in this volume.)

While each of the five community colleges that participated in this project represents a distinct population, together they depict the character of the community college student body nationwide. One campus is primarily urban and African American, and women make up 72 percent of its enrollment; three campuses are suburban, with white, international, immigrant, and African-American students all visibly present; the fifth campus is less racially diverse but serves rural students as well as urban and suburban residents. In total, these colleges enroll 60 percent women and significant numbers of older students, especially adults returning—often as single parents (usually mothers)—for training or retraining. Montgomery College, the flagship college of the larger collaborative project by virtue of its previous curriculum reform project, enrolls 15 percent of all the African-American students in Maryland community colleges, 53 percent of the Hispanic students, 50 percent of the Asian students, 25 percent of the physically challenged students, and leads the state in the number of students taking English for Speakers of Other Languages.

Principles

These two projects were based on seven principles that are important to any substantial curriculum transformation project in a community college. First, review of relevant scholarship and research is the essential starting point. Community college students have as much right to academic currency as university students, but because the community college teaching load does not provide incentive for research, faculty often need and welcome the opportunity to update themselves and to provide solid, newly conceived information to the students.[1]

Second, a focus on pedagogy is vital. Community colleges are teaching institutions, so good community college faculty are concerned about effective teaching. Because of the nature of these projects, feminist pedagogy has to be defined, discussed, and practiced. Feminist pedagogy creates active learning, uses as much collaboration as possible, respects every student as a learner, and expects students to assume responsibility for learning—ideas common to the writing-across-the-curriculum movement as well as to the community college mission. It is, in a word, a pedagogy of empowerment. The projects modeled this kind of pedagogy: Workshops were participatory, faculty actually changed courses rather than simply listening to presentations, they shared their work, and they were required to keep and submit journals tracing their work and thinking as they reformed their course or courses.

Third, changes must be appropriate to introductory courses and, simultaneously, introductory courses must be inclusive, accurate, and up-to-date. Introductory surveys establish the boundaries and key points by which students come to see the nature and scope of a subject. The language of a subject, the significance of its content, the influence of the subject on other subjects both current and past, the relevance of the subject in today's world, its major and minor issues—all are packaged in the introductory course, the staple of community college teaching. Today, students need to have the full view of a subject provided by the multiple vision that comes from scholarship which does not ignore gender, race, class, sexual preference, and ethnicity.

Fourth, both faculty and colleges must make substantial commitments. In these projects, faculty were compensated and were also accountable. They had to attend and participate; they had to submit revised courses; they had to keep and turn in journals, which showed their engagement and also evaluated all aspects of the project. Tight budgets make it difficult for colleges to find resources, but significant curriculum reform cannot occur without institutional support and funding.

Fifth, multiple views must be respected. The act of incorporating new paradigms reminds us that knowledge is constructed by people, that people are shaped by the knowledge that they study, that knowledge is usually expressed in language that cannot be fully accurate, and that the reformulation of knowledge is constant and continual.

Sixth, projects are only beginnings. Curriculum reform is a continuing process. Follow-up sessions for reports on how course revisions have worked and dissemination of revisions to other faculty need to be arranged. Participating faculty need opportunities to take revisions to the next stage.

Seventh, significant curriculum reform usually occurs in stages. Because these projects concentrated on scholarship on white women and minorities of both sexes, they followed a variation of the stage theories developed by Lerner, McIntosh, Schuster and Van Dyne, Tetrault, and others, all of which provide useful tools for evaluating the level of reformulation of a course.

Stage Theory

These projects defined the stages they went through as integration, transformation, and reconceptualization. Further, a course was understood as circumscribed by its content, language, and pedagogy, which are the components of all courses. At each of the three stages, the instructor considers content, pedagogy, and language, asking the same set of questions: Where are the women and minority men? Why are they missing? What are the effects of exclusion? How would this course change if it reflected the scholarship on women and minority men? How can the language be more accurate? How can I teach more effectively? Each question takes on a different texture and emphasis at stages two and three as the instructor gains perspective and information from each preceding stage.

The objective of the first stage, integration, is to begin consciously to use gender and race as categories of analysis and as subject matters worthy of study. The instructor will add material on women and minority men; add assignments that send students to multicultural and feminist sources; add awareness to the classroom through announcements of new books, lectures, or films; and eliminate sexist and racist language, metaphors, stereotypes, and norms. The instructor also moves toward feminist pedagogy, emphasizing collaborative learning. At the end of this stage, the course has been changed because material on and by women and minority men has been added, but the broad outlines and boundaries of the course remain the same.

In the second stage, transformation, the students and instructor develop bibliographies that include works by and about women and minority men. Here the course is changed by what is added *and* deleted. Instructors use new works and women and minority men as exemplars. They reperiodize and reorganize the course, fully incorporating the experiences of women and minority men. They ask, were the Dark Ages dark for all women? How did manifest destiny apply to American minorities? They include nontraditional genres like letters and diaries, and, in that process, validate forms that have been excluded. They change the course topics to reflect the fullness of the subject. In literature, for example, instructors include letters and orally transmitted folk tales; Linda Brent might replace Frederick Douglass in a crowded course outline. At this stage, the course is essentially transformed in that the key elements have been changed: Criteria of what is good are redefined; Lady Byron, Caroline Herschell, Aphra Behn are included as major contributors, not merely added as supplemental curiosities.

In the third and final stage, reconceptualization, the instructor gives the course new shape and vision, and challenges all assumptions: language, content, organization of knowledge, the politics and power structures of the discipline. Because of the breadth of this stage, project participants did not reach it during the span of the project, but they were at least able to grasp its concept.

Content

Dealing with new scholarship means, first of all, changes in the content of courses and attention to the methods by which content is established. Some of the content changes from these projects are no longer startling because of the accepted position these ideas have taken in some disciplines in the few years since these projects began. Textbooks by major publishers now incorporate scholarship on women and minority men, at least in literature, history, and sociology.

However, the changes made in course content, whether obvious or surprising, indicate how great the need was to balance the curriculum to provide instruction that validates the experiences of the majority of community college students. Courses in ten disciplines were changed in the following ways:

Arts:

- examining effects of the privileging of forms such as oil painting, symphonies, and operas—which often require expensive media, training, and civic support—as major, and classifying forms such as work songs, blues, ceremonial music of nonwestern cultures, ceramics, textiles, and jewelry as minor;
- exploring images of women and minority men in art, drama, film;
- determining the implications of valuing form, style, and technique over subject matter; abstraction vs. human concern;
- rediscovering female and minority male composers, painters, sculptors, photographers, patrons;
- including nonwestern scales, rhythms, and forms;
- seeing connections between values and progress ;
- asking, who are the tastemakers? whence their criteria?

Biology:

- examining the contributions of women scientists, such as Rosalind Franklin, Barbara McClintock, Martha Chase, Rachel Carson, Rosalyn

Yalow, Helen Taussig, and Candace Pert as integral parts of the course rather than as add ons;
• determining the evaluative point of view about research findings, methods, and applications: The aspirin/heart attack study using over 22,000 male physicians—why were women not included? Are the results applicable to females? Are conclusions which are based on small sample populations or relatively homogeneous groups, such as patients at veterans hospitals, valid generalizations to the whole population?
• acknowledging that science is not truly objective—that biases, personal animosities, rhetorical and metaphorical language, and contradictory views exist in science as well as in all other communities.

Business:

• adding specific material about women managers;
• increasing use of Labor Department statistics and other current documents about men/women/minorities salary and job categories;
• discussing working and family issues;
• discussing gender, race, and ethnic issues in advertising;
• discussing comparable worth.

Composition:

• considering textbooks for positive images of all groups, multicultural perspectives;
• increasing the use of peer editing;
• including journals and other informal writing both in the composition class and for use in other classes;
• sharing one's own writing;
• assigning topics dealing with race and gender;
• two concerns about teaching argument: lack of emphasis in textbooks on reaching consensus; students' unwillingness to challenge or take a stand.

Criminal Justice:

• analyzing depictions of judges, police officers, criminals, attorneys, and victims in pictures, drawings, and cartoons;
• considering women as offenders and professionals;
• reclassifying rape as a violent—not sexual—crime and the impact of such reclassification on offenders, victims, and the judicial system.

History:

- understanding how one group has been accepted as universal and normative, automatically marginalizing the others;
- using race, class, and gender as core themes, rather than including them as problems;
- questioning periodization and labels: asking how women, slaves, and workers experienced the golden era of fifth-century Greece or the stimulation of the Renaissance;
- looking at many human experiences in historical eras: for example, in the pre-Civil War South, looking at the master and the mistress of plantations, female and male slaves, men and women as yeoman farmers;
- examining the role of women in economic systems from the gathering/hunting societies to modern socialism, communism, and capitalism;
- increasing the use of primary sources and nontraditional sources, such as letters, diaries, advertisements: For example, a course unit on the Lowell Mill girls, using slides of photographs of the mills, a typical day's schedule, selections from the *Lowell Offering,* a magazine produced by and for the girls which both glossed over and revealed the realities of their lives.

Literature (American):

- including Native American, Hispanic-American, and Asian-American texts;
- paying more attention to slave narratives and seeing differences between female and male slave experiences;
- adding Zora Neale Hurston and other women writers to a course in African-American literature that has been dominated by male writers.

Literature (World):

- examining the myths of Eve and Pandora as models for images/ life patterns in the western world;
- providing gender analysis of the Iliad, the Odyssey, and the Aeneid;
- discovering insights into positions of women in the classical world through the dramas;
- pursuing a shift from exclusively European and North American texts to inclusion of African and Latin American texts;

• providing organization by themes: nature, love, family life, work, war/violence, with emphasis on multiplicity of views.

Nursing:

• adding cultural history of women as related to the development of nursing;
• considering the importance of gender in nursing;
• providing images of nurses in the media, arts, and literature;
• exploring the relationships between war and nursing;
• discussing the economic and political questions of equal pay and comparable worth;
• discovering the voice (or silence) of nurses in politics and policy.

Psychology:

• determining gender differences in mental illness;
• examining gender roles and mental disorders, such as depression, agoraphobia, eating disorders, alcoholism;
• considering the bias in scientific research—methodological bias in subject selection for psychological studies;
• exploring the implications of the use of male norms for evaluating women;
• discussing the cultural attitudes toward menstruation and menopause and the impact on women's self-esteem (contrast with attitudes toward male puberty and middle age);
• exploring the social dilemmas associated with prostitution and pornography.

Sociology:

• making race, class, gender, ethnicity more visible as tools of analysis;
• providing more critical evaluation of theories;
• comparing shopping malls that cater to different groups, noting differences in shops and services and racial assumptions about consumers;
• exploring gender stereotyping in children's stories and fairy tales;
• exploring considerations of domestic violence;
• examining novels about social problems.

Pedagogy/Active Learning

The Montgomery College Project and the Towson University/Maryland Community Colleges Project encouraged faculty to establish a participatory classroom atmosphere, one in which students collaborate with one another and with the instructor to enhance their learning. The primary goal is to move from "received" to "connected" and finally to "constructed" knowledge and passionate knowing.[2] Another goal is to construct courses that help students "integrate the skills of critical thinking with respect for and ability to work with others."[3]

Faculty included in their courses small-group work and student presentations, which build confidence as well as increase knowledge of course content. Instructors usually counted such activities in grading students. Faculty members also developed assignments, like journals and interviews, to increase personal involvement and to show students how their experiences and their worlds are the starting points for research into larger questions.

When they share classroom power through more student involvement, faculty do not abdicate their responsibility, nor do they make their jobs easier. Instructors still must transmit knowledge that defines their discipline; they must choose books and other materials; give lectures, tests, and grades; lead discussions; and carefully plan, monitor, guide, and evaluate student participation. Sensitivity, a great deal of flexibility, good humor, and much planning are essential when adopting inclusive teaching methods, but those methods are judged by both instructors and students as to whether they are worth the efforts. Transformation projects and writing-across-the-curriculum projects share this commitment to active, engaged learning.

Pedagogy/Teaching through Writing

Naturally, English faculty gave much attention to writing assignments as they revised their courses. Composition as well as literature courses were changed, so English faculty had special opportunities to apply composition research and to see its connections with feminist pedagogy. But faculty in other disciplines used writing in redesigned courses to a surprising extent. The required journals had shown clearly how informal writing can connect a learner with course material. In addition, many project faculty had participated in writing-across-the-curriculum efforts because they are the kind of faculty who are always interested in improving their teaching effectiveness.

In their revised courses, many faculty included writing in traditional modes, like research papers, case studies, summaries, essay exams, book/article/film/performance/exhibit reviews, and field trip reports. Increased time for drafting and revising was often scheduled, and more take-home assignments were given. One sociology instructor who wanted students to see writing both as a dialogue with him and as an instrument of learning stated this policy, which rewarded promptness and revision, in his course syllabus:

> All assignments turned in on time can be revised until you are sat-isfied with the results and your understanding of the material. Late papers will be accepted for two weeks, but they will not receive com-ments and cannot be revised. . . .

Faculty also used informal writing: journals, response papers, "think-ing" papers, reports of small-group discussion, one-minute writings, written questions about material or for use in examinations, and computer conferencing.

Two criminal justice faculty said that they increasingly find jour-nals to be "our most useful tool." They ask for some entries to be done at home and some written in class, and count journal writing in the course grade. Some of their prompts include:

- Describe yourself and your relationship to this course, including your course goals.
- Describe the effects of race, gender, age, social class, and physi-cal appearance on your own experiences with the criminal justice sys-tem and with crime.
- React to visual and print media coverage of crime issues (with which we are constantly bombarded). Write about the portrayal of victims, of offenders, of authority and power, of the victim-offender relationship.

These instructors said, "Almost all students have improved their writ-ing ability, perhaps more in terms of thoughtful expression than in style and form."

An instructor in hotel/motel management used what she called a reactive journal. She asked her students to write informally to such assignments as those listed below, and remarked recently that now she can't teach without this personal writing:

- In your work in the hospitality industry, have you ever experi-enced racism or sexism—either as a victim or an observer? Describe what you saw and felt.
- Analyze the climate of the organization in which you are working in terms of the presence or absence of sexist or racist attitudes.
- Write a work autobiography telling of jobs you have had in the

hospitality industry, how you acquired them, and what you learned from them.

• Analyze your managerial strengths and weaknesses. How would your management style differ from those of managers you have worked for in the hospitality industry?

• Do you think a person's management style has anything to do with his/her gender?

Two English faculty members, one in composition and one in literature, asked students to use journals as seedbeds for formal papers. The composition instructor joined her students in the process by developing one of her own journal entries into an article that she planned to submit for publication.

Pedagogy/Textbooks

Curriculum reform requires attention to textbooks and, in these projects, to analysis of the presence and treatment of women and minority men. Recently published books generally avoid overtly sexist language like the universal "he" and the misleading "man," but vestiges still remain. Nursing faculty worry about the continuing representation of nurses as "she's" and doctors as "he's." Philosophy faculty noted that the use of "man" and "men," especially in model syllogisms, can exclude women: All men are mortal. Mary is therefore a man . . . ? Social science faculty noticed that women and minority men are too often ghettoized into chapters as "problems" or "questions." Art faculty observed an improvement in a widely used text: In the book's 1963 edition, there were no plates of works by women or minority men; in a 1986 printing, among 1,079 plates, eighteen were by women and one was by a man of color. English composition and literature anthologies have become noticeably more inclusive in the last few years, in response to new scholarship and faculty insistence on its use.

Language

The language of a course defines its subject matter and values. Language is both the substance and the means of conveying substance. Obviously, such a complex issue is central to curriculum transformation. But just as project faculty could only be awakened to the issue in three semesters, language can only be touched on here. Focusing on language, project faculty looked for conscious and unconscious metaphors that establish attitudes: the taming of the wilderness, virgin land, settling of the West, Columbus's "discovery" of the hemisphere already populated by millions of people, labels of "progress" and "development," calling a community of female seals a "harem." All disciplines employ locutions that may not represent a concept accurately and that may, at the same time, perpetuate gender and cultural stereotypes.

The conceptual effect of common dualisms was also addressed. Polarities like masculine/feminine, black/white, active/passive make it difficult to conceive of the complex and more accurate patterns of reality. Faculty discussed the implications of using common metaphors and dualisms, and developed a heightened sensitivity to the power of language to either stifle or stimulate reader/student response.

Conclusion

The student body will continue to grow in number and diversity, and the curriculum will need reform, just as it always has. For the near future, it seems important for community college faculty and students to have the opportunity to update in the areas on which this essay has focused. The special mission of the community college, which is to empower its students by moving them from passive to active learning, verifies the need for more transformation projects. Finally, in their awareness of the constructing power of language, English faculty will continue to do research, to stay current in the growing body of research in composition and literature, to try to help students and colleagues understand how writing and learning are connected, to prepare students for writing in other courses, and finally to help students become independent, critical learners, as well as thoughtful members of their own communities and of that larger but increasingly fragile community, the world.

NOTES

1. Goldenberg, M., and Kievitt, F. D. "The Community College Scholar/ Teacher Revisited." *Community College Humanities Review,* 9 (1988): 108–115.
2. Belenky, M. R., et al. *Women's Ways of Knowing.* New York: Basic Books, 1986.
3. Shrewsbury, C.M. "What Is Feminist Pedagogy?" *Women's Studies Quarterly,* 15 (1987): 6–11.

The recipient of the ACCT 1996 William H. Meardy Faculty Member Award, **Myrna Goldenberg** *teaches English and women's studies at Montgomery College in Maryland. She is codirector of several local, state, and national curriculum transformation projects, including the Ford Foundation*

Curriculum Mainstreaming Teaching Initiative and the FIPSE Towson State/Maryland Community Colleges Project. She has published numerous articles on curriculum transformation, American Jewish women, and Holocaust studies, and she lectures frequently, both nationally and internationally, on women in the Holocaust.

Barbara Stout, *professor of English at Montgomery College, participated in Montgomery College's Balancing the Curriculum Institute and the Towson State/Maryland Community Colleges Project. She is secretary of the Conference on College Composition and Communication.*

Feminist Pedagogy and Techniques for the Changing Classroom

Shirley C. Parry

In the last five years, faculty at several community colleges in Maryland have experienced some major changes in the character of the classroom and in the way that education is conceived. Today, virtually all disciplines have classes that meet in computer laboratories, and faculty are increasingly being encouraged to learn the new technology so that they can teach in a variety of environments. Simultaneously, instructors and college administrators are acknowledging that the college's mission is not simply teaching, and must instead be reconceptualized in a relational way as teaching-and-learning.

This reconceptualization, especially, resonates with the basic notions of feminist pedagogy as it has developed over the past fifteen years. Happily, there are many techniques of feminist pedagogy that can be used effectively in both traditional and computerized classroom environments.[1]

Feminist Pedagogy

Feminist pedagogy promotes the awareness that knowledge is not a discrete body of "truths" that the instructor knows and imparts to students. It reframes the relationship between students and the course material by suggesting that students themselves are capable of active learning and that this, rather than passive receiving, is what works best. Feminist teaching encourages classroom interactions that emphasize students' ability to question and to explore issues deeply, and nurtures the development of motivation and skills that allow students to investigate ideas and evidence and arrive at meaning.

A slightly different version of this essay appears in *Community College Guide to Curriculum Change,* edited by Elaine Hedges, Myrna Goldenberg, and Sara Coulter (Baltimore, MD: Towson State University/Maryland Community College Project). Copyright © 1990 by Elaine Hedges, Myrna Goldenberg, and Sara Coulter. Reprinted by permission.

Feminist pedagogy also suggests a far more complex and dynamic relationship between students and instructors than is traditional. Feminist teachers often employ techniques that help students achieve mastery of material on their own or in groups. The goal is to give students the means to gain power and control over knowledge and, as a consequence, to have authority in the classroom. This, of course, means a shift among the relationships in the classroom. Although, initially, many faculty members were nervous about the idea of being "decentered," of sharing authority, in the long run we have found many important benefits. We are more able to relax and to be authentic in the classroom, and we, too, work in a learning mode that is exciting and encouraging to students. Fears that students would see us as less knowledgeable and that the content of the class hour would be diluted proved groundless. Students today seem more comfortable with this changed relationship than they were a decade ago. Then, some were uncomfortable and wanted the teacher to "teach." Now, my students thrive in this milieu.

A third dimension of feminist pedagogy is its emphasis on the cooperative and the collective. Again, there is a shift in relationships, here between student and student. As we become more skilled in devising effective structures for group work and collaborative exercises, the classroom becomes far less competitive and individualistic —and, students say, less intimidating and alienating. Students get acquainted with and learn from each other as they work together. They realize that they themselves can be sources of knowledge and aid to their peers as well as to the instructor, which gives them a sense of personal authority. In my experience, students' realizations that learning is genuinely a process comes most frequently from group work. Collaborating on tasks and projects and feeling connected and responsible to others in the classroom also helps create a sense of community.[2] This not only enhances learning in specific situations but, in addition, makes the experience of college a far more positive, less isolating one, my students report.

Feminist pedagogy also makes explicit that how we experience and understand things is rooted in our social position, based on a variety of factors, including gender, race, ethnicity, class, and sexual preference. Literary and artistic canons, psychological theories, legal principles, and historical interpretations based solely on the experiences and perspectives of privileged, white males have all come into question as feminist and African-American scholars, among others, have challenged an epistemology that asserts that there is one universal truth that can be known by a single group or apprehended from a single "place" or location. One way of incorporating our awareness of positionality in the classroom is to use techniques that help students, especially female and minority students, to identify their positions and to develop their own voices. Other strategies encourage and even emphasize multiple points of view in class discussions or written work, and help create an understanding of the dynamics of "difference" and of self/other.

Finally, feminist pedagogy affirms the value of personal experience as a central component of learning. Robert J. Bezucha suggests the importance of this undertaking:

> Resistance to feminism comes, in large part, from the fact that it seeks to undermine one of the most powerful and deeply held sets of distinctions drawn in Western thought and society: the separation of the public, the impersonal, and the objective, on the one hand, from the private, the personal, and the subjective, on the other. . . . Feminist pedagogy . . . challenges these established notions of teaching and learning from within the academy itself.[3]

Although some of us felt initial discomfort at the idea of sharing personal experiences with students, many have found that it has made the classroom more meaningful, allowing for less separation between ourselves and the material as well as between ourselves and our students. Instructors have developed exercises that elicit personal experience and that encourage students to use it to understand theory and to develop voice. Here again, students react very positively when they can use their own personal experiences and see them as valid elements in the learning process.

Exercises and Techniques

The exercises and teaching techniques that follow attempt to address one or more of the basic concerns of feminist pedagogy. Many techniques used by feminist teachers were not originally developed as specifically feminist methods. However, when they are used in the context of feminist reconceptualizations of knowledge and in classrooms where power relationships are being examined and realigned in consciously feminist ways, they become important tools of feminist pedagogy. The example of journal assignments—whether used in a traditional classroom setting or in a networked computer lab—is useful in this regard. Journals can be used to address central feminist issues—gender, for example—and can serve as important elements of feminist teaching. By providing a safe space for self-expression, journals can help engage students in the exploration of complex ideas, such as the relationships between gender, race, ethnicity, and class. Journals help empower students who are usually silent by allowing them to develop voice and mastery. Journal entries can also serve as bases for small or large group discussions, enabling students to participate in the structuring of the class period. Journal writing is also an effective means through which students can explore the relationship between their personal experiences and theory.

Although the assignments and classroom methods that follow are described in subject- or discipline-specific terms, virtually all of them can be adapted to any course, including skills courses.

Writing Techniques

1. "Quick" Writing. This adaptation of Cross and Angelo's "Minute Paper" helps foster student-student cooperation and a sense of authority.[4] The assignment, given after each examination, asks students to write for five minutes about what they did that improved their grade/score on a test. The students may read their responses aloud, put them on the computer network for their classmates to read, or convey them to the instructor, who will summarize the responses for the class. This student-produced information is also helpful to instructors as they counsel students.

2. Journals. Whether assigned in a notebook or on a computer, journal entries are used by many feminist teachers. The kinds of topics assigned can vary greatly, as the sample list below suggests.

• "You decide." Students explore different dimensions of a difficult or controversial notion. In criminal justice courses, for example, students are asked: What is sexual assault? What does a jury of one's peers mean in this context? In business classes, students are asked: Is protective legislation good or bad for women?

• Personalizing theory. In literature and women's studies courses, students write about their own social positions and the factors that determine positionality in their lives. In history and sociology, they write about personal experiences of prejudice. In literature, in conjunction with captivity narratives, they write about their own experiences of being captive or imprisoned in some way.

• Reflection. This expands the "personalizing theory" exercise by asking students to reflect at length about the meaning or impact of particular experiences. In psychology and women's studies courses, they write about how the experiences of sexism affect their thinking and their behavior. In science and engineering courses, students reflect on how their assumptions about gender affect their own self-esteem and success.

• Reading Response. In criminal justice courses, students react in journals to an assigned essay suggesting that female police officers make fewer but better arrests.

• Class Response. In acting classes, students write journal responses to a class exercise in which they play roles of the opposite sex. In nursing courses, students are assigned entries responding to clinical experiences.

• Specially structured journal writing. In philosophy, students use a modified version of the integrative learning journal when writing about readings or issues that have come up in class.[5] Their journals contain four sections: "diary," for subjective responses in a variety of forms; "notebook," for more thoughtful responses; "questions"; and "evaluation," for entries charting individual development as well as course progress. A different assignment, in Beginning Drawing, asks students to write daily for a month about the visual experience that made the greatest impact on them each day. This helps students develop voice as well as visual awareness. The instructor uses these entries to design individualized projects.

3. Other Writing. While there are countless other writing exercises to use and explore, two especially worth mentioning are the following:

• Imaginary letter. In a Human Sexuality class, male and female students are asked to write to a nine year-old daughter explaining menstruation. They are also asked to write in the voice of a middle-aged woman about menopause. In remedial writing classes, students tell a parent or friend in an imaginary letter something important about themselves they want the other to know.

• Interview. In Human Sexuality, students interview their mothers about pregnancy and gay and straight friends about their developing sexual preferences. In history, they interview females in the military, African-American women who were involved in the civil rights movement, and organizers in predominantly female unions.

Group Techniques in a Traditional Setting

Encouraging students to apply the principles of feminist group process in large class discussions and small group collaborations can make a significant difference in the success of collective work. In my classes, the students and I discuss the importance of giving each group member the opportunity to speak on major topics without interruption. Together we devise ways to implement this. In some cases, we go around the group and ask each person to either contribute or pass before beginning an open discussion. In others, the last speaker gives a special "speaker's designator" (chosen by the students) to the next speaker. Often we use these techniques for the first third of the semester and drop them as they become unnecessary—that is, when virtually all students feel comfortable participating and no one dominates. I also explain non-hierarchical methods of facilitating discussions and ask students to rotate facilitating functions in their groups. In addition, we discuss collective decision-making.

1. Expanded think-pair-share. Think-pair-share presents students with an issue or problem. They think about it individually for five to ten minutes, then pair off and discuss their ideas for another five to ten minutes. Finally, partners come back together with the rest of the class to share their discussions. This technique can be used in a variety of disciplines. In nursing, students analyze patient data provided by the instructor and develop three nursing diagnoses. In computer science, student pairs work on program modules.

Expanding think-pair-share can produce classroom exercises that are successful in helping students develop critical thinking skills, especially in relationship to topics about which they might have strong or deeply rooted opinions. In criminal justice, for example, the instructor assigns readings on pornography and censorship. She asks the class, "Should violent pornography be censored?" In response, students make three columns: pros, cons, and a third column of questions they want answered and information they want to have before they can come to a decision. At the end of a ten- to fifteen-minute period of individual thinking, the instructor lists on the board or a projected computer screen each item from the students' third columns. Without further instructions, students pair off and discuss the issue in pairs for fifteen to twenty minutes. When they come back together, the instructor focuses the discussion not on the pros and cons, but rather on students' questions and desired information.

This technique makes it possible to discuss charged subjects without extreme polarization. It requires students to think seriously about both sides of an issue rather than getting locked into particular opinions they might express during class discussion. It also makes them personally aware of how important it is to ask questions and be informed before making decisions. Significant interactions among students often result from this exercise.

2. Journal-based group discussions. Student journal entries can be used to structure class discussion. In English and social science courses, instructors can assign journal entries in a special format. They ask students to write either five very concrete observations about the text (e.g., "I observed that Rebecca Harding Davis suddenly injects color into *Life in the Iron Mills,*" or "I observed that the second generation of textile workers included many immigrants") or a mixture of observations and questions.[6] A separate part of the entry addresses students' personal responses to the reading.

At the beginning of class, the instructor asks each student to read aloud her/his most pertinent observation (or question) and writes it on the chalkboard. The class then decides the order in which they want to discuss the observations or questions, thus structuring the class period themselves around their own material. Later in the hour students decide whether there are important topics that have not yet been adequately addressed.

To the surprise (and relief) of instructors first employing this technique, students almost always focus on virtually every important point that the instructor would dwell on in a carefully planned class. When this method is used consistently, students seem especially motivated to keep up with course reading and participate in discussions. Most notably, they appear to take themselves more seriously as thinkers.

3. Group teaching. Students get into groups of four or five. Each group either is assigned or chooses an aspect of the material to focus on and discuss. In a literature class, groups may work on passages from a short story or a play; in remedial English, on different kinds of sentence fragments; in Human Sexuality, on different stages in sexual development; in computer science, on different Internet servers. Students work together to identify those things the other students most need to know about their group's material. After each member selects and designs a part of the presentation, the group as a whole teaches its unit to the rest of the class.

Results can be remarkable, not only in terms of the quality of insight and information presented. Students feel the group work aids their mastery of the subject matter, and the teaching format gives them an increased sense of authority. Following such an exercise, class members who are shy about talking often participate with greater ease and confidence in class discussions.

Feminist Pedagogy in the Computerized Classroom[7]

A networked computer environment can help instructors shift the
power relationships in the classroom and realize feminist pedagogy's
basic goals of encouraging cooperation among students, developing
voice and mastery, and promoting active learning. The instructor's
intention and approach to the technology are the determining factors.
If instructors are willing to share the technology—to give students
access to the available tools—and to create assignments tailored to
specific pedagogical goals, computer classrooms can be hotbeds of
feminist teaching.

Cooperation often develops as early as the second week of class, as
students forget how to do something on the computer and turn to
their neighbors for help. Three weeks into the semester, students
who had initially sat and waited for the instructor to aid them are
routinely working with their classmates. This creates an atmosphere
in which it is easy to move into collaborative work on assignments.

Networked computers also allow instructors—and students—to
communicate with each other. Because their work can be made available to the entire class, students get used to the idea that they have a
real audience who responds to what they put on the screen. As a
result, they begin to take their work more seriously. Conversations
and collaboration become accepted modes, and students feel responsibility for and connections with their classmates.

Instructors can encourage a combination of collaboration and
active learning by assigning group projects in networked environments
where students have access to a variety of resources. In American literature, for example, students read Charlotte Perkins Gilman's *The
Yellow Wallpaper,* discuss it in class, and then form groups to work on
aspects of the story, such as the characterization of the protagonist's
husband, the depiction of the marriage, and the changes in the narrative voice. The goal is group teaching: that is, for each group to
make a presentation on its topic to the rest of the class. Groups may
supplement their oral "lessons" with visuals that highlight main ideas,
perhaps by importing patterns and designs that resemble Victorian
wallpaper or images that evoke the enclosed nature of the setting.
Visuals can, in fact, be very effective. They are of particular help to
visual learners, and open up a creative dimension in students' thinking. The process of using outside resources—finding supplemental
information about women and depression, for example—becomes
habitual, and the instructor easily builds on this when assigning more
complicated projects, including research papers.

While collaboration is integral, computer classes also foster inde-

pendent learning. When students learn to use the computer tools—
the various software packages available, or specific aids like the the-
saurus or the spell check—their dependence on the instructor is
reduced. However, they need to know the limitations as well as the
benefits of the tools that they are using (the grammar check, for
instance). This knowledge gives them control and helps them make
individual decisions. The decentered instructor becomes both a
resource person and a co-learner, gaining new insights into the material from creative presentations and new knowledge about how to use
the technology from computer-skilled students.

Altogether, the computerized classroom has proved quite beneficial
to instructors employing feminist pedagogy. A recent study of computer-
assisted writing classes at Anne Arundel Community College showed
high degrees of collaboration, almost 100 percent participation in each
dialogue (group conversation on the computer), and an increase
in active learning behavior. Interviews with students conducted in
the second, eighth, and fourteenth weeks of class elicited responses
addressing issues that feminist teachers find important. The
researchers reported:

> Although some students initially feared that a classroom dominated
> by computers would be dehumanized, alien, and not conducive to
> learning, nearly all of the participants came to see the environment
> as a place for highly personalized collaborative learning. . . .[One
> said there developed] a "little community" within the classroom. . . .
> No student reported feeling that the computers had replaced the
> instructors; instead they saw that the environment served to enable
> rich communication channels among all of the class members, the
> instructor included.[8]

Conclusion

It is heartening to realize that feminist pedagogy is as relevant and
applicable to computerized classes as it is to classes in traditional set-
tings. In its capacity to alter power relationships in the classroom, to
model new ways of working and relating, to enhance student voices
and authority, and awaken us all to the complex effects of gender and
positionality on our lives, feminist pedagogy is a transformative
process whose influence extends far beyond the halls of academe.

NOTES

1. This article is a reworking of an earlier piece that was based in significant
   measure on conversations with and information provided by my colleagues in the Maryland Community College Curriculum Integration

project. My discussion of feminist pedagogy reflects ideas presented by Frances A. Maher and Mary Kay Thompson Tetreault to the project participants at a special seminar. Many of these ideas are developed in their excellent book, *Feminist Classroom* (New York: Basic Books, 1994).

2. Carolyn M. Shrewsbury discusses the importance of community in the feminist classroom in "What is Feminist Pedagogy?" *Women's Studies Quarterly* 15. 3 & 4 (1987): 9–11.

3. Robert J. Bezucha, "Feminist Pedagogy As a Subversive Activity," *Gendered Subjects,* edited by Margo Culley and Catherine Portuges (Boston: Routledge and Kegan Paul, 1985): 81–95.

4. See Thomas A. Angelo and K. Patricia Cross, *Classroom Assessment Techniques: A Handbook for College Teachers.* 2nd ed. (San Francisco: Josey-Bass, 1993).

5. See Ellen Berry and Elizabeth Black, "The Integrative Learning Journal." *Women's Studies Quarterly* 15. 3 & 4 (1987): 59–64.

6. Students are cautioned to make sure their observations address the text and not their own responses. An observation like "I observed that 'Diving Into the Wreck' is a difficult poem to read" focuses on the student's response ("difficult . . . to read") and not on the poem itself, and works less well in this exercise.

7. For information and insights into the computerized classroom, I am especially indebted to Anne H. S. Agee, Coordinator of Instructional Technology at Anne Arundel Community College.

8. Anne Agee, Marguerite Jamieson, and Cathi Mapes, "The Learning Environment in a Computer Classroom" (Arnold, MD: Anne Arundel Community College, 1995): 8.

Shirley C. Parry *participated in the Towson State/Maryland Community Colleges Curriculum Integration Project. She is professor of English and director of women's studies at Anne Arundel Community College in Arnold, Maryland; she has done extensive work on the fiction of Paule Marshall.*

Identity and Diversity:
An Exploratory Assignment

Anne M. Wiley

Several years ago, three colleagues and I embarked on a journey that would enrich us professionally and engage our students in understanding their own identity while exploring the diversity of women's lives. We had begun our curriculum transformation efforts after we had attended the Wheaton College Curriculum Transformation Conference in 1983. Following that, we had begun to integrate diverse content into our courses to experiment with feminist and more inclusive pedagogies. Now we wanted to find a way to share those experiences with each other and take control of our own professional development. While we came from different disciplines, including early childhood education, English and literature, and psychology, the language of feminism—content and pedagogy—acted as the crossroads to our many discussions regarding our various disciplines. As the process evolved, we focused on a manageable assignment that we could each implement in our courses. Our first groups of students knew that this assignment was being used in other courses and we permitted students who were in more than one of our courses during the same semester to submit the same work.

While each of us implemented the assignment slightly differently, we all assigned the same four basic topics:

- Explore a time when you felt like "other" (when you were made to feel invisible, excluded, too visible).
- Explore a time when you perceived someone or some group as "other" (when you noticed someone or some group was outside or excluded).
- Explore a time when a connection was made between you and an "other."
- Describe your understanding of how you will continue your explorations and connections after this semester.

One of the challenges that emerged in our discussions was the language we used to describe the assignment to our students. The language of this project helped us work toward greater classroom awareness. We used terms such as noticing "others," noticing differences, visibility and invisibility, and marginality, yet we knew that, at times, we are all "other." And we continually questioned the concept of "other" since it is always measured against something. Throughout all of our philosophical debates and discussions, students related to these concepts as you will see in the student excerpts.

To plant the seed of the project, we went on a thirty-six hour retreat to Maine in November, 1992. The actual original notes for ideas were written on the back of a checkstub and a restaurant napkin! After the retreat, for the next three months, we met for an hour about every two weeks as we prepared our course syllabi and the assignment guidelines. We began figuring out how we would develop assignments that would help students come to a better understanding of themselves and the diverse world around them. As the assignments evolved throughout that first year, we continued to meet every three weeks. We often met over food—usually breakfast, sometimes dinner. We shared reactions from students. We strategized about how to manage our workloads and, in general, we provided support for each other. This sharing and dialogue were integral and important parts of our process. In coming together, we asked questions and prompted each other to be more reflective. We probed different areas: how and what we teach and why, and how this transformation work was changing us personally as well as professionally. Since this effort became a faculty renewal process for us, we assembled a framework of questions to guide us:

- What happens in this assignment for our students?
- What happens in this assignment for each of us as teachers?
- Why do we continue to do this project?

Faculty Renewal

Initially, as we embarked on this endeavor, we were interested in faculty renewal. All of us were seasoned teachers in a community college, with experience ranging from fourteen to twenty-six years. We needed to take charge of our professional development. Like other community college faculty, we had noticed, first gradually and then more dramatically, a shift in the demographics of our students. In addition to traditionally aged college students, we were finding in our classrooms increasing numbers of students from diverse backgrounds, refugees and recent immigrants, returning adult students, first-generation college students, and even students still in high school. Feeling a sense of urgency about how and what we should teach in such a rapidly changing world, we questioned the meaningfulness of our teaching. We wanted to promote authentic learning and assist ourselves and our students to make connections between academic and daily lives. Since we had begun individually to change the content and pedagogical strategies of our courses, we seized the opportunity to work with each other. We posed these questions to ourselves:

- Why do we teach?
- Why do we teach at a community college, particularly at our rural community college?
- What do each of us need to do differently in our teaching and in our classrooms to connect our content with our students' lives?
- How do we each promote authentic learning?
- How do we make connections between everyday lives and the academy?
- How do we honor the everyday lives of our students?
- What has this assignment and process taught each of us?
- How do we grow in our own lives and in our teaching?
- How do we acknowledge what our students teach us?
- How do we teach so that our classrooms promote extended conversations?
- How does this assignment help us pose questions in class discussions and in our response on assignments?

Focus on Psychology of Women

Psychology of Women is a course that I had taught each semester for seven years. The course enrolled about twenty-five students each semester, many of them returning adult women. Originally I had taught the course from a developmental psychology perspective, chronologically. Over the years, the course content and approach had shifted. At first I added an overview of the basic concepts of feminism and the psychology of gender. Then, I explored issues of aging and psychological relational theoretical frameworks.[1] To assist students in understanding the diversity of women's lives, I then moved to explore issues including black motherhood, white privilege, and heterosexual privilege. The diverse readings, including poems, articles, essays and literature, as well as the class discussions, explored the challenges facing psychology to become more inclusive of all humans. In class, students often discussed information about women missing from the curriculum. In addition to the supplemental readings, I used videos to augment the primary course texts: *Women and Gender: A Feminist Psychology* by Mary Crawford and Rhoda Unger and the reader, *Women's Growth in Connection: Writings from the Stone Center.*

As in many other women's studies courses,[2] the course assignments included a weekly reflective journal, an in-class midterm, a take-home final, and a term paper that included interviewing and reporting on the interview.[3] Most of the journal entries were weekly reactions to the assigned readings but there were also a few guided and specific journals. One such guided journal included an exploration of each student's own ethnicity/race/class background, and often prepared students with some preliminary thinking prior to initiating the identity and diversity assignment. (See appendix.)

The teaching strategies were also typical of many women's studies courses and included small and large group discussions and in-class exercises. I often used some specific circle exercises as well as small groups with guided questions.[4]

In completing the identity and diversity assignment in Psychology of Women, most students wrote four journal entries, each of them approximately two pages long, using a personal narrative approach to describe their experiences. Over the years, the assignment changed somewhat and guidelines were altered accordingly. Because the Psychology of Women course explored issues of identity and examined how identity changes over the lifespan, the students' responses often included: an account of the personal journey and exploration that examined the process of identification of what it means to be labeled "other/different"; an exploration focused on critical incidents/turning points in their lives, often at the vulnerable periods of the preteen and teen years (ages eleven through fifteen); and an examination of past incidents and their lives through reflection, questions, and analysis.

Since students submitted responses to the first and second questions by midsemester, I was able to respond and guide their reflections. My guidance often involved asking questions to encourage further analysis. For some students, the questions provoked them to take action—to communicate across differences, to build towards empathy, tolerance, acceptance, and ultimately to build alliances with other women different from themselves.

When asked to describe an incident of "feeling like 'other' *or* noticing 'others,'" students often described an incident from their own adolescence. For many students, this assignment provided an opportunity to reflect on critical moments in their lives. Generally, students responded to the assignment favorably, offering intimate reflections and writing in sophisticated fashion with both feeling and analysis. The assignment also enabled students to write term papers that were rich and deep.

The writing that was produced in response to the diversity exercise was filled with nuance and self-examination. For example, Janice—white, married, in her late twenties and raising a toddler son—wrote about moving in seventh grade from a small nurturing private grade school to a large, impersonal public school:[5]

> In a school such as the one I attended, I quickly came to notice that certain people had been labeled "other" and were correspondingly ostracized. This was the fate I tried to constantly avoid. . . . I had gone to grade school with a girl named Martha, who . . . even in grade school used to get teased, and upon entering junior high, she instantly achieved "weirdo" status and was constantly getting harassed. . . . I felt very sorry for Martha . . . yet, standing up for her would have meant risking losing the shaky ground of acceptability I had just barely gained and I didn't want to do it. Our school was very violent. One of the dangers of not being accepted by the "in" crowd was that you became a prime target for the beatings up that occurred regularly in the park across the street from the school. . . . One day word spread that a group of girls had Martha in the park and that she was "gonna get it." We all went running over, as was the tradition. I guess an audience was required. They stood in a circle around Martha, not severely beating her, but terrifying her, and certainly hurting her with a kick here, a punch there. None of us went to get a teacher, or defended her. We just stood there and watched. She was crying, not just from the pain, I'm sure, but also because of how humiliated she must have felt. We watched her suffer from being "other," and felt relieved it wasn't us. Excluding her gave us a sense of belonging. It was sick. . . .

Peter, a white male about twenty years old, wrote about his transfer experience from a public elementary school to a private high school:

> I was soon overwhelmed by the fact that my fellow students were for the most part extremely wealthy and from all parts of the world as it is primarily a boarding school. My response was to be quiet and shy, an attempt to be anonymous which failed miserably. I was small, unconcerned with how I dressed. . . . There was a great deal

of hazing at this school and I certainly received my share. I was picked on a lot and beaten up a few times for no reason at all. . . . I felt unable to fight back for two reasons. I was smaller than most of the people who gave me trouble and I thought if I simply endured it, it would be easier than if I put up a fight. I hated this experience and even now I cannot understand it completely.

Jackie, a woman in her forties and a single mother of a preteen daughter, wrote about her experiences as the teenage daughter of a bisexual mother:

When my friends found out that my mother had a woman lover and that she lived with us, things changed drastically. I guess I never really had been pushed to examine how I felt about my mother's bisexuality until this time. In fact, it was something I never really even acknowledged to myself, as if it were this vague awareness beneath the surface of everything else. When I was confronted with friends, however, I was forced to acknowledge it to myself and to them. People's attitudes changed towards me overnight. I was no longer included in social activities that I usually was. My girlfriends stopped spending the night; they were always too busy all of [a] sudden. And gossip and rumors spread throughout the school. I felt so ashamed and exposed. And I was confused since I hadn't done anything wrong. I was the same person they had all liked and accepted before. I hadn't changed. It was a very painful way to learn about [what] "other" is all about. And it can divide people that would have otherwise been close.

Another white student, Linda, a single mother, in her forties, the first in her family to attend college, wrote about connections with the international, refugee, and immigrant students that she tutored. At first she noticed differences and then she began to make connections:

I have come to know the students I tutor as special, honest, loving, and honorable people. I quietly observe them as they struggle to make a life in this country, on our terms. They face oppressions of the like that not many Americans can comprehend, both here in America and from whence they came. I am exposed to various cultures and still have difficulty distinguishing the cultural differences . . . but I realize that this is mostly ignorance on my part . . . these students are here in our school, walking the halls, and sitting in the cafeteria . . . excluded. This is partly our doing, and partly because they do not yet feel like they quite belong. . . .

Another student, Joyce, a second generation Korean-American woman in her twenties, discussed the differences between being a boy and being a girl in her family:

> The eldest boy in an Asian family is supposed to take care of the aging parents. Since my brother was not only the eldest boy, but also the only boy on my father's side of the family (to carry on the family name), he was held in the imagery of a demi-god. . . . When I was eleven years old, there was, in the living room on the book-shelves, a showcase of every single trophy that my brother had ever won. In the center of this hideous display was an 8 x 10 framed photograph of my brother in the various uniforms that he had worn. The bookcase resembled a Korean funeral where offerings are brought to the burial site along with a picture of the deceased where popular Buddhism and ancestral worship fuse neatly together. . . . Substantiating imagery of myself was absent. My trophies from various karate events and honor rolls were restricted to my room. My mother caught me bowing to the trophies in the living room and did not appreciate the sarcasm; but she failed to change the circumstances. . . .

Another response came from a white, lesbian woman named Maria, in her late twenties. She wrote about being in a relationship with an African-American woman and how she had never considered the idea of white skin privilege and its impact on relationships. About a restaurant experience, she recalled:

> I had never stopped to look around me and notice that she was the only black woman in a roomful of people. She later brought to light another factor, which I was so oblivious to. She was in a restaurant, where many Italians worked and also patronized. . . . I was so comfortable there, ordering food in the language of my people. I was thrilled by the atmosphere and the menu and just assumed Valerie was too. . . . I now understand why she was so indecisive when selecting her dinner, she had no special preference, this was not her food, or her people for that matter.

Maria explored what she perceived as her lover's two identities, a public one and a private one, and related how she came to understand the complexities of race and sexuality:

> It all felt so disintegrated. I accused her of being homophobic and asked her to explain her different behaviors. She would tell me it

was not that simple. That I had no idea what it was like to be a black lesbian. She was so right. I came to understand through time and experience that the issues she faces as a black lesbian were far greater and more complex than the issues I face as a white lesbian. I do not say this to diminish my struggle or invalidate the white lesbian experience, but just to make a delineation. As a black lesbian, Valerie must never let her lesbianism overshadow her blackness. If she is affectionate in public with a white female lover, she opens the door to be labeled as a traitor from the black lesbian community as well as the black heterosexual community. What does her choice to be a lesbian reflect into the black community about black men? How is that viewed and possibly used to further oppress the black community? . . . . Reflecting back to our first date, I now ask myself, why did the waiter look at me when he asked what will we be having for dinner? Why did he hand me the check at the end of our meal? It could have been because I assume an assertive presence and maybe not. These and many more are the questions that African-American women must ask themselves daily when these situations occur. Pretty soon, you are questioning yourself, and this is how racism infiltrates and destroys the psyche.

In conclusion, the benefits of collaborating with colleagues and providing students with opportunities to reflect and to tell their own stories about difference have been at least threefold. First, engaging in this endeavor with students and with colleagues, I was able to explore how and what I teach on a daily basis. The collaboration broadened my understanding of the complexity of students' lives. It strengthened my resolve to continue to identify ways to provide community college students with opportunities that bring the curriculum to bear on their daily lives, to give students the opportunity to tell their own stories and reflect about their past experiences—to bring those past experiences to bear upon their present lives.

In this particular course, perhaps because of the theoretical exploration of psychological identity development in adolescent girls and women, many students were able to reflect on critical experiences during their own adolescence. The exercise which called for them to notice others and see themselves as "other" resulted in a richer, deeper understanding of the complexity across differences in all women's lives. Providing students with the opportunity to explore these connections helps individuals make bridges and collaborations across those same differences.

A second but equally satisfying outcome of the effort was the collaboration with my three colleagues. The sharing, both of the creation of the assignment and the ongoing discussion of effects, was important. As we shared, we gained a sense of collegiality and we enjoyed cross-disciplinary dialogues. These dialogues enriched the teaching of our individual classes. They also provided all four of us with the opportunity to discuss daily teaching dilemmas, to ground our teaching in the real lives of our students, to take risks in our teaching efforts, and to engage actively in conversations with our students.

Out of this we came to believe that institutions need to provide time for faculty to come together in small groups to discuss their teaching, their students, and their curriculum. All too often, institutions, including my own, emphasize large institutional professional development activities, or they emphasize off-campus conferences and workshops. While these are important professional activities that need to be offered, the benefits of promoting small, interdisciplinary, interdepartmental dialogues in small groups of faculty merit more attention than has been given.

Finally, and coming full circle, the experience of the assignment and the ongoing discussions provided me with the courage to take risks about both what and how I teach. I was enabled to suspend ideas about teaching based on how I was taught and to try new ways of teaching and facilitating learning. The experience led me to conclude that students cannot be encouraged to take action, to challenge the status quo, without grounded opportunities to reflect upon their own past experiences. Students need to reflect upon their past experiences of injustice and intolerance and they need ways to integrate those experiences into their current lives. The identity and diversity assignment reaffirmed my belief that the content of our classes must be connected to the daily lives of the students in our classrooms.

IDENTITY AND DIVERSITY ASSIGNMENT GUIDELINES, PSYCHOLOGY OF WOMEN COURSE

Purpose

The purpose of the assignment is for you to show evidence and document your understanding and your own exploration of what it means to be "other" and how you have made connections to "other." Since this course deals with the psychology of women, your exploration will most likely focus on how you felt like an outsider or "other" or invisible or too visible as a woman. The assignment primarily asks you to reflect on when you felt like " other" and when you perceived someone or some group as "other." Finally, the assignment asks you to describe a time when you made a connection with "other(s)" and asks you to reflect upon how you will keep these explorations going in your life.

Basic Questions

These questions can assist you in this personal journey and reflection:

1. Explore a time when you felt like "other": when you were made to feel invisible, excluded, too visible.

2. Explore a time when you perceived someone or some group as "other": when you noticed someone or some group was outside or excluded.

3. Explore a time when a connection was made between you and "other."

4. Describe your understanding of how you will continue your explorations and connections after this semester. (Additional guidelines and in class writing will prompt this response.)

Some Notes and Thoughts

How do I go about doing this assignment? Try to consider when you felt invisible, excluded, or too visible in the broadest sense: your family background, your race, your ethnicity, your religion, your schooling, your work, your size and looks, your socioeconomic class, your age, your choice in intimate partner, your politics, where you live now or lived in the past, your cultural background, your linguistic background, your physical abilities/challenges.

You will continue to read materials that will help these reflections over the semester. You will do a guided journal on exploring your ethnicity and cultural background which will assist you in this self-exploration. This project assignment is in process and continues to change each semester. I welcome your feedback as you attempt these personal self-reflections.

What Do I Hand In?

Since this is a very personal and reflective journey, what you will hand in will vary. At the very least, each of you needs to submit evidence of your reaction to the four (4) questions above. For many of you the evidence will be in the form of a one-two page reaction paper or journal entry, answering each question. Some of you may want to demonstrate the evidence through a piece of poetry, art, music, and so on. We will do some writing in class to help prompt your memories and we will certainly be discussing these issues in relation to some of the readings and content in the course.

A Quote from Johnnetta Cole, President of Spellman College

> How do we get under each others' skins? . . . I hate to be ordinary, but I don't know anything other than education that has worked to create human empathy. If I cannot through human intelligence come to say, "My God, what must it be like to be in that condition?!," what hope is there for the human race?

Try to think of the word *education* in this quote as broadly defined, as both academic/school experiences *and* experiential education, life experiences, and everyday life that has influenced how you think about yourself in relation to "other."

Ethnicity Journal

This is a focused journal assignment and is graded pass/fail. We will spend some time in class in small groups sharing our backgrounds in context with the assigned readings on diversity and gender. Your journal entry needs to focus and reflect on your upbringing and early schooling and life experiences. As you do this entry, think particularly of your family's attitudes towards learning new concepts and ideas. Also try to think of specific incidents in your life. In addition, you are expected to have read the assigned readings and integrate your thoughts about the readings as you do this focused journal.

1. Identify your ethnic, class, and racial background of both sides of your family. (If you were adopted or raised in foster homes and don't know much about your birth parents and family, put information about your family/parents who raised you.) As you are writing this section, you might consider the neighborhood you lived in, the types of schools you went to, the influence of religious activities, influence of cultural and ethnic festivities you participated in, family income, educational level and jobs your parents had. Also consider identifying some information about your grandparents if you know it.

2. Identify at least two positive aspects of your background and how these positive influences shape who you are today. Think about how these positive influences shape your values, your attitudes, your behavior. Try to be specific and cite examples. Consider completing the sentence, "I am most proud of the influence that my family had on me concerning. . . ."

3. Identify at least two negative aspects of your background and how those influences shape your values, your attitudes, your behavior. Try to be specific and cite examples. Consider completing the sentence, "If I could change two things about myself that were influenced by my family, they would be. . . ."

It is important to spend some time with this journal assignment. If you carefully reflect and write this journal assignment, it will nicely lead into questions one and two in the diversity assignment.

NOTES

Special thanks to the generosity of my colleagues: Kate Finnegan, Mary Ellen Kelly and Phyllis Nahman. Their collaboration, conversations and mutual efforts ensured this project. Special thanks to my Psychology of Women students, especially those from 1992–1996, who willingly provided me with their excerpts. This article was previously part of panel presentations made at an October 1993 Gender and Higher Education conference, in Burlington, VT and at the National Women's Studies Association conference at Ames, IA in June 1994. Conference presentations were supported by the GCC Foundation and the Ford Foundation, respectively.

1. For more information, read Crawford, M. and Unger, R. *Women and Gender: A Feminist Psychology.* NY: McGraw Hill, 1995; Jordan, J. V. et al. *Women's Growth in Connection: Writings from the Stone Center.* NY: Guilford Press, 1991.

2. For example, see special issue on feminist pedagogy, *Women's Studies Quarterly, 15,* (3 & 4).

3. Disch, E. and Thompson, B. (1990). "Teaching and Learning from the Heart." *NWSA Journal,* 2 (1), 68–78. Maher, F. A. and Tetreault, M. K. *The Feminist Classroom: An Inside Look at How Professors and Students are Transforming Higher Education for a Diverse Society.* NY: Basic Books, 1994. Schniedewind, N. (1987). "Teaching Feminist Process." *Women's Studies Quarterly, 14* (3&4), 15–31. Shapiro, A. H. (1991). "Creating a Conversation: Teaching all the Women in the Feminist Classroom." *NWSA Journal, 3* (1), 70–80.

4. Thompson, B. and Disch, E. (1992). "Feminist, Anti-Racist, Anti-Oppression Teaching: Two White Women's Experience." *Radical Teacher, 41,* 4–10.

5. All names used are pseudonyms.

REFERENCES

Crawford, M. and Unger, R. *Women and Gender: A Feminist Psychology.* NY: McGraw Hill, 1995.

Disch, E. and Thompson, B. "Teaching and Learning from the Heart." *NWSA Journal,* 2, no. 1 (1990): 68–78.

Dunn, K. "Feminist Teaching: Who Are Your Students?" *Women's Studies Quarterly, 15,* nos. 3 & 4 (1987): 40–46.

Fisher, B. "The Heart Has Its Reasons: Feelings, Thinking, and Community Building in Feminist Education." *Women's Studies Quarterly, 15,* nos. 3 & 4 (1987): 47–58.

Fisher, J. "Returning Women in the Feminist Classroom." *Women's Studies Quarterly, 15,* nos. 3 & 4 (1987): 90–95.

Jenkins, M. M. "Teaching the New Majority: Guidelines for Cross-Cultural Communication between Students and Faculty." *Feminist Teacher, 5,* no. 1 (1990): 8–14.

Jordan, J. V., Kaplan, A. G., Miller, J. B., Stiver, I. P. and Surrey, J. L. *Women's Growth in Connection: Writings from the Stone Center.* NY: Guilford Press, 1991.

Lather, P. *Getting Smart: Feminist Research and Pedagogy with/in the Postmodern.* NY: Routledge, 1991.

Luttrell, W. L. "The Teachers, They All Had Their Pets: Concepts of Gender, Knowledge and Power." *SIGNS: Journal of Women, Culture and Society, 18,* no. 3 (1993): 505–546.

Luttrell, W. L. "Working-Class Women's Ways of Knowing: Effects of Gender, Race and Class." *Sociology of Education, 62* (1989): 33–46.

Maher, F. A. *Cross Cultural Perspectives and Women's Experiences.* NY: Norton, 1987a.

Maher, F. A. "Toward a Richer Theory of Feminist Pedagogy: A Comparison of 'Liberation' and 'Gender' Models for Teaching and Learning." *Journal of Education, 169,* no. 3 (1987b): 91–100.

Maher, F. A. and Tetreault, M. K. *The Feminist Classroom: An Inside Look at How Professors and Students are Transforming Higher Education for a Diverse Society.* NY: Basic Books, 1994.

Maher, F. A. and Tetreault, M. K. "Frames of Positionality: Constructing Meaningful Dialogues about Gender and Race." *Anthropological Quarterly* (1992): 118–126.

McCollum, A. B. "Grading in the Classroom of Inclusion: An Invitation." *Transformations: The New Jersey Project Journal, 2* (1991): 19–25.

Pagano, J. A. *Exiles and Communities: Teaching in the Patriarchal Wilderness.* Albany, NY: SUNY Press, 1990.

Rountree, J. and Lambert, J. "Participation in Higher Education Among Adult Women." *Community Junior College Quarterly, 16* (1992): 85–94.

Schniedewind, N. "Feminist Values: Guidelines for Teaching Methodology in Women's Studies." *Learning Our Way: Essays in Feminist Education,* edited by C. Bunch and S. Pollack. Trumansburg, NY: Crossing Press, 1983.

Schniedewind, N. "Teaching Feminist Process." *Women's Studies Quarterly, 15,* nos. 3 & 4 (1987): 15–31.

Shapiro, A. H. "Creating a Conversation: Teaching all the Women in the Feminist Classroom." *NWSA Journal, 3,* no. 1 (1991): 70–80.

Thompson, B. and Disch, E. "Feminist, Anti-Racist, Anti-Oppression Teaching: Two White Women's Experience." *Radical Teacher, 41* (1992): 4–10.

Thompson, M. E. "Diversity in the Classroom: Creating Opportunities for Learning Feminist Theory." *Women's Studies Quarterly,* 15, nos. 3 & 4 (1987): 81–89.

Tokarczyk, M. M. and Fay, E. A., eds. *Working-Class Women in the Academy: Laborers in the Knowledge Factory.* Amherst, MA: University of Massachusetts Press, 1993.

Ventimiglia, L. M. "Cooperative Learning at the College Level." *Thought and Action: The NEA Higher Education Journal,* 9, no. 2 (1994): 5–30.

Weiler, K. *Women Teaching for Change: Gender, Class and Power.* Boston: Bergin and Garvey Publishers, 1988.

Weis, L. *Between Two Worlds: Black Students in an Urban Community College.* Boston: Routledge and Kegan-Paul, 1985.

Wiley, A. *Working-Class Women in a Women's Studies Course from a Community College: Awakening Hearts and Minds.* Doctoral dissertation. University of Massachusetts, Amherst, MA, 1993.

Zandy, J. *Calling Home: Working-Class Women's Writings: An Anthology.* New Brunswick, NJ: Rutgers University Press, 1992.

Anne M. Wiley *is a professor of psychology and women's studies at Greenfield Community College, Massachusetts, and an adjunct professor in women's studies at Keene State College, New Hampshire. She served as the Inclusive Curriculum project coordinator and is coordinator for the women's studies option at GCC. She recently completed her dissertation, entitled* Working-Class Women in a Women's Studies Course from a Community College: Awakening Hearts and Minds. *She serves on a local school committee and the advisory board of the local Vocational Gender Equity Center and is active in her teacher's union.*

Teaching in (Puerto Rican) Tongues: A Report From the Space In-Between

Liza Fiol-Matta

When I first read *Hunger of Memory*, Richard Rodríguez's narrative of his education, I felt both saddened and angry. This was not my story, I thought. The alienation between public and private selves that he records had not happened to me. However, after reflecting on his book for ten years, I can admit that so much of what he wrote was also true for me. Like him, I learned mixed messages of selfhood and power along with the English of the Catholic schools I attended, as my father, a Puerto Rican career Army officer, was transferred from one posting to another. At Loretto Academy in El Paso I learned that the less I associated with "the Mexican girls," the better (that is, more "American") I was. At Pauline Memorial in Colorado Springs I learned that the better my English was, the better would be my relationship with my teachers. On the weekdays at St. Joseph's in Columbia, South Carolina the better I memorized lines from my seventh grade reader ("Speak for yourself, John," Evangeline rebuked her reluctant lover), the greater the distance between the mother for whom I translated/spoke on weekends and myself.

Rodríguez decided to go "all the way down the path to full Americanization;" I decided instead to change the agenda, to work toward transforming the curriculum that had told him, a Chicano boy, and me, a Puerto Rican girl, that we and our families were flawed in our skins, our accents, our histories.[1] Why didn't I accept that the cost of the American education we received—the individual loss and angst, the loss of home and community—was worth the redemption promised us from our outsider status?

First, this country never represented home for me; it was never the only one in which we had a right to live. My mother had made it quite clear that our sojourn in the United States was temporary and that upon my father's retirement we would go back to Puerto Rico. My

A version of this paper was delivered at The New Jersey Project Summer Institute in June 1995.

mother's overriding commitment to our nation—to Puerto Rico—
meant, in fact, that we could go home again—home to a *terruño,* a
plot of land, "all our own," though shared with millions of other Puerto
Ricans. Second, just as the United States was never our Promised
Land, English was never our language of redemption. We went home
every night to Spanish.

What does it mean to be a Puerto Rican English teacher? One
answer is that it means both an awareness—and a responsibility to
that awareness—of the potential racist, classist, sexist, and hetero-
sexist lessons that can be replicated and taught even inadvertently.
It means knowing that uncritically handing down the equation
"knowledge is power" can obscure the real power scenarios that are
enacted every day in the streets, offices, factories, stores, and classrooms of this country. I never want to recreate for a student, whether
in my curriculum, my pedagogy, or my encounters in the hallways,
the education I received by having had pointed out constantly to
me the deficiencies of, as one of my teachers phrased it, those of my
"cultural temperament."

> *Her mouth smiled at me*
> *sweetly, feigning concern;*
> *another mistake highlighted*
> *in the red ink of her scorn.*
> *I heard her cluck, her voice*
> *reeking with sympathy,*
> *"Now, now. You're not going*
> *to start crying, are you?*
> *Like all those of your*
> *cultural temperament?"*

Of course, I cried. Then I disappeared from her classroom, becoming one of the many students who "inexplicably" one day just don't
come back. Children may learn early on about the location of their
social-political selves in the classroom, but there is precious little
power that knowledge gives them if they swallow whole the notion
that they must live a covert cultural/ethnic life to succeed there.[2]

The story of my Puerto Rican consciousness is a story of recovery
of/from language, of/from dislocation and exile, of/from displacement and marginalization. It is a story of surviving disruption and
invalidation, and of putting into words the possibility of wholeness
despite interruption and erasure. It is this sense of wholeness—along
with an understanding of the process of coming into consciousness—
that I bring into the classroom, that informs my teaching, that students

hear in my voice, that establishes the pulse of a syllabus or a new con-
figuration of a course.

Education—by which I mean something as narrowly defined as
what is learned in the classroom and as broadly conceived as that
which we receive as information from profit-making news sources—
more often than not erases the student and attempts to replace her
with the proper consumer, the proper worker, the proper cog in the
wheel. This is as true of the middle-class, white, young man majoring
in business at the state university as it is the woman of color in an
urban community college office technology class, living on public
assistance. The constant remembering of the rupturing, alienating
pain felt by so many students focuses my teaching.

Rican-Figuring the Classroom

In several ways reconceptualizing the teaching-learning continuum
affects the geography of the classroom. As a Latina I am conscious of
my location in an "in-between space" created by colonialism: in-
between languages, in-between topographies, in-between racial
discourses. When one teaches from the place "in-between," the
importance of creating links that extend outside the classroom space
becomes clear.[3] The island of the classroom does not have to create
isolated individual students; feminist and critical pedagogies have
given us many tools with which to reconfigure classroom space.[4] But
what I call Rican-figuring includes reconfiguring the intellectual and
emotional spaces that surround the student, placing the "formal"
education in a context that does not deny the reality of the "outside"
world. Students do not need to leave their selves at the door, nor do
they have to leave the world to learn.[5] In order for the teaching I do
to be effective students must bring the outside in, for one of the central points in my philosophy is that upward mobility or social and economic advancement does not have to be based on "escapist" notions
of education (escape from one's family, class, neighborhood, community, language, ethnicity, and so on). The learning community of
the classroom can help make sense of the communities from which
students come, their needs, and how best to give something back.

Rican-figuring the classroom includes leaving the "island," constructing the geography of the "classroom" differently, making a
classroom of the world and the body. This is why I devise projects that
include moving out of the classroom space. One such project is the
trip to nowhere. We get on the subway and ride for 45 minutes, during which we observe and think and write and connect and try out

figurative language and juxtapositions. We locate our bodies within the movement of the train and in relation to the others on the train. We take note of ads, decipher the messages around us, and allow our senses to be engaged. We record the specificity of our environment and name the concreteness of our world. Later, back in the classroom, we recall sensation and sights. We write subway poems or city scenes. I have seen previously vague expository writing become full of rich detail. Descriptive paragraphs in novels become easier to read carefully than to skim past; the perfunctory parsing of *Cliff Notes* into plot and character summaries ceases to satisfy when the rhythms, colors, and sounds of language are no longer invisible.

Rican-figuring means knowing that the borderlands are places that are inhabited and full of knowledge and meaning, places where one can work and learn, the space in-between that defies easy definitions of territoriality. When students encounter me as a professor of Latin American Studies, or Puerto Rican Studies, or Latina Writing, or Caribbean Studies, the obvious relief that shows on their faces that I am Caribbean, Latina, Puerto Rican mirrors their receptivity to my claiming knowledge of the area covered by the course. Extrapolating from their reactions, I know that my "ethnicity" must mean something as well to the students whose English I "correct." When I walk into the classroom as a professor of English, I carry with me the authority of another kind of knowledge. The number of basic writing and composition texts published each year by a thriving textbook industry is proof that in U.S. college classrooms, paragraphing, capitalization, and sentence endings are notions as seemingly arcane as unraveling rhetorical modes, scansion, and figurative language. However, I have noticed that students are less resistant to my expertise now than even ten years ago. Has it become easier to accept that one's English teacher can be found in her office chattering away with a visitor in Spanish, that when she reads her poetry it is in Spanish, that her bilingualism is not antithetical to her expertise in English? Do they know that for me English is a tool, not a trade-off, and that I will not ask them to barter their selves in order to gain proficiency in a language?

Salsa Pedagogy

What I know about teaching in the in-between space is that things are always more complex than they seem, that there is always a question behind the question at hand, and that, in the U.S., it is simultaneously true that "You can be anything that you want to be," and "You cannot be anything other than what you are."

My job is to teach my students how to look for connections, how to encounter the image, how to do both their improvisational riffs and their well-rehearsed solos. In salsa, which is African-derived Puerto Rican polyrhythmic music, the musicians depend on something called the *clave* to play together. It is the rhythm tapped out on a cowbell or sticks which is heard continuously throughout a piece. I see my role in the classroom as keeping the *clave* steady through a lesson. I listen for the *clave* and tap it out for them. I try to give students the security that they will hear/feel/know the *clave,* so they can engage in their primary task in my classroom, a task not dissimilar to that of the intellectual as described by the cultural critic Edward Said: exercising, rehearsing their specific voices, learning how to represent themselves and their ideas, how to dispute the "official narratives" and standard images of their lives, how to unmask and create "alternative versions" of their truths and selves.[6]

Defining the concept of "American," and insisting on putting Puerto Rico's historical reality at the center of my pedagogy are important for me because the rhetoric of higher education in this country configures the college classroom as an "American" and/or "Americanizing" space.[7] The work of curriculum transformation is that of democratizing education, striving to create an inclusive curriculum that mirrors the multiple experiences of those of us who inhabit this continent and our planet.[8] When *this* Puerto Rican enters the classroom, I am in the ironic position of invading a gendered, racialized, legislated American space, a fact recognized by designations of Affirmative Action hirings or Targets of Opportunity. However, it is *my* action—my entering the space of instruction as a Puerto Rican woman conscious of the contradictions of what place, language, class, and race mean in the United States—that is affirmative.

So, I continue to search for ways to help students recognize both the beat and the counterbeat, the *clave,* in a lesson. To contextualize Gloria Naylor's *The Women of Brewster Place* for a composition class, I include lessons on community organizing, and on urban renewal. We visit City Hall and sit in on a City Council session. To learn how New York City politics works students are required to attend a meeting of their school or community board, or a public hearing on an issue that will directly affect their neighborhood. All of these activities fill in Naylor's story of Brewster Place and demonstrate the intersections of the personal and political in all our lives. This is just one example of how to illustrate for our students the underlying pulse that organizes the music of learning.

A few months ago I was struck by an episode of the television drama, "In The Heat of the Night," in which one of the white citizens

of the small town of Sparta gets upset when Sheriff Gillespie's driver, a Puerto Rican woman, speaks in Spanish. "Why isn't she speaking American?" he asks Gillespie. The Sheriff responds, "Oh, it's
American, all right. It just ain't English." If hearing the *clave* doesn't
come naturally for us, it is enough to remember that keeping a
steady *clave* can be as "simple" as remembering that "'speaking'
American" doesn't necessarily mean "speaking" or "acting" or "thinking" in English.

There is no need to go through the education process and feel a
discontinuity, a void or rupture with the self. Richard Rodríguez's
story is not the only one of the education of a Latino/a. His way does
not have to be the way for all. I teach as if my students' survival
depended on it. I know that my own does.

NOTES

1. *Hunger of Memory,* 177. José David Saldívar presents an excellent critique
   of *Hunger of Memory* in *The Dialectics of Our America: Genealogy, Cultural
   Critique, and Literary History* (Durham, NC: Duke University Press, 1991),
   135–138. Catherine E. Walsh's study of the dynamics of language acquisition, power, and pedagogy is also useful in this context [*Pedagogy and the
   Struggle for Voice: Issues of Language, Power, and Schooling for Puerto Ricans*
   (New York: Bergin and Garvey, 1991)].

2. Although referring to a different type of situation, I think Patricia J.
   Williams' idea of "editing" oneself in order to survive whole describes this
   survival strategy well. See *The Alchemy of Race and Rights: Diary of a Law
   Professor* (Cambridge, MA: Harvard, 1991), 183.

3. I first encountered this phrase in Homi K. Bhabha, "Introduction:
   Narrating the Nation," in *Nation and Narration,* ed. Homi K. Bhabha
   (London: Routledge, 1990), 4.

4. The literature of critical and feminist pedagogy is growing daily. Among
   some of the more useful resources are: Lynn Becker, Carolina Mancuso,
   and Sharon Shelton-Colangelo, "The Connected Classroom: A Conver-
   sation on Feminist Pedagogy," *Critical Issues* 1.1 (1993): 1–22; Margo
   Culley and Catherine Portuges, eds., *Gendered Subjects: The Dynamics of
   Feminist Teaching* (Boston: Routledge & Kegan Paul, 1985); Elisabeth
   Dumer and Sandra Runzo, "Transforming the Composition Classroom,"
   Teaching Writing: Pedagogy, Gender and Equity, eds. Cynthia L. Caywood and
   Gillian R. Overing (Albany, NY: State University of New York Press),
   45–62; Laurie Finke, "Knowledge as Bait: Feminism, Voice, and the
   Pedagogical Unconscious," *College English* 55.1 (January 1993): 7–27;
   Susan L. Gabriel and Isaiah Smithson, eds., *Gender in the Classroom: Power
   and Pedagogy* (Urbana, IL: University of Illinois Press, 1990); Henry A.
   Giroux and Peter McLaren, eds, *Between Borders: Pedagogy and the Politics of
   Cultural Studies,* (New York: Routledge, 1994); Jennifer M. Gore, *The*

Struggle for Pedagogies: Critical and Feminist Discourses as Regimes of Truth (New York: Routledge, 1993); Alice Kessler-Harris, "The View from Women's Studies," *Signs* 17.4 (1992): 794–805; Cameron McCarthy and Warren Crichlow, eds., *Race, Identity and Representation in Education* (New York: Routledge, 1993); Peter McLaren, *Critical Pedagogy and Predatory Culture: Oppositional Politics in a Postmodern Era* (London: Routledge, 1995); Ira Shor, *Critical Teaching and Everyday Life* (Boston: South End Press, 1980); Christine E. Sleeter, "Multicultural Education as a Form of Resistance to Oppression," *Journal of Education* 171.3 (1989): 51–71; Kathleen Weiler, *Women Teaching for Change: Gender, Class and Power* (New York: Bergin and Garvey: 1988).

5. Paulo Freire has long stressed the importance of this connection. See *The Pedagogy of the Oppressed,* trans. Myra Bergman Ramos (New York: Continuum, 1982), and *Education for Critical Consciousness,* trans. Myra Bergman Ramos (New York: Continuum, 1983). Ross Talarico describes writing projects that take students into their streets and living rooms in *Spreading the Word: Poetry and the Survival of Community in America* (Durham, NC: Duke University Press, 1995).

6. *Representations of the Intellectual* (New York: Pantheon, 1994), 22.

7. I have had my share of conversations with college teachers and education professionals who have told me that it is irrational for me to expect that "Americans" should learn about Puerto Rico. I have wondered if they would tell someone to go back to, say, New Jersey with quite the same nationalistic arrogance with which I have been told to go "back to Puerto Rico if you don't like it here"? I recall the look of incomprehension of one participant at a conference for English Department chairpersons where I was a guest speaker when, in response to a similar statement, I remarked that actually by living in New York I was already living in the largest Puerto Rican city in the world. Surprisingly, many people do not understand that even going back to the island would still leave me in an American space. The absurdity of the colonial situation was recently illustrated by Juan Mari Bras, a leading independence activist in Puerto Rico, when, upon renouncing his American citizenship, it became obvious that one of the alternatives the US State Department had in resolving the case was to deport Mari Bras . . . "back" to Puerto Rico! See, "Un boricua extranjero en Puerto Rico," *El Diario/La Prensa* Nueva York 5 enero 1996, 4–5.

8. "Democratizing" is a major theme in education debates and can be employed in both liberatory and repressive practices. Donaldo Macedo reveals the convoluted thinking behind the latter in his *Literacies of Power: What Americans Are Not Allowed to Know* (Boulder: Westview, 1994). Elizabeth K. Minnich picks apart the "faulty abstractions" and generalities that created the 18th-century notion of democracy upon which government and education is based in this country and continue to pervade political and intellectual discourse today [see "From Ivory Tower to Tower of Babel?" *The Politics of Liberal Education*. Eds. Darryl J. Gless and Barbara Herrnstein Smith (Durham, NC: Duke University Press, 1992), 187–200].

Liza Fiol-Matta *is an assistant professor in the English department at LaGuardia Community College at the City University of New York. She was project coordinator of the Ford Foundation Mainstreaming Minority Women's Studies and codirector of the Ford Foundation Curriculum Mainstreaming Teaching Initiative. With Mariam K. Chamberlain, she coedited* Women of Color and the Multicultural Curriculum: Transforming the College Classroom *(New York: The Feminist Press, 1994). She is also active in Puerto Rican Studies and Latina Feminist Studies. She is a poet and a fiction writer and is currently working on a manuscript titled* Ni de aquí, Ni de allá: A Meditation on Puerto Rican Identity.

Rethinking the "Southern Lady"

Sara W. Smith

Like many of us, I was educated in classrooms heavily influenced by
critical estimations that ignored the experiences and the writings of
women and people of color. They were the subjects, but almost never
the originators, of discourse. As I began the difficult task of rethinking and transforming my courses at Montgomery College, what I discovered—which was not unusual—was that I had been replicating in
them my own somewhat imperfect education. My progress through
the stages of curriculum transformation occasioned a painful recon-
sideration of my own education, and as I reevaluated what I had been
taught and what I had been taught to value, I experienced a profound sense of regret and loss.

As a white southern woman educated almost exclusively in the
South, I was taught to have pride in the literary tradition of the
region, but that tradition encompassed little more than the writings
of William Faulkner, Tennessee Williams, Thomas Wolfe, and Robert
Penn Warren. All of these are good writers, but, as Adrienne Rich
observes in *Blood, Bread, and Poetry: Selected Prose 1979–1985*, "beautiful language can lie . . . the oppressor's language sometimes sounds
beautiful" (123). This beautifully written literature that I was taught
was partial and incomplete because it presented its myths through
the prisms of white male writers and through white male critics, who
exaggerated their own tastes and common experiences as universal.
The images of women, particularly southern women, were both marginalized and distorted.

If one of the avowed purposes of literature is to reveal to ourselves
our own reflections, imagine how hard I had to search to see my
experiences mirrored in the required readings. Imagine the detec-
tive work some of our students must still engage in! The literature of
the canon forced me to confront not my own reality, but the beliefs,
fears, inadequacies, and philosophies of male writers. Today many of
our students still find an incomplete or skewed presentation of life in

A slightly different version of this essay appears in *Community College Guide to
Curriculum Change,* edited by Elaine Hedges, Myrna Goldenberg, and Sara Coulter
(Baltimore, MD: Towson State University/Maryland Community College Project).
Copyright © 1990 by Elaine Hedges, Myrna Goldenberg, and Sara Coulter. Reprinted
by permission.

what they are assigned to read. If literature is a mirror of our existence, the reflection of women has been distorted and cracked.

During my college years in the late 1950s and early 1960s, the canon attempted to teach me my place in the world. I had to understand and interpret the myths of womanhood and, most particularly, the myths of the southern woman almost solely from a male point of view. Most readers, I imagine, could without hesitation call up in rich, descriptive detail an image of a southern woman. I am not that mythical woman, nor am I acquainted with anyone who is. How much more distressing it is to consider what the southern woman of color must encounter in the canon. If she is not a "mammy" or a "whore," she is invisible.

As a student, in order to understand subjugation of the powerless and the pain of dislocation felt by many rural southerners, I read *Grapes of Wrath*. How much more instructive Harriette Arnow's *The Dollmaker* would have been. I would have recognized that the horror Gertie felt was as desolate as that felt by Kurtz in *Heart of Darkness*. I might also have come away with some understanding of female imagination and creative urges. As a working-class, untheorizing, inarticulate artist, Gertie would have much in common with the slaves and daughters of slaves in Alice Walker's essay, "In Search of Our Mother's Gardens." However, nothing I had read informed me of the suppression of female artistic desire, of what it must feel like as a woman to sacrifice one's only means of expression. I had been left to conclude that female expression was incomplete, inconsequential, and inferior because I had seen so few examples of it.

Perhaps I could see parts of myself in Temple in *Sanctuary* or Addie Bundren in *As I Lay Dying* or even Emily in "A Rose for Emily." Faulkner wrote movingly of a particular South, but it was not the only South. While my understanding of the South and of African-Americans was based primarily on Faulkner's complex and ambiguous treatment of them, Ralph Ellison, James Baldwin, Richard Wright, and Zora Neale Hurston were being silenced by the thunder of the canon which had only recently discovered Faulkner. College students of southern literature were beginning to explore the relationships of African Americans and whites but only through the experiences and understanding of white men. I understood the institution of slavery from Faulkner, not from Sojourner Truth, Linda Brent, or Margaret Walker. I learned the so-called southern gothic tradition and the incongruity of the southern experience from Tennessee Williams, not Carson McCullers or Flannery O'Connor.

I might have seen a reflection of a real southern woman if we had read Eudora Welty as someone other than an incidental regional writer of short stories, or if we had been encouraged to see her work as a powerful rendering of the human condition rather than a set of quiet, ironic sketches about struggles with female domesticity. Might both the men and women in my classes have better understood the inequities of conventional marriage and the suppression of female sexuality had we read Kate Chopin rather than, or at least in addition to, Tennessee Williams? If so, we would have had works to counter the literary myths of what a woman, particularly a southern woman, was; and we could have learned how destructive those myths could be.

In "Saving the Life That Is Your Own: The Importance of Models in the Artist's Life" *(In Search of Our Mother's Gardens)* , Alice Walker explains that she was forced to "write all the things *I should have been able to read.* Consulting, as belatedly discovered models, those writers —most of whom, not surprisingly, are women—who understood that their experience as ordinary human beings was also valuable, and in danger of being misrepresented, distorted, or lost" (13). Our body of literature is enriched by Walker's necessity to write, but how distressing that some of what we should have read and what our students should be reading is still not recognized as worthy by some. As Carolyn Heilbrun observes in *Writing A Woman's Life*, "It is a hard thing to make up stories to live by. We can only retell and live by the stories we have read or heard. We live our lives through texts" (37).

As a reader and a teacher, I acknowledge the power of literature, not only to reflect our culture, but to shape it. I teach to give my students an understanding of themselves and some hope for the future, as well as a relationship with ideas from the past. I think that students learn best if we teach classes where reason is not divorced from feeling, where students do not suffer the loss that Richard Rodríguez describes so movingly in his memoir, *Hunger of Memory*. If I teach the restricted canon, I deprive a significant number of students of some hope for achievement by limiting their expectations. To read the responses of my students, both black and white, male and female, to Toni Morrison's *The Bluest Eye* is to know that I have provided them with opportunities that I never had as a student. I know that the women in my classes do not have to become men to see themselves, that people of color do not have to become white to understand the human condition. I also know, contrary to what Alan Bloom would have had us think, that when I include writings by women and people of color or when I teach the "classics" from a feminist perspective, my literature courses lose none of the academic rigor I experienced as a student.

WORKS CITED

Heilbrun, Carolyn. *Writing a Woman's Life.* New York: Norton, 1988.
Rich, Adrienne. *Blood, Bread, and Poetry: Selected Prose, 1979–1985.* New York: Norton, 1994.
Walker, Alice. *In Search of Our Mother's Gardens.* New York: Harcourt Brace Jovanovich, 1983.

Sara W. Smith is professor of English at Montgomery College; she served as the coordinator for Montgomery College and participated in the English workshop in the FIPSE project, "Integrating Women and Minorities into the Curriculum." Her current interests include contemporary Native-American writings by women.

Integrating Scholarship on Minority Women into Health, Physical Education, and Dance

Carole M. Cascio

As a dance and nutrition instructor participating in seminars and conferences sponsored by the Curriculum Mainstreaming and Teaching Initiative, I began to see that I needed to become familiar with feminist thought, concepts of beauty, and the thinking and ideas of African-American feminists. I became interested in various forms of expression in addition to movement and dance, and then decided to include resources in the arts, literature, film, and poetry in my reconceptualizing of the dance curriculum. Much of my energy was directed toward gaining enough information and the awareness needed to formulate diverse approaches to my task. Discovery of journals such as *Signs* helped me identify sources for future reading.

Participation in the project also brought to my attention the ways in which race, class, and gender function in my classes. I have therefore made a concerted effort to identify opportunities that provide diversity and individuation to women in my classes. In Basic Nutrition, for example, I have provided food examples which are expressive of the races and ethnicity represented in my class. At one time, I had students who were Nigerian, Bajan, Asian-American, and French. I invited each student to speak about food choices, preparations, and factors that control access to food in their cultures. As a result, students were eager to share and became more active and invested in the class. The experience was especially satisfying, since their own diets proved to be generally more nutritious than most of the typical, fast-food-centered diets of the other students. The experience made clear the ways in which economics and culture change lifestyles and affect health through patterns and habits of eating.

After I attended the University of Delaware Women's Studies Conference, the idea of identity became still more interesting to me. There I heard a panel on food preparation and the preservation of cultural identity, which led to my including the topic in my class. The use of food as an expression of self and culture led to such lively

discussions and interesting discoveries of socially and culturally determined attitudes, that these topics and activities will continue to be
part of my course outline in the future.

I also wanted to explore the role of the body in self-perception, so
I presented a movement workshop for students in a Psychology of
Women class. After providing experiences to create an appropriate
atmosphere and to bring to the students awareness of their bodies, I
led a series of directed improvisations which allowed the students
access to internal initiations of posture and gesture. I also encouraged them to look for mergers in movement patterns which would
integrate and give dimension to their actions. Students explored how
to become known to themselves by activating weight through motion.
In addition, I asked students to bring in a picture of a person they
would like to *look* like and one of a person they would like to *be* like.
Brief discussion led me to understand that this idea of outer/inner
reflection was a difficult concept to acknowledge and that issues of
external beauty constitute a painful reality for many students.
Students' papers reacting to these experiences provided insights into
the ways in which self-consciously developed thought movement is
valuable to the formation of self-concept and self-esteem.

As chairperson of the Dance Department and as a project participant, I have reviewed the department's courses and curriculum and
subsequently made certain decisions. The dance history course will
be revised to reflect more accurately and adequately African-
American influences and works; and the functions of gender, race,
and class will be integrated more fully into the curriculum. In addition, the existing Folk and Ballroom Dance course content will be
revised to more adequately contextualize race, class, gender, religion,
and ethnicity, as expressed by the forms and styles of the dances
performed. I have recommended the following new courses for
inclusion in our offerings: "African-American Ethnic Dance" and
"Dance: An Artifact of Culture," in which dance will be explored as
an expression of race, class, gender, religion, art, and ethnicity.

In addition, I have asked faculty to consider more fully their
choice of music and movement vocabularies in order to represent
cultural differences of their students. Workshops have been planned
to design creative activities and pedagogy which may allow more
access to and identification with the course materials for all students
in our classes. And finally, I have encouraged faculty to design more
opportunities for individuation in their classes. Although certain
techniques are driven by particular styles and forms, students need to
find and define themselves within the content of courses.

As a member of the Health, Physical Education and Dance Division and as a result of participation in this project, I plan to recommend reviews of the ways in which the content of all the division's courses are taught with respect to gender and race. For example, we may not be considering carefully enough the potential for negative impact on the individuals in our classes when we present issues of obesity, fitness, and health. The emphasis on body weight seems gender-biased against females. Courses such as "Slimnastics" and the emphasis on body composition seem to promote "weightism." Furthermore, consideration needs to be given to the manner in which co-educational movement activities are presented and organized in order to avoid the appearance of male superiority. In addition, data and the content of health-related courses need to be evaluated so that they include the concerns of all minority students.

As a result of my participation in this project, I have now developed a vocabulary that demonstrates feminist thought. My library has expanded to include authors who are women of color and my car's cassette tape player reflects the voices of minority women. I realize that, until recently, I knew little about the quality of life of women who are not white. I recognize the existence of weightism, ageism, sexism, and racism. I was always interested; now I am beginning to recognize the extent of my desire and need to know more.

See *"Resources: Bibliographies" in this issue for an annotated bibliography, "Minority Women and the Dance Curriculum."*

*As chair of the dance department at Essex Community College in Baltimore, Maryland, **Carole M. Cascio** developed these ideas and materials through her participation in the Ford Foundation Grant to Integrate the Scholarship on Minority Women into the Curriculum. Although she retired from teaching in 1996, she continues to explore the way in which diversity and pluralism can be infused into the curriculum. She is also a member of the grant team of the College in the American Commitments Project, sponsored by the Association of American Colleges and Universities.*

Achieving Gender Equity in Science Education

Wendy Eisner

Science has traditionally been a predominantly white, middle-class male profession, but a turning point may be near. Currently, there is a shortage of American scientists and, at the same time, an increasing number of female students in higher education. Therefore it would be beneficial to invite women into the field of science, both to meet the demand for scientists and to enrich the content of science. Sue Rosser claims, "As more women and people from differing races, classes, and ethnic backgrounds become scientists, the science they evolve is likely to reflect their rich diversity of perspective" (Rosser, 1990, p. 111).

Evidence shows men have slightly better cognitive skills (mental rotation, disembedding figures, and field independence) than women and that, among adolescents, males have higher self-esteem and more interest in science than do females. There is also evidence supporting sexually differentiated brains at birth, partially due to hormonal activity, but further studies show the human brain is also open to modification by experience. For science educators, the question arises: What experiences will increase the probability that females will be motivated, confident, and competent with respect to science?

In order for change to take place regarding women in science, deep-seated attitudes toward women pervasive throughout American culture need to change. The belief that, while generally physically, emotionally, socially, and/or cognitively different from some men, women are worth *as much as* men must replace the belief that women are worth *less than* men. Because science is socially constructed, and "science reflects the bias of the powerful within the society" (Hubbard, 1983, cited in Rosser, 1990, p. 28), the attitudes, actions, and priorities of lawmakers regarding the equality of women need to change. In this regard, government needs to fund more female-friendly science research projects (e.g., with constructive social benefits in health, education, and welfare areas) and to fund childcare and paid parental-leave programs to help resolve the career vs. family conflict that contributes to the attrition rate of women in science, especially at the undergraduate level.

In the home, parents can encourage infants and children to play with gender-neutral toys. Parental attitudes, expectations, and behavior can also change to reflect the belief that their daughters are worth as much as their sons. It is important that parents effectively communicate that belief to their daughters, and that they believe that their daughters are as competent in science/math abilities as are their sons. Overall, parents must pay attention to their daughters, and support assertiveness and independence in their daughters' thinking and behavior.

In the schools, at all grade levels, recruitment efforts can be geared to increase female enrollment in science/math courses. Female participation in after-school and/or summer extracurricular and enrichment science/math programs should be promoted. Schools can make science/math careers attractive both by emphasizing that such careers enable women to influence social effects of scientific research, and by explaining that employment in the sciences earns relatively high salaries. Teachers should discuss stereotypes of the physical scientist as male and impersonal, and encourage female-friendly attitudes by including female scientists as role models. They can also provide science mentors who will encourage female students to become scientists.

In the areas of instruction, pedagogy, and classroom atmosphere, teachers' attitudes and expectations must change so that they value their female students as much as they do their male students, believe their female students are as competent as the males, and encourage females to take academic risks as well as to accept responsibility for their academic successes. Science and math teachers should be trained to communicate both verbally and nonverbally in a gender-neutral manner and to treat female students as competent and able to succeed in the field. Faculty can also provide a meaningful context for a given topic, showing its use in real life and its relationship to other topics. Presenting the material with enthusiasm, in comprehensible terminology, and with the use of personally meaningful examples so that it comes alive and is accessible and engaging to the students are necessary steps toward gender-neutral teaching. Administering untimed tests (the Mills College model cited in Rosser, 1990, p. 69) and contextualizing questions about a given concept in relation to other ideas are also female-friendly practices.

Perceptions that women students are less assertive or active in science and math classrooms can be addressed by training teachers to call on female students as often as they do male students; to give females as detailed and constructive feedback as they give males; to comment on the academic progress of their female students; to support independent problem solving by females; and to set up small, noncompetitive study groups/lab teams that are either single-sex or coed with at least two females in each group.

In science laboratory exercises, instructors can expand the kinds of observations beyond those traditionally done in scientific research (e.g., to study female-female interactions in a given species). They can undertake experiments related to problems of social concern rather than to those of the military. They can formulate hypotheses and design experiments using gender as a variable. They can include females as experimental subjects, explain the contexts of lab exercises, and use gender-neutral language when interpreting the data (Rosser, 1990, chap. 5). Female students should be given the opportunity to develop science-related cognitive skills that have been shown to be problematic for them: spatial visualization, including graphing; numerical problem solving and applications; logical reasoning; and scientific investigation (Skolnick et al, 1982, in Rosser, 1990, p.74). To revise the science education course content and curriculum, instructors should use a phase model (See, in this volume, Shirley C. Parry, "Feminist Pedagogy") to incorporate scholarship on women's contributions into one's discipline and women's experiences into one's course syllabus. Texts need be chosen that use gender-neutral language and that include female achievements, roles, and experiences in both the text and illustrations.

Two-year colleges have a special role to play in community outreach. Several have bridge programs with county high schools, enabling high school students to take courses at the colleges. These programs could be used to invite women to science/math courses. Another outreach activity could involve running workshops for both pre-college classroom teachers and administrators that show how to make science/math instruction female-friendly for nine- to eighteen-year-olds. Colleges could invite parents through local PTAs to hear a guest speaker or a panel of speakers discuss ways to effect gender equity in the home and school. Math/science departments could generate lists of local female scientists, including those at the colleges, who would be willing to give female students tours of their labs and to advise them regarding careers in science.

College activities could include producing and distributing to science/math faculty booklets containing key articles and suggested readings on gender equity in science education and curriculum transformation. Outreach across the disciplines could be fostered by meeting with humanities and social science faculty to discuss effective ways of educating women applicable across the curriculum (e.g., Belenky et al., 1988). It is important for faculty to discuss ways of initiating instructional and curricular reform in their classrooms in addition to those of science/math. A mentoring program for female students in the science/math departments would assure that students interested in and performing well in science/math would be assigned advisers for their entire college career. This one-to-one interaction between a student and an individual in the field who shows genuine concern for her career direction has been shown to affect positively women's decisions to enter science. For colleges like Nassau Community College, which has implemented a community learning program, communities and/or interdisciplinary courses enabling students to appreciate connections between science/math and other disciplines would also do much to open the path towards science careers to women.

WORKS CITED

Belenky, Mary F., et al. *Women's Ways of Knowing.* New York: Basic Books, 1988.
Rosser, Sue. *Female Friendly Science.* New York: Teachers College Press, 1990.

Wendy Eisner, *assistant professor of psychology at Nassau Community College, participated in the 1994 Ford Foundation program entitled "Examining Gender in Math, Science, and Technology." She received her doctorate in biopsychology from the City University of New York in 1987; her research interests concern the neural basis of visual preferences, and she is currently coediting an anthology,* Pathways to the Self, *for the introductory psychology course at the community college level.*

Transforming Required English Composition

Suzanne S. Liggett

Since 1979 I have taught English 102 every semester at Montgomery College, sometimes as many as three sections per semester. English 102, a second-level freshman composition course and a general education requirement for graduation in most curricula, emphasizes library research techniques, including note taking and documentation methods; reporting on, interpreting, analyzing and evaluating source material; the study of inductive and deductive logic; and the writing and analysis of reasoned arguments.

For the past decade, I have assigned my students to research and write their major paper on the "American Frontier: The Pioneer Spirit in American History and Letters." For topics, students could choose from many places and periods. Chronologically, the first period began in 1607 and the final one ended in 1905, when the last land run was held in the Oklahoma Indian territory. Geographically, they could move from the eastern shore to the far west, from the northern borders to the south—so long as they dealt with the locality during the time it was a frontier. Topics could include popular culture personages of the frontier past such as Jesse James, Butch Cassidy, and Calamity Jane, lesser-known figures such as Belle Starr, John Charles Fremont, and Aida Jenkins, and writers, painters, and early photographers. Or they could cover experiences unique to pioneering events—crossing the country in wagons, hostage situations between pioneers and Native Americans (the captivity narrative genre unique to American letters), the immigrant experience, military episodes in Indian Wars, political decisions, law and order issues, and so on.

Traditionally, I used the first three weeks to focus on the background to this research. I presented the Frederick Jackson Turner

A slightly different version of this essay appears in *Community College Guide to Curriculum Change*, edited by Elaine Hedges, Myrna Goldenberg, and Sara Coulter (Baltimore, MD: Towson State University/Maryland Community College Project). Copyright © 1990 by Elaine Hedges, Myrna Goldenberg, and Sara Coulter. Reprinted by permission.

theory that the winning of the West was the central forming experience for the national character. The class discussed how the emigra-
tion to the U.S. of peoples from all over the world, especially in the
nineteenth century, reshaped not only this country but central and
western Europe.

To contextualize this assignment for individuals, we discussed the
students' majors and tried to find topics related to their fields of
study. Students then received their first assignment for the course, a
library search which would introduce them to reference sources on
many frontier topics. A term paper workshop followed, in which we
studied a polished model and discussed citations, and so on. Students
were also responsible, within the first six weeks, for announcing their
topics, providing a preliminary bibliography, doing independent
readings, and creating an articulate thesis and strategy for their
papers. All in all, at the time I was pleased with both the topic—its
contribution to general education, and the rigor of the task—and
with the course organization—the search assignment and the steps I
had set up to monitor individual writing projects.

After the first three weeks of class, we would leave the research
focus and commence a study of general semantics (using Hayakawa's
Language in Thought and Action) as a preface to reasoned argument.
General semantics invariably took more class time to cover than had
been calculated, since students needed to experience, understand,
and behave as if they understood an enormous paradigm shift: sepa-
rating the symbolic world of language, verbal and nonverbal, from
the phenomenal world of non-language events. Hence, at the end of
the semester we were usually rushing to fit in the reasoned argument
section of the course, consisting of some systematic coverage of
inductive and deductive reasoning. Major papers in the course
included: a library search assignment of 1000–1250 words, with citations and works cited; a formal summary of chapter 2 from *Language
in Thought and Action*, 4th ed.; an analysis/general semantics essay of
750 words, with citations based on class reading assignments; an argument analysis of 500–750 words, written in class based on a reading
from the argument analysis reader; a general semantics essay examination; and a research paper/reasoned argument of at least 2000
words in length.

After I had developed the course along these lines, which took
about five semesters, I proceeded to teach the course uncritically
until 1989 when I began the FIPSE curriculum transformation project work. At that time, I was already beginning to be vaguely dissat-
isfied with the topic of the frontier, not so much because we couldn't

find material on women and minority men in the seventeenth, eighteenth, and nineteenth centuries, since materials published especially on women increased exponentially during the years I taught the course, but because of the reactions to the topic from African-American students and students not born in the U.S. African-American students were faced with a shortage of material that focused on African Americans on the frontier; students born in other countries, whose population at my college has increased each year, believed that, because they were not native to this country, they could not find enough information about even a limited topic to write on it with much insight.

I had joined the curriculum transformation project intending to assemble a textbook of readings—journals as well as fiction and poetry selections—consisting of authors exploring the frontier experience from more personal perspectives. I also wanted to include readings about experiences of Native Americans, and Africans, Europeans, Asians, and others coming to the U.S. I had hoped that such a book would encourage students to explore different kinds of materials within the topic area and, ultimately, to feel their own life experiences were relevant to the course.

My initial reaction to the enormous amount of reading assigned by the project coordinators was frustration and impatience: I wanted to get on with my own work. The flow of material continued, however, and even though I made minor additions and revisions to my syllabus for the Fall of 1989, by that time I was no nearer my goal of assembling a reader than when I had entered the project.

Not until I began writing the last journal of 1989 (the journal writing that faculty in the project were asked to do was another of my frustrations) did I finally allow myself to express all of the misgivings I had been accumulating about this English 102 fortress I had built for myself and taken a fair amount of pride in. For a number of reasons, I had been resisting any careful course scrutiny. Not only had I put a large personal investment of time in the course development, but I had also been invited into the project on the promise of supplementing the course with a collection of readings: So someone else was investing time and money in the course as well!

But once I had really examined the course and located its fundamental weaknesses, I knew I wanted to change the "issues" content. The stack of project articles that I had been cursing included course syllabi transformed by other instructors as well as discussions of course design and workability. These were helpful, although they didn't completely address the problems I was confronting. While on break and away from fellow project members, I felt at liberty to transform my course in the particular ways I felt necessary.

I began by examining the problems of my course. First, the essential elements of the course were partitioned, not integrated; after being introduced, the research topic was discussed only privately with each student on paper or in my office. Although my students' historical knowledge was sketchy and uneven, no historical issues were raised later in class or tested according to the techniques of analysis or evaluation which we were learning in the argument segment. Many general principles of semantics trickled down into the analysis of persuasion and argument, but the readings for the segment on argument, introducing yet another new issue, required another mental re-orientation.

Second, African-American students and foreign-born students had difficulty relating even to the issues raised in *Male/Female Roles: Opposing Viewpoints Series,* which I had added for the autumn of 1989. Why? These issues were explored from the point of view of a white American population and did not deal with black feminist perspectives at all. The foreign-born students, most of whose cultures operate under different gender role constructs, felt excluded both from the class discussions and also from the arguments about gender and sex made by the contributing authors. Problems in finding relevant research topics for the African-American and foreign-born students became acute and added layers of anxiety to their research projects that white, U.S.-born students did not have to contend with.

Having identified these misgivings, I realized how deep were the problems of integrating the current course materials and how ill-suited was the research topic for students not well-schooled in American history and American culture. I knew I wanted to change the topic matter of the course. English 102 is the kind of writing course that requires teaching certain skills and content in matters of research, argumentation, and persuasion, yet allows each instructor to choose the intellectual matter on which to develop and practice these skills.

Two priorities governed my consideration of a new topic. First, the topic had to be accessible to every conceivable English 102 student. Second, the topic had to meet the requirements set up by the department for English 102—research and documentation, reasoned argument, and persuasion analysis and evaluation. When events beginning in November 1989 riveted everyone's attention toward Eastern Europe, and when Washington's political pundits, conservative and liberal alike, waxed on about how freedom and justice were finally to make a home in the Eastern bloc countries, I knew I had found the intellectual territory for a new English 102 research topic and the intellectual matter for in-class discussion of general semantic issues, reasoned argument, and persuasion analysis and evaluation.

The syllabus assignments themselves do not reflect the depth of change that has resulted from this shift in the research topic and the incorporation of the same topic into the teaching of general semantics and reasoned argument. However, the revised English 102 syllabus, which I ran in 1990 as a pilot, did begin to show the possibilities for a total class ecology. By this I mean that I am trying to make of the class an ecosystem in which everything supports and reinforces everything else, skills and content always working in an integrated way. Fortunately, the paper assignments can remain essentially the same in type and number, with one exception. Assignments #1 and #2 will be reversed so that students can receive instruction in formal summary writing before the library search assignment. The library search (now #2) will integrate ten individual writing and critical thinking tasks along with the search questions.

Below is one writing assignment and samples of course elements that can be integrated within it:

Research Assignment 1. Journalists and social critics have been talking throughout the 1980s of two serious social conditions: the "feminization of poverty in America" and the black male as "an endangered species" in American society. Choose one of these conditions and locate at least three articles in newspapers or journals or reports which would either explain such an idea or support its credibility.

Writing Task: Turn one of the two quoted phrases above into a declarative claim and, using the source material, support or deny the claim in a short argument (approximately 150 words).

Research Assignment 2. Identify the novel you plan to read as a companion to your research project. Justify your choice by locating at least two reviews of the book in which literary critics discuss the insights and the value of your author's work.

Writing Task: Write a paragraph of justification or recommendation for the novel of your choice, using the critics' responses as well as your own as support.

Research Assignment 3. What percentage of the male population of Montgomery County is African American? What percentage of the population of Rockville is women?

Writing Task: Pretend that you are on the County Council. Using either one of these statistics as one of your several reasons, make an actuative claim and argue for revised county policy or planning for the future.

My hope, with this transformed course, is that issues of social, political, and economic justice in America will appeal at some level and in some guise (historical? legal? literary? philosophic? artistic? psychological?) to every student. Toward this end, I also revised and added to a packet of materials which a colleague and I originally assembled in the summer of 1989 and first used in the Fall 1989 semester as a basic text. The first half of the packet contains materials for teaching reasoned argument, including: 1) the language of fact, inference, and judgment; 2) making and recognizing assumptions; 3) the scope and structure of argument; 4) making claims and organizing evidence; 5) modes of reasoning; and 6) evaluating arguments. The second half contains 48 articles, arranged in four sections, directly related to the research topic, which is now called "The Coming of Freedom in and to America." The sections are: 1) advertising claims and imagery; 2) male and female roles in American life; 3) the legal status of women and people of color in America; and 4) the immigrant experience. These sections include articles on cultural and racial stereotypes and their commercial and political uses; sex and gender clarifications and issues; an historical overview including legal documents on the status of women and people of color in the U.S.; immigration issues, arguments, and experiences. These are our "seed" articles for other writing assignments and for the study of argument and general semantics. Equally important, these articles contain useful bibliographies and raise issues which might very well launch students into their research "orbit."

On the other hand, I may be the one launched into orbit! Although at this writing it is too early in the semester to predict any outcomes, it is somewhat ironic that my only English 102 class this term contains only white Americans, and that over 60 percent of them are male. If this transformed course works with this population, it will work with any at Montgomery College.

Suzanne S. Liggett, *professor of English at Montgomery Community College in Rockville, Maryland, continues to revise the curriculum for her English courses. Currently her classes are studying the present-day influence of language, images, and symbols as they are used by mass media in the formation of popular culture.*

Changing Style, Changing Subject: The Required Composition Course

Dianne Ganz Scheper

I'd like to preface my summary of curricular changes with a line from one of my favorite Wallace Stevens' poems: "Every change in style is a change in subject." Such an insight is creatively ambiguous since "subject" here can mean both "person" and "subject matter." In this double sense, Stevens' poem helps locate the dynamic of change that has transformed my teaching as a result of the FIPSE curriculum project: What I gained from my FIPSE experience is something like a new style of thinking—a change in perception that governs the way I approach, appreciate, and evaluate texts of all kinds, not only written texts, but social and cultural events as texts as well.

"Epistemological shift" might be too grandiose a term to describe this change in perspective, and yet, in a modest way, there has been a real shift in my interpretive position, and as a result I made changes in the structure and subject matter of my courses beyond what I had anticipated at the outset of the project. I introduced a new research topic in our advanced composition class, changed the selection of readings in my World Literature class, and realigned the emphasis in the honors course, "Contemporary Modes in Western Spirituality." Let me summarize these latter two shifts briefly before giving a more comprehensive description of the changes made in my advanced composition class.

The first changes that I made in World Literature were clearly "stage one" changes, simply adding works by and about women. We read Flaubert's *Madame Bovary,* Chopin's *The Awakening,* and Ibsen's *The Doll House,* and students wrote personal essays on the ways in which, respectively, Emma, Edna, and Nora defined their roles as women. Hardly a challenge to the canon! Yet I had never before

A slightly different version of this essay appears in *Community College Guide to Curriculum Change,* edited by Elaine Hedges, Myrna Goldenberg, and Sara Coulter (Baltimore, MD: Towson State University/Maryland Community College Project). Copyright © 1990 by Elaine Hedges, Myrna Goldenberg, and Sara Coulter. Reprinted by permission.

taught *The Awakening,* and I admit to having never made gender issues a central topic for class discussion or student papers. Then in the fall of 1989, I entered the second phase of curriculum change, when I made gender, class, and racial issues part of the critical evaluation of such texts as Pope's "Essay on Man," Dostoevsky's *Notes from Underground,* Freud's *Civilization and its Discontents* and Conrad's *Heart of Darkness.* More recently, I have also added Anita Desai's *Clear Light of Day* and Toni Morrison's *The Bluest Eye* to our readings. My intention is to look at these two texts alongside Kafka's *Metamorphosis* to compare the way three writers from different times and cultures explore the drama of family disintegration, and to study as well how each writer deals with issues of individual alienation, dysfunctional families, and the impact on families of changing social conditions.

I revised the honors course, "Contemporary Modes of Western Spirituality," using new insights gained from my reading during the year in the project. Originally, I had designed the course as an examination of four contemporary modes of Western spirituality that have arisen in response to the social changes and global dangers of the twentieth century: creation spirituality, liberation spirituality, women's spirituality, and the Buddhist movement in the West. I retained this structure, but what I discovered in my reading is that a nexus of shared values connects all of these spiritualities. All four are trying to transcend dualistic thinking, to heal the division between body and mind, person and social "place;" to liberate people from oppressive ideas and conditions, and to promote a philosophy of interdependence. It's very exciting to see the interrelatedness of creation, Buddhist, liberationist and feminist spiritualities, and I will include in the readings at least one text, perhaps Joanna Macy's *Thinking like a Mountain,* that makes a point of this interconnectedness.

Second, as a result of my reading in feminist spirituality, I have broken away from the exclusive "spiritual giants" model used in most classes in western spirituality (at least in the classes I have taken and/or heard about). Not only does the "giants" model include very few women, it also perpetuates a conception of spirituality that I now believe faulty: the spiritual quest as the solitary, mystical "flight of the alone to the alone." Carol Ochs, in *Women and Spirituality,* goes to the heart of the matter when she suggests that most models of traditional spirituality are extensions of male-centered developmental models which emphasize individuation and "coming into selfhood" rather than relationship and nurturing, or "overcoming separation." Ochs points out that, although there have been female mystics in the Western tradition, she was not able to find even one spiritual text written from the perspective of a happily married woman! Ochs redefines spirituality as a "process of coming into relationship with reality," emphasizing that it is a way of being and doing as well as knowing, and that it is a process that is active, participatory, and transformative. Feminists suggest a model that replaces or at least supplements "otherworldliness" with experiences that traditional writers on spirituality have chosen to neglect: love, joy, birth, nurturance. In feminist perspectives, the focus shifts from idealizing the extraordinary to valuing the ordinary, paying close attention to present circumstances as material for spiritual growth.

In line with this feminist shift, I have adopted as a supplementary text in the honors course a writing manual called *Writing Down the Bones,* by Natalie Goldberg, a poet and practicing Buddhist. Her manual recommends keeping a journal as a spiritual practice, a daily discipline in keeping still for a few minutes, freeing ourselves from distractions, and paying the sort of close attention that develops insight into our ordinary experience. To regard journal writing as a form of spiritual process solves a dilemma for me. It is a hermeneutical axiom that at least some slight acquaintance with spiritual practice is a necessary grounding for the understanding of spiritual texts. Unlike denominational forms of spiritual practice, journal writing is entirely appropriate to an academic setting. Thus, I recommend that students use Goldberg's manual to guide their journal writing during the semester, and that they regard their journal writing as a modest sort of spiritual discipline that will help provide a grounding context for their understanding of the spiritual texts we examine in class.

The most extensive curricular changes have been made in my advanced composition course, which stresses the study of semantics, critical thinking, and research techniques. The "magnum opus" of the course is the student research paper. Although some teachers consider the research project a strictly individual, independent student endeavor and thus give students *carte blanche* in choosing research topics, others choose a broad research topic for the class as a whole and ask students to address this common topic from variously chosen individual perspectives. Some research topics that have been used by teachers in the past include the American frontier, American literary naturalism, fairy tales, and the American work ethic. I have found most successful those research topics that can be explored using the critical tools that students develop during a study of semantics, especially their new understanding of how language constructs our personal and social realities.

When I entered the project, I was using the somewhat amorphous research topic, "American Values." Students read a text called *American Values* (from the Greenhaven Press *Opposing Viewpoints* series) as a basis for class discussion on social, religious, and business values, and then chose individual issues to explore further in a research paper. After the first semester in the project, I realized that some of the project readings might be adapted to the design and aim of the composition course. During the summer I gathered together a series of essays, stories, articles and poems to use as a classroom text. I named this packet PR/ISM because the readings explored the ways in which hidden ideologies—"isms" about gender, class, race, and even species—act as "prisms," shaping our views of the world and our behavior. The following excerpt from my introductory syllabus explains how these readings were to function as a basis for class discussion and as a sort of "starter pack" for student research.

> To My Students: Welcome to what I trust will be a rewarding semester of shared study. Our work is organized around three areas of investigation. First, we will focus on general semantics, the study of the relationship between language, thought, and action. Second, we will concentrate on the highly organized language of reasoned discourse, which forms the foundation of critical thinking. Third, we will share background readings that will help us to understand the formative influence of hidden assumptions about human nature, race and gender roles. Specifically we will be looking at three ideologies, three "isms": racism, sexism, and what might be called "speciesism"—the assumption that human beings are the only really valuable form of life on the planet. In each case we will examine how the "ism" acts as a "prism," shaping our view of the world and structuring our social reality. From these discussions, students will select particular perspectives to explore further in their research papers.

I began using PR/ISM for the first time during the fall 1989 semester, not at all sure that it was a smart idea to plunge so deeply and all at once into the murky waters of sexism, racism, and "speciesism." I especially had trepidations about addressing matters of gender, class and race, on a weekly basis, in the classroom discussion. However, my worst fears—of angry insurrection, unmanageable class discussions, students' unwillingness to think critically about emotionally loaded issues—never materialized. At the same time, neither did my greatest hopes that some students would experience the same intellectual paradigm shift that I had experienced. Nevertheless, students did seem to acquire a greater sensitivity and sophistication in thinking about issues of race, gender, class and species, and they were very positive about the value of class discussions and their research endeavors.

I was especially pleased by the way the PR/ISM readings dovetailed with our studies in semantics and critical thinking. For example, as students were learning to distinguish among fact, inference, and judgment, they were also trying to distinguish between the biological and cultural determinants that create male and female roles. As they were learning to identify definitional and descriptive assumptions, they were also reading Friedan and Schlafly on the "nature" and role of women, and Margaret Andersen on sex and gender in human culture. They read Hayakawa on "Language as a Classification System" while also reading Robert Moore on "Racist Stereotyping in the English Language." They learned to recognize value assumptions and to locate a priori premises while reading an excerpt from Carol Gilligan's *In a Different Voice* and Duncan Taylor's "Nature as a Mirror of Changing Human Values." They practiced analyzing argumentative claims and evidence while reading de Gobineau, Hitler, and Elijah Muhammed on racial superiority. And along with induction and deduction, they examined "ecological thinking" as a possible mode of reasoning.

In about the fourth week of class students chose individual research topics in one of the three areas (sexism, racism and speciesism), and proceeded to meet throughout the term in seminar groups with others working in the same general subject area. Among the many rich and informative papers that emerged were a study of Georgia O'Keeffe's experience as a "woman" artist, an investigation of female roles in Greek mythology, a study of Richard Wright's *Native Son*, an evaluation of Dian Fossey's life and work, and a critique of the Indian Removal Act of 1830.

I subsequently revised the student packet, deleting some readings and adding others. I modified the list of suggested research paper proposals, narrowing the range of suggestions so as not to overwhelm students with possibilities (a mistake I had made previously) and to encourage them to focus earlier on a specific topic. I will undoubtedly make further changes to fine tune the material and the approach, but I am happily persuaded that an advanced composition course is an ideal forum for the study of gender, class, and racial issues. Furthermore, students testified in their course evaluations that they appreciated spending their energies investigating matters that they recognized as being relevant not only to their personal and social lives, but also to our shared planetary future.

Dianne Ganz Scheper *is professor of English composition and literature at Montgomery College, Rockville, Maryland. She reviews books about women and nature for* Belle Lettres *and is completing a dissertation on Annie Dillard.*

Writing the Self in a Changing World

Liza Fiol-Matta

One of the most powerful types of writing we can elicit from students in a first-year composition class is the autobiographical essay that analyzes the self in relation to the world in which we live. Despite rumblings by back-to-basics adherents, self-reflective writing need not be solipsistic nor lacking in academic rigor. Certainly, the personal essay has long been a rhetorical form to frame both insight and knowledge. Writing in the first-person about their lives in family and community, or about their understanding of local and/or global debates, allows students to examine prejudices and assumptions, address gaps of knowledge, and rehearse their public voices. In the assignments which I detail here I have attempted to integrate critical and creative thinking, and to demonstrate the importance of developing a complex notion of "self"—one which acknowledges the ways that history, politics, economics, and other institutions and systems work in our individual lives.

The power of Margaret Walker's essay, "On Being Female, Black, and Free," stems from her incisive ability to generalize about her individual experience, weaving her personal narrative through a scathing indictment first of American, then of world-wide, white male-dominated society. When teaching this essay, it is important to explain and discuss the device of generalizing from private experience as a tool for establishing one's right to comment on broader issues. When Walker's essay is compared to the more traditional "Once More to the Lake," by E. B. White, Walker's different use of the generalizing device is apparent. Students are quick to point out that the difference lies in the politicizing nature of Walker's insight into her life and life choices. This aspect of her essay illustrates forcefully the political reality of personal experience. Walker is not offering cliches or facile observations of black women's struggle in society, nor of women in general, but uniquely personal insights stemming from her private experience.

When teaching this essay, the instructor may find that among the questions students raise is the obvious but difficult one centering on

Walker's concept of freedom. Students have perceived what they feel are contradictions in her analysis. How can she feel free in the society that she describes? How is she free within the personal life she has chosen, unable because of family and work commitments to write when and where she pleases? An interesting idea that has come up in classroom discussions of this essay concerns the opening passage where she says of her birth certificate, "I have no wish to change it from being female, black and free." What, students ask, is freedom in this context? When one is tied to a place and conditions of birth that negate certain freedoms (as she illustrates from her own life and in her examples of world-wide struggles and internal strife), how can one restate a birth certificate in this manner? Her concept of freedom as a "philosophical state of mind and existence" is also debatable. Can one be truly free only in the mind? Isn't that a cop-out? How can it be a satisfactory existence? Drawing students through Walker's growing awareness of the various types of discrimination that have affected her helps clarify how she became an agent of change in her life. Furthermore, as she names and defines those values that shape her as an individual (her religion, her concept of motherhood) the seeming contradictions both of her personal choices ("Why opt for a life that takes time and energy away from what you really want to do? Are our life choices as cut-and-dry as that?") and of her definition of freedom begin to be resolved.

After students ask themselves how truly free Margaret Walker is, the extended question becomes, how truly free is anyone who must meet the exigencies of a complex structured society where most people are supposed to "know their place," whether because of gender, race, class or ethnic origin, or simply as a consequence of growing up in a family less supportive than Walker's? Experientially centered discussion, then, raises questions of definitions of personal freedom, relative freedom, and political freedom in a format accessible and not intimidating for students. For example, fruitful discussions come from asking: What do you feel makes Walker free? That she is a writer? a woman? black? Often the answer has come from the conclusion that what makes her free is her own strength and conviction of worth, her sense of self.

The other concept that Walker discusses is that of the multiple expectations and duties of women's lives. Specifically, class discussion can revolve around her enumeration of the various traditionally ascribed female tasks that she has had to take on, and, moreover, her obvious success both in these and in her teaching and writing. The idea of the superwoman is a challenging one. First, Walker debunks the myth of glamour and financial success as the birthright of the writer. She points out that she chose not to circumvent marriage and work, but that work and family have dictated how and when she can write. Could Walker, or any woman, have been successful were she not seemingly a superwoman? Yet, she never refers to herself as one. Her references to feminine principles are those of creation, reproduction, and healing. She is neither bitter nor regretful and, when she is angry, hers is not an idle, wasteful anger. In fact, her anger is the very real and universal anger that comes from her perception of the historical process at work in the "sexist, racist, violent and most materialistic society," the United States. Her anger is the political personal anger of one who knows that the "syndicated world system" can literally blow us to bits and make of us "anonymous dust and nonentity." It is in this context that she affirms that women writers write of the "human potential," and tap into the "annealing" power of women's spirit.

Teachers might want to point to specific elements of Walker's language and prose style. Walker uses straightforward prose, strong with conviction and unapologetic. A few of her sentences can be examined for her use of repetition and phrasal cadences. For example, "Always I am determined to overcome adversity, determined to win, determined to be me, myself at my best, always female, always black, and everlastingly free." The essay contains many of these eloquently moving, forceful sentences, and the effect of this style can be discussed. Similarly, the teacher can point out the firm voice that is heard throughout. The honesty of the sentiment and voice is "real," not only because a personal story weaves it together, but because the tone and style never falter. Discussions of rhetoric and style can also include the effectiveness of Walker's use of the personal narrative, how it works alongside a more generalized polemical commentary on society, and in what ways the narrative strengthens or detracts from her argument.

Finally, this essay has yielded memorable discussion and writing when read in conjunction with the last chapter of Richard Wright's autobiography, *Black Boy*, which has been given the title in at least one textbook of "The Library Card." Both the writing activities that follow can be adapted to include that reading as well.

Writing Activities

While any of the questions posed by the preceding example can result in appropriate essays, the following two topics have elicited particularly thoughtful writing from students:

1. *"Every day I have lived, however, I have discovered that the value system in which I was raised is of no value in the society in which I must live."*—*Margaret Walker.* Write a 500-word essay discussing all or some of the following: What were the values with which you were raised? How free or limited have these values (of your family, your generation, your religion, etc.) made you? Do you still live by these values? What changes or compromises in these values have you had to make in general or in any specific circumstances? Why? How has this affected you? (You might find you will want to limit the discussion to one or two of the most important or significant values that apply in these contexts.)

2. In this essay Margaret Walker shows that she is an intensely political person. Yet she begins by offering a personal narrative of her life, her education, and how she became a writer. Toward the end of the essay she divulges that she is writing this at the age of 63. From where you are now in age and experience, how do you see yourself and your life choices in relation to the society and world around you? Where are you heading and in response to what? Within the framework of this society, do you feel you will have the freedom to get to where you want to go? What changes, if any, do you think society will have to undergo for you to reach your goals? What changes will you have to undergo?

Poetry in the Composition Classroom

Using poetry in the freshman composition classroom is rare. Most textbooks are either guides explaining the composing process and its component stages, or they are readers and anthologies of prose models—essays or excerpts from longer pieces, usually nonfiction. Poetry is usually absent. However, poetry can offer structures and illustrations of concepts that are transferable to the prose-writing situation, while stimulating discussion and generating writing topics.

A useful essay which addresses the importance of poetry for voicing women's experiences is Audre Lorde's "Poetry is not a Luxury," (in *The Future of Difference,* Eisenstein and Jardine, eds. New Brunswick: Rutgers University Press, 1985, 125–27). In the poetry of "revelation or distillation of experience," Lorde says, women can "give name to the nameless so it can be thought." She rejects the male "I think therefore I am" for the female "I feel therefore I can be free." And, she states, "Poetry coins the language to express and charter this revolutionary awareness and demand the implementation of that freedom." Finally, she asserts that in expressing feelings distilled from experience, poetry makes real the possibility of change and action towards change, for "our poems . . . give us the strength and courage to see, to feel, to speak, and to dare."

What follows are two lessons using the poetry of the Puerto Rican poet Julia de Burgos (1914–1953) and the Iranian poet Forugh Farrokhzād (1935–1967). Both of these poets are presented in translation, but the focus of the discussion of these readings is not so much literary (which could raise thorny questions about translation) as the rendering of experience and insight. The first poem discussed illustrates the need for definition of self in individual-encoded terms. The second poem is appropriate for discussion about being a part of the larger political world around us.

The need to name, or encode, one's own world is an important issue in language and gender theory. In the writing classroom this issue is especially important since we are asking students to think through their experiences and draw on their lives to define themselves, to describe their worlds (both public and private), to take and defend a position on contemporary issues—in effect, to conceptualize in language and codes which more often fetter rather than free their attempts to transpose feelings, ideas, and perceptions into writing. This concept of encoding, or naming one's world, can become an intriguing lesson in the writing classroom, as words and definitions are the stuff of written expression.

One of the strongest statements made in Puerto Rican poetry of a woman rejecting societal restrictions of individual definitions of self is Julia de Burgos's "A Julia de Burgos" ("To Julia de Burgos"). Reading her cathartic rejection of the categories, or male-encoded registers, which traditionally define women is an appropriate way to introduce the concepts of definition of identity and self through poetry.[1]

De Burgos often struggles with issues of self-definition, seeing the process, as she states in one poem, as *"un juego de escondite con mi ser"* ("a game of hide-and-seek with my self"). In "A Julia de Burgos," she declares her independence from the external societal-(male)-defined trappings of womanhood. Instead of the rejected categories:

> cold doll of social prevarication
> honey of polite hypocrisies
> like your world, selfish
> the prim ladylike lady
> belong(ing) to your husband, to your master
> curl(ing) your hair, paint(ing) your face *[artificially]*

a housewife, resigned, submissive
ruled by the prejudices *[categories]* of men

De Burgos offers her own terms:

the living spark of human truth
baring my naked heart in all my poems *[painfully honest]*
risk(ing) everything to be what I am
I am life, strength, woman
belong(ing) to no one, or to everyone *[through poetry]*
hair curled by the wind, face painted by the sun
[like Quixote's horse running headlong] a runaway Rocinante
sniffing at horizons *[her own categories]*

This listing is not exhaustive, but it illustrates for students some problems in finding language adequate for the naming of experience. For example, in the Spanish original the line translated here as "the living spark of human truth" reads *"el viril destello de humana verdad."* The male-encoded word "viril" jumps out as contradictory in a feminist reading of the poem, as does the need to selflessly, painfully bare one's soul to be free from the hypocrisy forced on de Burgos by society. Yet here is a woman in the mid-twentieth century, from a culture that strictly defines women's lives, attempting to find liberation through language that redefines her self by exposing her inner and inward perceptions. Significantly, she offers no apologies for not conforming to the dominant view of woman. This poem illustrates perfectly Lorde's thesis that poetry is a place where women can first express the possibility of action, for it is true that de Burgos is still struggling with the fact that only in poetry can she fight against the categories that she consciously rejects.

For a successful lesson using de Burgos's poem, a writing assignment or class discussion should first introduce the concepts of dominant-encoded registers and definitions, thus addressing the issues of naming one's world in experiential terms. In this way, the exercise can allow students to explore their experiences and concepts of self in contexts that reflect what they truly know to be their realities.

In the writing activity that follows I leave open the question of rhetorical mode because an important part of understanding the functions of language and self-expression is the students' active participation in choosing a mode appropriate to their stories. This does not mean, however, leaving them out on a limb after making them climb the tree. Obviously, de Burgos explores her definition of self by contrasting what society expects from her (behavior, roles) with what she feels deeply to be her own reality. Discussion could take place to determine what expository mode or modes would be appropriate for this kind of analysis. Obvious possibilities include narration, description, comparison and contrast, and enumeration. One could also discuss how narrative and descriptive details might function in writing prose structurally similar to de Burgos's poem. Also, the function of a metaphor or symbol used in a prose piece could be discussed, for example, as a thematic thread running throughout the piece, or, as in the poem, as a concluding element.

Finally, Sandra María Esteves's bilingual poem "A Julia y a mi" ("To Julia and to Me")[2] makes an interesting companion reading to de Burgos's poem. (Using Esteves's poem will be more effective if there are Spanish-speaking students in the class, since roughly half of the poem is in Spanish.) The poem is of particular interest because it presents a reply to de Burgos from a Latina poet from New York who angrily rejects de Burgos's life and verse as suicidal and despairing. Esteves refers to the body of de Burgos's work and declares that *"te perdiste en palabras no en vida /* you let the dragon slay you." She concludes, *"a ti Julia, ya será tarde / pero a mi no, yo vivo / y grito si me duele la vida / . . .* my fist is my soul / it cuts into the blood of dragons /and marks time with the beat of an Afro-Cuban drum."[3] As a caveat to those unfamiliar with Puerto Rican poetry, many readers may feel they do not agree with Esteves's assessment of de Burgos's life and work, but that could add texture to the discussion. Students researching de Burgos's life and the circumstances of her death will shed light on Esteves's personalizing the poet's life. I have suggested "A Julia y a mi" not for its evaluation of de Burgos, but as an example of one woman's experiential declaration of a concept of Latina self in reply to another's.

Discussion Questions and Activities

1. Julia de Burgos names various ways in which she acts to conform to her society's concept of womanhood. What are these ways, and how do they differ from her internal perceptions of self?

2. In what ways are you expected to behave in your work, family, or social environment that you feel are different from who you *really* are?

3. Explore various ways you are categorized, as Julia de Burgos does in her poem. Which of these do you think are better defined as personality traits, and which could be thought of as culturally determined? Which of these categories do you reject, and with what parallel behavior, or concept of self, would you contrast it?

4. Julia de Burgos has a specific audience in mind. To whom is she addressing her poem? What is the significance of this choice? Why didn't she address the external parties (her husband, for example) who she feels are to blame for placing the roles upon her?

5. What is the allusion in the final stanza? How does that metaphor describe her concept of self? What metaphor or symbol would you choose to describe your relationship to the world around you?

Writing Activity

Choose an area of your life in which you feel you are called upon to act in a role that feels uncomfortable within your concept of who you are. It may be for, example, your role as parent, as worker, as student, as sibling, or as friend. Explore this role through writing, presenting both sides of the coin as de Burgos does in the reading. Try to include a generalizing symbol or metaphor that presents you as you see yourself.

• • •

The poem, "I Feel Sorry for the Garden," by the Iranian poet Forugh Farrokhzād[4] has been a successful vehicle in my classes for framing discussions of the concept of family and how the roles of different family members change as all grow older. Furthermore, besides being a poignant treatment of a daughter's and sister's perceptions of change among the values of the families in her neighborhood, caught as they are by the threat of impending war, it vividly illustrates how the spheres of one's private world and that of the outer world can inform each other.

When teaching this poem, one can point out how its structure has much in common with an expository essay. First, there is an introductory segment in which the poet presents the symbol of her family's past (the garden) and how it is now no longer cared for. The four segments that follow—father, mother, brother and sister—elaborate on the changes that each of these family members have gone through by focusing on the poet's observations of their lives now. The dissolution of the image of the happy unified family is symbolized in the change in their attitudes towards the garden:

> My father says, "My day is past
> . . . When I'm gone, what's it to me
> if the garden's there
> or ceases to be—"

. . .

My mother's whole life is a prayer rug
. . . looking for traces of sin
[she] thinks it's the curse of some hidden fault
that's blighted the garden

. . .

My brother calls the garden a graveyard
He laughs at the way the weeds have taken over

. . .

My sister, who used to be friends with the flowers,
. . . Whenever
she comes to see us
and her skirt brushes against the poverty of the garden
she bathes herself in eau de cologne

As they lead their lonely despairing adult lives, the garden no longer matters. Finally, she expands in the concluding segments on the idea that all the gardens around her are being transformed, quite literally, into bunkers ("our neighbors are all planting their gardens / with machine guns and mortars / in place of flowers"). She distills her personal vision in the midst of such collective despair: "I am frightened of a time that's lost its soul / . . . I'm as much alone / as a schoolgirl crazy about geometry / I think maybe the garden could be saved. . . ."

Though the speaker is alone in her conviction, she refuses to abandon the idea of peace, just as she alone refuses to abandon the garden. So, the poem moves from the speaker as a member of a particular family with its specific problems (and with their own specific garden to symbolize their increasing alienation) outward to the speaker as an observer/participant in a world going mad, with the garden becoming the collective symbol of a peaceful time forever lost (". . . slowly the garden's mind / grows empty /of memories of green"). Like the schoolgirl, crazy to be crazy about geometry in a society where technological and intellectual domains are still circumscribed by men, she is alone in the end. Even the schoolchildren "fill their school bags / with homemade bombs."

One of the writing issues to consider exploring here is that of point of view. The joining of the personal/private and the personal/observer (public) roles succeeds in Farrokhzād's poem because of the informing and organizing first-person point of view. Is the speaker/observer

an adult or a child? In what voice is she speaking? The speaker seems
to have been a mature witness to the time-wrought changes within
her family and to the garden, yet the voice is reminiscent of a child's.
What evidence is there that a child is speaking? One might suggest,
perhaps, a concern for the small things, the details, in the garden;
the innocence of believing in the garden; the references to the
schoolchildren and the schoolgirl. What is the contrary evidence?
One could name the poet's insights into the motivations of her family members, some of the vocabulary, and the rather adult-informed
sense of reality as the garden slowly dies. How does the point of view
illuminate the speaker's role in the poem? Students have pointed out
that insights of both the adult and the child are being drawn upon.
The teacher could suggest that students try to weave into their writing both stances, as an experiment. Another student comment has
suggested that perhaps children see far more profoundly than they
are given credit for and that indeed it is a child speaking but "with a
wisdom beyond her years."

While there is much to discuss in this poem, I have found three
general categories of writing activities in particular that can be developed from it. The first is the most personal, stemming from the following questions: As you have grown older, how would you describe
the relationships between your family members and you? Have the
roles that each had assumed over the years changed in any way?
When did you first notice a change in your perception of the family
structure? Has "growing up" affected your relationships with your sib-
lings? The teacher might remind students that, although this poem
depicts alienating factors, relationships can also change for the better. Students should be made aware that the poem's insights don't
have to dictate the tone or content of their essays.

The second writing activity for this reading focuses on the poem
itself. What are the types of alienation or apathy (or other attitudes
and experiences) that the characters in the poem experience?
Students have drawn from this question material for discussing, for
example, how work environments can set one up to experience the
kind of feelings the father has in the poem. His reasoning is that one
gives everything to a job for so long and retirement comes so late in
life that it is not enjoyed but produces the father's current attitude of
apathy: "I've carried my load, / and done what I had to do / . . . all I
want's my retirement check." The mother's religious fanaticism also
has been discussed as an alienating factor. The narrator's subsequent
feelings of isolation and alienation are described sharply. While she
is obviously in a personal and political situation that is very different

from that which we may experience in the United States, it is instructive to remind ourselves and our students that the speaker's situation is not uncommon; a great number of people throughout the world experience political fear and danger as everyday realities. Whether from repressive governments or ongoing wars or deep poverty and famine, they wake up daily to situations analogous to those described in Farrokhzād's poem.

A less personal essay can be fashioned from the issues of the self as observer of the world around us as it changes and causes us, if not to change along with it, at least to contemplate those changes and try to understand them in some way. Questions to explore along these lines can include: What changes in the immediate world around you (the neighborhood, community, hometown, or home country) have affected you? How do you feel in the face of these changes? Are you a part of them, or are you excluded from them? Are they positive or negative changes? Is there anything that you can do, or have tried to do, to stop them? To help them along? In the U.S., the possibilities have included gentrification, urban decay of neighborhoods, and increasing drug-influenced economic structures in the community. An elementary way to phrase this, for a brainstorming type of session, could be, "If you had the power to change one thing in your neighborhood and/or community, what would it be?" The questions that stem from that inquiry vary: Why do you choose that aspect? What has been the effect of that element on the life or quality of life of the neighborhood? Why are you particularly interested in that element? How does it affect you personally? How do others feel about it? Do they share your concern, or are they apathetic? Have you reached out to try to effect change? What have been the results if you have? Why haven't you if you haven't?

As a last suggestion, for this autobiographical and political essay, the idea of the garden as the generalizing element (the symbol of the changes in both the family and the community) is an intriguing one to follow up. Can students produce a similar image from their environments as a metaphor for the aspect of change (or stability) they are writing about? It might be a particular building or landmark that has or hasn't changed over time, a store or spot that has gone the way of gentrification, and so on. For any classroom and student population, this can be a fruitful and imaginative exercise, since students can learn to see in their own environments and experiences the raw material for their writing.

The texts discussed here have in common an analysis of how social and political realities play significant roles in determining one's ability to name one's world. Margaret Walker's essay is a nuanced critique of the gendered and racial conditions she confronts as an African American woman writer. Julia de Burgos gives voice to the otherwise silent inner self, the woman covertly struggling against her society's limiting definitions of femininity. Sandra María Esteves's voice rings out defiantly, clearing a space in Latino culture for the strong loud *mujer* of the inner-city. Finally, the mourning speaker in Forugh Farrokhzād's poem may be unable to stem the tides of war and time, but her critique of society's complacency and acceptance of the seemingly inevitable betrays no resignation.

These writers illustrate how powerful the combination of self-knowledge and political consciousness can be. Introducing students to strong women's voices such as these—and facilitating through writing activities that join autobiography with self-reflective analysis a critical awareness of the places these students occupy in their families, neighborhoods, social circles, and other institutions—produces thoughtful, engaged, committed writing. And isn't this what English Composition should be about?

NOTES

1. For a bilingual presentation of the poem, useful, if there are Spanish-speaking students in the class, see *The Defiant Muse: Hispanic Feminist Poems from the Middle Ages to the Present,* edited by Angel Flores and Kate Flores, 78–81. New York: The Feminist Press, 1986.

2. In *Herejes y mitificadores: Muestra de poesía puertorriqueña en los estados unidos,* edited by Efraín Barradas and Rafael Rodríguez, 114–115. Río Piedras: Ediciones Huracán, 1980.

3. These brief examples from Esteves' poem also illustrate how she, and many Latina/o poets, mix Spanish and English interlingually. This mirrors the code-switching of everyday speech; the lines quoted here are not translations. For readers needing translation: *"te perdiste en palabras no en vida,"* you lost yourself in words not in life; *"a ti Julia, ya será tarde / pero a mi no, yo vivo / y grito si me duele la vida,"* for you, Julia, it might be too late / but not for me, I live / and cry out if life hurts me.

4. In *The Other Voice: Twentieth-Century Women's Poetry in Translation,* edited by Joanna Bankier, Carol Cosman, et al, 141–44. New York: Norton, 1976. An alternative translation, accompanied by the original Persian, can be found in *A Lonely Woman: Forugh Farrokhzād and her Poetry,* by Michael C. Hillman, 119-122. Washington, DC: Three Continents Press/Mage Publishers, 1987.

Liza Fiol-Matta *is an assistant professor in the English department at LaGuardia Community College at the City University of New York. She was* *project coordinator of the Ford Foundation Mainstreaming Minority Women's Studies and codirector of the Ford Foundation Curriculum Mainstreaming Teaching Initiative. With Mariam K. Chamberlain, she coedited* Women of Color and the Multicultural Curriculum: Transforming the College Classroom *(New York: The Feminist Press, 1994). She is also active in Puerto Rican Studies and Latina Feminist Studies. She is a poet and a fiction writer and is currently working on a manuscript titled* Ni de aquí, Ni de allá: A Meditation on Puerto Rican Identity.

Revising an Interpersonal Communication Course

Catherine T. Motoyama

It has been both a privilege and a distinct pleasure to coordinate the Ford Foundation Curriculum Mainstreaming and Teaching Initiative Project at the College of San Mateo. In addition to making valuable contacts with kindred spirits on campus and at Cañada and Skyline Colleges, I was able to revise my basic course in Interpersonal Communication.

Speech 120 is a transferable course within the California State University system and serves as a requirement for many majors, such as nursing and architecture. Given the speech communication field's grounding in classical rhetoric, curriculum transformation is difficult. Many communication premises grow out of the Aristotelian tradition. One example is the communication model in the textbook I currently assign, Adler and Towne's *Looking Out/Looking In.*[1] The model is speaker-oriented—privileging the speaker as initiator of messages and reducing the listener's role to that of reactive agent. Moreover, the model does not account for the positions of the communicators. The identities of the speaker and listener, if they are considered at all, are essentialist and reductive in nature. Finally, the important notion of contexts which give rise to, inform, and constrain communication is absent. Context is equated with physical setting, a simple idea, rather than with the intersection of cultures— some consonant, others dissonant, still others distant—invoked by the communication act. For instance, if I as a feminist teacher were to talk with a conservative student, our gender, ethnicity, sexual orientation, age, role, political affiliations, and so on would enrich and complicate the discourse. Yet these cultures are not considered in the current communication model.

Looking Out/Looking In admittedly improves upon the bias against, and invisibility of, women and persons of different classes and color in older textbooks, but is unsatisfactory in providing a balanced curriculum. Myra Sadker, David Sadker, and Lynnette Long, calling for appropriate representation of women, describe fragmentation as an approach in which our contributions or conditions are treated as "unique occurrences" instead of being integrated into the main body of the text.[2] In this sense, the textbook is fragmented. It is problematic also because it does not adequately represent women, gays and lesbians, or persons of color as constituting the mainstream; instead, these communities are presented as marginalia, incidental points of interest, or they are boxed into separate "viewpoints."[3] Consequently, my revisions have developed mostly in the area of pedagogy, or, in other words, the ways in which I facilitate the course.

Prior to the transformation of Speech 120, I had taken a lesson from Paulo Freire and re-thought my role in the classroom as that of teacher-learner.[4] My students became learner-teachers—more responsible for sharing their insights, coming up with different views, and learning and teaching themselves as well as me. I incorporated opportunities for students to get to know each other, to depend on one another, to cooperate with one another, and to trust one another. This came about by designing collaborative exercises and debriefing sessions to move the locus of classroom authority away from me, as a traditional professor, to one more equitably distributed among the students, or learner-teachers. In addition, I gave the class a great deal of feedback on their writing, oral presentations, and group projects. Not only were graded quizzes (representing one-half of their cumulative grade) a part of the Speech 120 experience, but individual conferences and revision of papers with both myself and smaller groups of classmates were an integral part of gaining communication competence.

As part of the transformation of the course and pedagogy, I included more writing assignments. Each writing assignment was an essay on a chapter of the text, which was designed to relate to concepts presented in the readings and focusing on issues of gender, identity, and power. Each of the three papers had two stages: the first, an in-class draft which was shared with a small group of classmates; the other, the final paper which was to be turned in to me. I had hoped the in-class read-throughs would help my learner-teachers to recognize their biases towards others and towards issues covered in class. I wanted them to become invested personally in the course without undue fear of being judged by a grade. Many students enjoyed the writing assignments and considered them a review for the quizzes. They mentioned to me that they also enjoyed expressing themselves and learning about other people's positions, experiences, and "takes" on the assignment. Some students, however, admitted that they did not enjoy writing under any circumstances.[5]

One problem I encountered was that attendance was always lower on read-through days than it was on lecture days. This shows, I think, the students placing a higher value on a teacher's lectures than on collaborative work; or it could show my inexperience in promoting the value of student-centered learning. Another difficulty was that the class was not always equipped to provide productive critiques. This was remedied by stressing the importance of rewrites and devoting more time to show students how to read the papers critically.

This issue of student preparation, or the lack of it, brings up a larger concern I have regarding speech communication faculty being marginalized within language arts faculties. While many English programs have reading and writing laboratories, few speech programs have, for example, videocameras for recording speeches or speech laboratories for additional tutoring. Speech communication has not been accorded equal respect or treatment as, say, literary studies. How many Speaking Across the Curriculum programs are implemented compared with Writing Across the Curriculum programs? While I prepare (minimally, I admit) my classes to support theses in essays or to critique papers, I know of few—if any—English teachers who teach their classes to put together or rehearse their required oral presentations.

But going back to my class revisions, the second change that I made was to give one of my quizzes to groups rather than individuals. This was an interesting experience in instituting collaboration as an integral part of coursework. The learner-teachers were put into study teams one period prior to that of the quiz. They were to divide up the review among themselves and collectively take the test. In taking the test, some groups chose to consolidate their responses on one sheet, while others took exams individually and then compared results. The study teams turned quizzes in to me and learned *how many* answers were incorrect—however, I did not tell them *which* answers were incorrect. If they did well, they could choose to keep their original grade; if they did less well or poorly, they could revise their answers. The class seemed to enjoy this and everyone scored well on this assignment. Even those who usually did not fare well on examinations had an opportunity to benefit from others. Moreover, it seemed as if this assignment encouraged fuller participation because, being accountable to a group of peers, all students were better prepared for the examination.

Still, I needed to continue helping students through the process of understanding the contexts of the assignment. I had earlier introduced the difference between competition and collaboration, mentioning that our educational system is based on the former. I put the question to the class: What would your study team do if I were to choose one person to take the exam for all of you? They laughed and replied that it depended on whether that person was smart or not. I asked, what if that person were you? They then agreed that they would help one another regardless of who was selected to be the test-taker.

The final change that I made in my Speech 120 course was to introduce a mandatory course critique which received full credit regardless of what was said. I then compiled the comments, which were all positive with some preferences stated (such as, "Give us two papers instead of three," or "I hate writing.") and made a list of advice for new Speech 120 classes. I felt the course critique was excellent in lending closure to the class, in my learning how to improve the administration of the class, in giving next semester's newcomers some expectations from seasoned learner-teachers, and in offering a sense of continuity to the individuals who made up this class.

In summary, the changes in the area of pedagogy for the Speech 120 class focused on decentering the locus of authority in the classroom and making revision a necessary part of all assignments, foregrounding collaboration as the standard mode of operation. These changes not only addressed to some extent the omissions and silences contained in the course textbook, but brought stronger, more authentic voices to both individuals and the class as a whole.

NOTES

1. Ronald B. Adler and Neil Towne. *Looking Out/Looking In,* 7th ed. Fort Worth: Harcourt Brace Jovanovich, 1993.
2. Myra Sadker, David Sadker, and Lynette Long, "Gender and Educational Equity," in *Multicultural Education: Issues and Perspectives,* 2nd ed., edited by James A. Banks and Cherry A. Banks, 112–13. Boston: Allyn and Bacon, 1993.
3. I am not implying that women, gays and lesbians, and persons of color are mutually exclusive categories. This is a semantic difficulty which needs to be rethought. Even within our Ford Foundation Project, I was uncomfortable with the idea that "women" might position me, a woman of color, in a "default" category. Similarly, I wanted the definition of "women" to include lesbians, bisexual women, and transsexual women.
4. Paulo Friere. *Pedagogy of the Oppressed.* NY: Continuum, 1970.
5. Speech 120 is a diverse class in many ways—notably, there are many learners of English as a second language in various stages of their study of English and students enrolled in remedial writing and reading courses.

A Japanese American from Hawaii, **Catherine T. Motoyama,** *Ph.D., codirected the Ford Foundation Curriculum Mainstreaming and Teaching Initiative Project for the San Mateo Community College District. She wishes to thank her* issei *mother and her* nisei *father for her education.*

Changing the Dance Curriculum

Diana Evans Cushway

As a result of my participation in the Ford Curriculum Transformation Project I designed a questionnaire to guide modern dance students in reevaluating and assessing their perceptions of dance through considerations of culture and gender. One question, for example, that generated a lot of class discussion concerned the appropriate size, weight, and shape of a dancer's body. We discussed the current obsession with the anorectic dancer as well as the way in which Western cultures split the performing dancer from the audience. We compared this to Congolese cultural dance, where everybody of all sizes and shapes dances from infancy to old age.

In another activity I asked students to list movements that are traditionally performed by women and those traditionally performed by men. I asked them to consider whether dancers of each gender could transgress such traditional movements or steps (for example, women lifting men into the air or women lifting women). Following up on students' complaints that women's movements in MTV videos are usually oriented toward sexually stimulating the male viewer, I asked the class how they would choreograph a dance expressing female sexuality or sensuality differently from what they have seen on MTV. Two female students who volunteered then created a duet in collaboration with a student poet. Three other female students worked on a dance that requires lifting and maintaining each other's body weight. Meanwhile, two male students addressed the peer pressure against men taking a dance class at all. They elected to choreograph a duet for themselves, included in the class's final dance performance, to demonstrate the feasibility and importance of men dancing.

Such a performance of choreographed work by beginning modern dance students is produced at the conclusion of each semester. With the project informing my thoughts and intentions, I wanted to include many different cultural forms without trivializing them. Since I am not professionally trained in world dances, I found that the best way to present these was with the use of the PBS videotape, *Dances From Around The World*. My concern, however, in using this resource is that it is only a crumb, a small offering of different forms of dance, not unlike hosting a workshop of Congolese dancing and drumming for just one dance period. The department needs specialists in different forms of dance, not to make single guest appearances, but to teach semester-long classes. For instance, in the fall we could have flamenco and in the spring *capoeria* (a Brazilian form of martial arts and dance). It is essential that each dance form be taught by a resident expert. It is insulting to think that someone trained in Western European dance forms can, after one semester of flamenco or Congolese dance, teach it to students.

Although I cannot afford to hire guest artists, I have discovered that many of my students dance with performing groups from such other countries as Mexico, Samoa, and Ethiopia. Recently, after I had asked these students to perform in an informal dance event, we created a college multicultural dance company. We will be performing works from the modern, jazz, and ballet classes, in addition to an Ethiopian pre-wedding dance, a machete and a Mexican hat dance, and a traditional dance from Haiti and Samoa. This group of dancers and dances has elicited such interest that the students will also be performing for PTAs, for elementary schools, and in libraries, in addition to our regular college program.

I also decided to discuss gender issues with my independent studies class. This group of Skyline College students assists me in the elementary schools by teaching creative dance to third-grade children. My students were asked to keep a journal recording how many girls' names they had learned as compared to boys' names; how many girls as compared to boys were selected to demonstrate an activity or answer a question by myself, the classroom teacher, or their peers; and lastly, which sex received the most positive attention. Each of my students teach one class at the end of the semester, and they were evaluated by their peers on their management of gender equality.

Attention to this topic is essential; in working with children, I have observed both myself and many of my colleagues, subtly and overtly, preferring boys over girls. I am very aware of the problems that young girls face. Yet I find that gender bias is so pervasive that I have to be aware of it constantly and to monitor my behavior in the classroom. My awareness of gender bias in the classroom came about after reading studies about how elementary school teachers often call more on boys and spend more time answering their questions.

In one young class, although the girls followed directions and proceeded to do the activity promptly and quietly, some of the more rambunctious boys needed to be corralled and demanded more of my attention. After the class, I discovered that I had learned more of the boys' names than the girls' names. It is a bad habit that I had not been aware of until I spent some time in self-reflection. To correct this habit, it is important to validate and reward the girls' behavior by exclaiming, for example, "Look at so and so, she was really listening and is already working on the project." Giving an equal amount of attention and praise to both boys and girls corrects this problem.

In another class several years ago, the children were involved in a creative group activity. Once again a very loud group of boys was getting all my attention and positive feedback. My assistant had to get my attention to observe a group of girls who were working very quietly and were creating group sculptural designs that were intricate and complex in shape and form. They were some of the best students I had ever seen. I realized that if my assistant had not brought them to my attention, I probably would have missed their work entirely. I was shocked. I still hear dance teachers today remark about how wonderful the dynamic energy of boys is compared to the girls, and I wince each time. (I need to do more than wince, however; I need to be more proactive by verbally and explicitly explaining my viewpoint.) Too much emphasis is put on the showy and flashy dives to the floor or high leaps and turning jumps and not enough on all the parts of movement and its inherent subtleties. Sometimes it seems as if the girls are expected to move like the boys, that as teachers we perceive the boys' movement as the "norm." The predicament for girls may be that while they are perfectly able to do flashy jumps and dives, in addition to all the other wonderful things they do, they are generally taught to be less assertive than boys. To correct this, girls should be encouraged to move assertively while also being equally appreciated for their other abilities.

Making these changes takes conscious effort. I point out to my student assistants how in every class I am always aware now of choosing an equal number of boys and girls to demonstrate, to answer questions, to be leaders, and to receive praise. In addition to encouraging and praising young girls who move energetically, in every class that I teach I choose one quiet, shy girl who is really focused. Then I learn her name, point her out, and refer to her throughout the class as an excellent example of a good listener. (A good technique to use for any exceptionally shy and quiet student: Offer extra attention and encouragement.) Whenever I ask a classroom teacher to choose students for a demonstration, I always preface my remark with, "Pick an equal number of boys and girls." If I don't do this, I invariably end up with more boys. To further advocate gender equality, it is important to resist sex-segregation in the classroom by having even ratios of boys to girls work together in groups and lines when traveling across the floor.

In one of my residencies a few years ago, I worked with and learned a great deal from a classroom teacher who was trained at a Montessori school. He treated his students so equally that I found the girls more assertive about speaking up and answering questions, moving through space and choosing to be leaders, than I have observed in any other class. It is important that the children do not perceive that they must move in or look a certain way to get approval. The dance instructor must spend time reviewing, challenging, updating, and critiquing individual pedagogical styles in and out of the classroom. I have been even more vigilant in my equal treatment of the children. I have discovered that either the girls are now doing more fabulous and wonderful dancing, or that I am now really giving them the attention they deserve and thus am more aware of their talents.

Questions About Dance:

1. What is beautiful?
2. Do you and your family and friends agree on what is beautiful?
3. Is beauty culturally specific?
4. Why do some cultures describe something as beautiful and other cultures describe the same thing as ugly?
5. Could you make a dance with empty detergent boxes?
6. Can a short, overweight person/dancer be beautiful to watch dance?
7. Who decides how heavy a dancer should be?
8. How old can you be before you should stop dancing?
9. How can you perform a dance other than in a theatre?
10. Where should you *not* perform a dance?
11. What idea would you be least likely to make a dance about?
12. Is it possible to move too slowly, too quickly, or to get too twisted in a shape?
13. What part of your life have you never thought about expressing through dance?
14. What part of your life have you thought about expressing through dance?
15. How could you create an MTV dance of the future that is radically different from the dance that you see on MTV today?
16. How do MTV images of women help you feel good about yourself? feel bad?
17. Please add a question that you would like to ask.

MODERN DANCE 110AA, SYLLABUS

Attire: Please wear leotard and stirrup tights, bare feet or flat dance shoes. Hair must be worn tied up, away from the face. No large jewelry or perfume in class. Five minutes will be given before and after class to give you extra time to change and prepare, please do not be late. If you miss part of the warmup you are more susceptible to injury.

This beginning level modern dance class will focus on good postural alignment, as well as strength and stretching exercises, from Jose Limón and Merce Cunningham techniques. The class will learn technical dance movements and phrases; center floor and across the floor. Emphasis will be on students' own development of creative expression and practice in improvisational movement.

Grading Policy

1. Full participation in fitness testing program, completion of pre- and post-tests.

2. Attendance = 15 pts. 2 absences = A; 3 = B; 4 = C; 5 = D; 6 = F. Please keep track of your absences!

3. Failure to withdraw properly from the course will result in an F.

4. MIDTERM—execute dance phrase that I will teach you with proper technique and rhythm (15 pts.)

5. Participation and improvement in fitness testing—situps and flexibility (5 pts.)

6. Center and across floor, and alignment—overall improvement (20 pts.)

7. Final choreography project including supporting art work and paper (35 pts.)

8. Vocabulary test (10 pts.)

Available in the library please read: Humphrey, Doris. *The Art of Making Dances.* New York: Grove Atlantic, 1987.

Diana Evans Cushway *participated in the Ford Foundation Curriculum Mainstreaming and Teaching Initiative Project, and is an instructor at Skyline College, San Bruno, California. She is the director of the Skyline College dance program and the founder and artistic director of Skyline's Eclectic Dance Company, a multicultural, community-oriented performing group. She is currently completing a book on teaching creative movement in artist residence programs.*

Transforming a Criminal Justice Curriculum

Marie Henry and Vicky E. Dorworth

What began as an effort by two colleagues to address a few problems within their criminal justice program, as well as an effort to refresh and stimulate their own ideas on scholarship and pedagogy, has become a major turning point in the direction of the participants and the program. The journey has not been without pain, but it has always been without regret. It continues undaunted toward a more inclusive, humanistic and fulfilling approach to the study of criminal justice within a community college environment.

The Criminal Justice Program at Montgomery College was developed as an occupational degree program simultaneously charged with preparing students for entry level jobs in law enforcement, security, and corrections; and with preparing students for transfer to four-year programs in criminal justice, criminology, other social sciences, and pre-professional programs. The program's students, faculty, and advisory board reflected the employment field's pervasiveness of white males in population, content, and orientation. A five-year program evaluation showed that women and minority men taking the introductory criminal justice course tended to drop out of further course work at rates disproportionate to white male students in the program. Wondering why this was happening, we used a projective technique to investigate our students' perceptions of professionals in the criminal justice field. The results showed that the student body overwhelmingly perceived police officers, wardens, college professors, and judges to be male and white. Students perceived social workers and high school teachers, on the other hand, to be female or effeminate males. They saw victims as female and offenders as male. Finally, in spite of recent criminal justice job recruitment posters portraying a wide diversity of employees, actual employment

A slightly different version of this essay appears in *Community College Guide to Curriculum Change*, edited by Elaine Hedges, Myrna Goldenberg, and Sara Coulter (Baltimore, MD: Towson State University/Maryland Community College Project). Copyright © 1990 by Elaine Hedges, Myrna Goldenberg, and Sara Coulter. Reprinted by permission.

statistics reflected the white male stereotype as basically true in all areas. We found likewise that introductory criminal justice texts largely reinforced the old stereotypes of white male dominance in the field of law enforcement, including courts, and corrections. Females were disproportionately characterized as victims, and males of color were portrayed overwhelmingly as offenders. The few exceptions to this rule were often ghettoized in sections focusing on affirmative action or recent innovations.

We became interested in the curriculum transformation project after participating in two separate summer institutes sponsored by Montgomery College. The only female faculty members in a program taught predominantly by white males (two full-timers, and approximately six part-timers per semester, all male), we often sought a sense of community with each other on issues when we disagreed with our colleagues. While we had yet to identify any specific problems, we did feel an amorphous sense of being left out, devalued, denied, and trivialized. Our goal in attending summer institutes was to modify a specific criminal justice course, and we were both ready, when the opportunity arose, to expand upon this initial endeavor. We had already begun to wrestle with some broad pedagogical issues, such as authority in the classroom, self-directed and self-responsible learning, collaborative learning, and alternative criteria for student evaluation. We were also changing content areas, such as adding women both as offenders and as professionals in the field, as well as seeing them as victims; and looking at gender as a factor in differential definitions of crime, selective law enforcement, and preferential treatment by the courts and corrections. In the different stages of course transformation discussed by Schuster and Van Dyne in their article, "Placing Women in the Liberal Arts: Stages of Curriculum Transformation," we were probably at level two out of six, mostly still adding and stirring, while striving to develop a changed perspective.

On the surface, the project gave us both the opportunity to continue our work and to learn more about integrating women into all of our criminal justice courses. We each looked forward to concentrating on a new course to transform. To our surprise, the first semester of the project involved massive reading, little of which had anything directly to do with criminal justice. At times it seemed irrelevant, redundant, esoteric, and, especially, overwhelming. In spite of ourselves, however, a subtle yet intense osmosis was occurring. We found ourselves talking together a lot and confronting strong feelings—

anger, depression, frustration, more anger, determination, defensiveness, and guilt—about what we were reading. We learned two important lessons about curriculum transformation during this early part of the journey. First, there could be no real course transformation without our confronting a more challenging personal transformation, constantly exploring, questioning, and redefining not only our teaching roles, but all of our social relationships and positions. Second, the value of regularly sharing these experiences with an empathic colleague or group was irreplaceable in helping us cope with the strong emotions and the sometimes seemingly insurmountable obstacles identified by our readings and discussions.

First Thing First: Changing Course Objectives

In the second semester of the project, we were each asked to select a specific subject section of our chosen courses, Introduction to Law Enforcement and Criminal Law, to concentrate on researching and modifying with our newly acquired and still tentatively fitting "feminist" perspective. In addition to questioning the labeling of our changes as feminist (since we were beginning to feel strongly the need to focus on course inclusion by other social stratification factors as well), we both needed first to step back and redefine our objectives for the courses we were teaching. Redefining course objectives was probably the most important single turning point in the transformation process. It was also the most challenging because it forced a new perspective for teaching all parts of the courses. This process of redefining naturally carried over into all of our other courses as well and demanded a completely new set of criteria for developing course content, method, and success. The following list of objectives, which grows and changes as we do, includes ideas and issues which were left largely ignored by our earlier, more traditional approach to teaching criminal justice courses:

1. Recognizing the inadequacy of presenting only a status quo, "objective" overview of the criminal justice system, criminal law, enforcement, corrections, and the courts;

2. Inspiring questions and critical evaluation of the goals, methods, and effectiveness of the criminal justice system.

3. Defining the law and criminal justice from a more sociological perspective, recognizing the relativistic nature of criminal law and justice, and their relationship to the social system and power structure of which they are a part.

4. Exposing the role that discretion within the criminal justice system plays in reinforcing social norms.

5. Employing a cross-cultural and interdisciplinary perspective in the exploration of criminal justice and criminal law issues.

6. Redefining criminal justice and criminal law in broader, less ethnocentric terms, that recognize human rights in a more generic sense.

7. Integrating sexual, racial, social class issues and other forms of inclusiveness within a learning environment that also encourages the development of skills cited by criminal justice employers as needed by job applicants—critical thinking skills, improved verbal and written communication skills, awareness of ethical dilemmas, exposure to technological developments in the field, familiarity with the insights of the behavioral sciences.

8. Recognizing the limitations of the "objective" scientific method as applied in a chauvinistic society; identifying our own biases and concerns and communicating them to students; and encouraging students to explore their personal biases, concerns, and goals.

9. Developing the concept of "privilege" as it applies to criminal law and the criminal justice system.[1]

10. Selecting resources, including texts, readings, audiovisuals and guest speakers, which explicitly or implicitly sensitize students to social stratification issues, raising questions rather than merely presenting information about the criminal law and criminal justice system; which provide role models for different groups of students; and which expose the differential treatment of "outgroups" (women, people of color, noncitizens, mentally and physically disabled, socially and economically disadvantaged) by the criminal justice system.

11. Encouraging active student interest, participation, responsibility, and learning in a classroom environment that supports respect for diversity and individualized styles of learning.

12. Recognizing the potentially chilling effects of classroom climate on student participation, personal investment and learning; and encouraging a classroom climate that better empowers all students as students, criminal justice professionals, citizens, and people.

Course Changes: Experimenting with a New Perspective

During the final two semesters of the project, we began to introduce and evaluate changes in our course requirements developed from our newly altered course objectives. Since then, we have been experimenting with a variety of methods for translating these goals into classroom realities. Before instituting any of these changes, we first prepared ourselves for several potentially disheartening outcomes, recognizing that not every attempt would be successful. We anticipated, for example, resistance from students and colleagues, ridicule, lack of cooperation, and defensiveness; the generation of painful emotions which could not be fully explored and resolved within the scope of one class or one semester; and a lack of security felt by students who had successfully mastered the rules of more traditional courses. And yet we also had high hopes for positive results that would far outweigh the negatives. We both felt that the best approach to implementing the transformation in the classroom was to begin our courses with a full disclosure of purposes and expected risks and benefits, and to solicit either an "informed consent," an open-minded acceptance, or at least a conscious suspension of judgment until the semester's end. In one instance, we invited students to share their goals in taking the course and to reconcile or integrate their goals, the goals of the instructor, and the goals of other students in the class. Here are some of the practices we have introduced, all of which we shall continue to expand and refine according to feedback from students, each other, and other interested faculty.

Journals

Both of us were required to keep personal journals as part of the project. Project directors explained the benefits of keeping journals, sharing examples of journal application for the classroom. At first glance, although we had each kept journals for other purposes at different times in our lives, we questioned the utility of such a requirement for criminal justice courses. Over the course of three semesters, however, we have discovered and expanded upon the functions of a journal requirement in three criminal justice courses. Increasingly, we both find the journals to be our most useful tool in accomplishing a myriad of transformational goals. We have varied the journal entries, with some entries being assigned for work at home, and some for in-class writing. Journal assignments have included the following:

1. Describe yourself and your relationship to the course you are taking, including your course goals.

2. Describe the effects of race, gender, age, social class, physical, and mental attributes on your life experiences and privileges, and more specifically on your involvement in crime and with the criminal justice system.

3. Choose between changing your race or sex, telling why.[2]

4. Identify, analyze, and react to visual and print media coverage of crime issues (with which we are constantly bombarded!). In addition to looking generally at a media item, look for more specific issues as they come up in class; for example, the role of social stratification factors, the role of discretion, the role of the public in defining crime control policies, the portrayal of victims, criminal justice procedural issues, the portrayal of authority and power, and the victim-offender relationship. (Sometimes current media presentations are brought in by the instructor for immediate written reaction and comment; for example, the headlines and accompanying coverage, "Manhunt For Police Chief" and "Man Gets Three Days For Rape.")

5. Think about, react to, and decide critical issues within the field that relate to gender, racial and social class biases inherent in the criminal justice system and our society. These issues are presented, often with some short summary of research results, editorials, essays, or audiovisual stimulus, throughout the semester, and responded to in the journals. Some of the issues have been framed in a "you decide" format, first appearing in Joel Samaha's text, *Criminal Justice,* and have covered such topics as racial, gender, and social class aspects of determining employment competency, use of deadly force, sentencing disparity, use of the death penalty, the use of violent predator profiles, differential treatment of repeat offenders, definitions of sexual assault and other crimes, and ethical issues on the job. The most sensitive area of discussion in both written and verbal formats has been the area of sexual preference: should sodomy and "unnatural" sex practices be decriminalized, should homosexuals and lesbians be employed as police officers and correctional officers? More recently, physical and mental abilities and disabilities have become a concern for us in the context of criminal justice issues, and these have yet to be integrated.

6. Write reactions to classroom discussions that have become heated, emotionally charged, or stalemated. Evaluate the content as well as the process involved in these discussions.

Small Group Discussions

Primarily in an effort to relinquish authority and to broaden the base of student input, small group discussions were added to the courses and to the evaluation of student performance in the course. Small groups of three to six students were asked to solve consensually criminal justice problems such as the following examples: Several situa-

tions were presented requiring groups to discriminate between con-
senting sexual activity and sexual assault; at another time, groups
were asked to rank by seriousness a set of criminal offenses and to
assign appropriate sentences; still another time, elements of criminal
liability were identified in a series of fact situations; finally, groups
were asked to resolve ethical dilemmas presented to defense attorneys, prosecutors, judges, and juries. While the topics were still
assigned by the instructor (sometimes in response to student interests generated by the earlier journal entries), the discussions were
left solely to the groups. Students' requests for guidance from the
instructors were met with calculated nondirectiveness, such as, "Well,
what does your group think the answer should be?" Small group
debriefings were sometimes held to compare small group resolutions
to those of current legal, practical, and professional associations.

Evaluation Alternatives

We made a conscious effort to diminish the importance of traditional
objective examination-style questions to evaluate student success. At
the same time, both instructors tried to offer a variety of evaluation
tools so that different student learning styles could be accommodat-
ed. In one class, students chose their preferred style of examination.
In another class, students could choose between in-class quizzes or
take-home reaction papers for each major content section of the
course. Writing and revision opportunities were increased, and take-
home assignments expanded. We evaluated journals and small group
participation and gave substantial credit to these practices in the
course.

Integration of Social Stratification Issues into Traditional Assignments

Each transformed course included at least one assignment "left over"
from the more traditional approach to the course. Into these assignments, which we still considered essential, we integrated social stratification issues. For example, in the introductory course, both instructors
have regularly required students to analyze a criminal justice journal article in order to study the use of scientific methodology in
research. To introduce the new approach to this traditional assignment, we first had students analyze in small class groups a research
article that dealt with gender differences in the selection of a law

enforcement career. Students were then asked to find and critique a research article of their own and to look specifically for evidence of gender/racial/social class bias as they examined the usual issues of methodology—topical selection, sample selection, and interpretation of research results. In the criminal law class, students were asked to "brief" one criminal court opinion and were given cases in class to summarize. The cases chosen included legal issues related to the differential treatment of offenders by age, race, social class, and gender.

Integration of Social Stratification Issues into Traditional Resources

Social stratification issues were also used to choose new films, texts, readings, and speakers and were integrated into traditional content areas. For example, the film, *Women in Prison* (Penn State Audio-Visual Service) was shown to stimulate a discussion of prison conditions and of the goals and effectiveness of crime control measures in general. *Machismo* (Films for the Humanities) was used to generate discussion of the pros and cons of allowing cultural background to be a defense for criminal behavior. Discussion naturally followed, speculating on differential treatment, problems, and concerns of incarcerated men and women in the first film and in the second, on the perpetuation of social differences in the treatment of various groups by the criminal justice system.

The Results: What Difference Have We Made?

At times within the span of our personal and course transformations, the results have been questionable, or at least obtained at what appeared to be a high price. For every added subject, perspective, and method, we stole time from other areas once considered critical to our courses. Decisions about including or excluding content were agonizingly made after much discussion and thought. This was particularly true of the introductory survey course, which was already so broad in nature. Departmental confrontations increased, as we no longer complied with previously accepted policies, treatment, and trivialization. We exacerbated the dissension in our department by erroneously expecting colleagues, who had yet to experience the transformation process, to embrace our perspective. Heated arguments have also erupted in the classrooms, and confrontations have sometimes deadlocked in frustration and anger. Time necessary to complete even the simplest tasks has multiplied because decision making has demanded more student input, course modifications keep evolving according to students' needs and interests, and time spent reading student papers has at least tripled.

Yet, in retrospect, none of these difficulties can tarnish the real contributions and important positive differences evidenced by our personal and curricular changes. While women and minority men are not yet flocking to our doors in droves for jobs in criminal justice and for acceptance into our program, they are, based on student performance, student comments, and enrollment in our sections, increasing both in numbers and participation. We indeed recognize a trickle-down effect, as students compare our courses to other more traditional orientations in other college classes. Almost all students have improved their writing ability, though perhaps more in terms of thoughtful expression than in correct style and form. Even classroom discussions have improved. There are fewer unsupported, emotion-laden, bombshell-attack responses. Increasingly, students appear to be more accepting of a diversity of opinions and more sensitive to other students' needs and perspectives over the semester. In addition, students and teachers enjoy coming to class and look forward to the experience. Many conversations have continued in the hallways after class, and student groups have initiated out-of-class meetings to discuss assignments and issues. Students have also been more willing to integrate personal experiences, sometimes painful, into small group and classroom discussions. In almost all cases, a closer group cohesion and empathy have emerged, and students seem more willing to facilitate one another's learning and understanding. Evidence of an increase in sensitivity to gender, racial, and social class issues has been seen in reaction paper discussions, in students' choices of media items, journal articles, and law library cases, and in classroom discussions.

In conclusion, our odyssey has created nothing short of personal and professional crisis. As in any crisis, we have become at times disoriented and insecure, at times defensive and angry, at times overwhelmed and afraid. But in facing and exploring the roots of these feelings, and in giving our ideas a chance to succeed or fail, we both wholeheartedly agree that we have empowered ourselves, our relationships, our students, and our program. And, as in any odyssey of revelation, there is no turning back.

BALANCING THE CURRICULUM—COURSE CHANGES IN PROGRESS

Area Addressed	Pre-FIPSE Institutes	Current Additions/ Changes
Teaching Values	Objectivity; eclecticism; value-free presentations; comprehensive coverage of material; fair hearing for all sides; facts.	Identified bias toward role of social stratification on person's status as person, offender, victim, criminal justice professional; ethical choices/dilemmas; critical thinking; issues; process.
Self-Concept as Teacher	Expert; authority; guide; competent professional; detached observer.	Personal investment; growing learner; involved participant; collaborator; colleague; instigator; negotiator.
Student Role	Receptacle for learning/thinking; questioner; audience; individuals.	Interactive learner/teacher; experienced participant; filter; responsible actor; group support.
Course Content	Traditional outlining of a "given" US CJ system with some questioning of status quo; isolated units of study in subject areas (police, courts, corrections, juvenile justice); theory of system operation; examples of system	More integration of topical areas; less isolation; more cross-cultural references and comparisons; more relativist presentation of laws and process; law and crime in a sociological context; role and examples of discretion in the law and its application.

	variations in operation; expounding of principles of criminal liability, procedural steps, and specific offenses by law.	
Classroom Style	Lecture; guided discussion; questions; semi-formal.	Addition of student collaboration; small groups and work efforts; more informal; personal; experiential.
Assignments and Evaluation	Objective and short essay; examinations, informational papers; "correct" answers; some field exposure; awareness of research, scientific method; "objective" coverage of topical issues.	Recognition of social stratification as variable; more choice; class participation; writing assignments— reasoned answers, position papers, reading reviews, editorials; field and media observations; critiquing of research, scientific method.
Readings	Textbook; some current media coverage.	Smaller core text with issue-related readings; editorials, commentaries; more emphasis on current local examples.
Selection of Audio-visuals and Texts	Currency and interest; additional supportive source of information about system.	Role modeling as major selection criterion; raising of issues and problems in system; sensitivity to social stratification variables.
Student Response	Passive with some questions ("Will this be on the	Fuller participation; personal involvement; more freedom of

| exam?"); active "elite"; coerced participation. | expression, more self-confidence; emotional investment in issues; greater cohesion as a group and respect for other students, diversity. |
| Saturated. | Hungry for more. |

NOTES

1. This concept is discussed in "White Privilege and Male Privilege: A Personal Account of Coming to See Correspondences through Work in Women's Studies" by Peggy McIntosh, Working Paper No. 189, Wellesley College Center for Research on Women, Wellesley, Mass., 1988.
2. Borrowed from the "forced choice" exercise developed by Paula Rothenberg, author of *Racism and Sexism: An Integrated Study,* the exercise graphically illustrates sex-role and race-role stereotyping and diversity. Discussion of the general results leads naturally into a discussion of the impact of these stereotypes on criminal justice processing.

Marie Henry, coordinator of the criminal justice program at Sullivan County Community College, New York, participated in the FIPSE-sponsored community college transformation project in Maryland. She is currently involved in developing course materials that incorporate technology, collaborative learning activities, self-assessment, and portfolio evaluation.

Vicky E. Dorworth, Ed.D., is an associate professor at Montgomery College in Rockville, Maryland. Her research interests include the representation of women in the criminal justice field and in various forms of popular culture. She is also interested in techniques to improve teaching and learning in the classroom through the identification of different learning and teaching styles.

Revising Economic History: Self-Integration and Course Integration

Barbara Bourne Murray

I have always believed that teachers are empowered to change lives by changing thought processes. We have the opportunity to expose our students to new information that could destroy life-long myths and misconceptions about events, people, and possibly about students themselves as individuals or as members of a group. The transformation project to integrate the scholarship on women into the curriculum was an opportunity for me to assess my academic and personal commitment to women's issues, especially those of African-American women, as well as to revise an economic history course to address the specific role and status of women in our economy. The project empowered me with content and methodologies necessary to change my students' (and my own) thought processes about women in society, and challenged me to rethink my understanding of the relationships between history and racism, sexism, classism, and ethnocentrism.

Soon after the project began, I realized that I had to consider the extent to which my personal experiences were—or were not—reflected in how and what I taught. I needed to evaluate critically whether I used my life and my experience to limit my students' views of the world, expand them, move them to the right or left, or keep them in the middle. How has my life as a member of race, gender, and class groups determined the content and context of the courses I was teaching and was about to revise? To my amazement, I realized that I may often have been teaching as if I were a non-person, in a mode that separated my personal experiences from the course content. I thought about the content we didn't discuss—or conveniently didn't have time to discuss—and about discussing safe, "nonpolitical" issues.

I realized that if I taught, and continued to teach in any of these ways, I was being dishonest with myself and with my students.

As I became more conscious of the methodology of my teaching, I recognized that it wasn't enough that I knew I was an African-American woman. I had to feel comfortable with the process of interweaving who I am, where I came from, and the whole of my experience with my work as a teacher. If I had been accomplishing this to any extent, as some of my colleagues had told me I had, I was taking it for granted. I needed now to become conscious of the process and use it to its fullest capacity. In the 1960s, as an undergraduate in a primarily white institution, I had tried, as a protective device, to be raceless and sexless. My experiences in graduate school, including being in charge of a dormitory corridor of Black and Puerto Rican students, and then at the Community College of Baltimore, where I arrived at a time when students were demanding Black instructors, had certainly helped me develop my sense of my African-American identity and to bring it into the classroom. But even at the community college, I now realized, although I taught some of my courses out of the awareness that I was a Black woman, including the college's short-lived women's studies courses in the mid-1970s, my racial and gender identity had not seemed related to what I taught in courses in economic theory, where most of the students were white. In an important way, the curriculum project let me say clearly to myself that I teach from an African-American woman's perspective. Working in the project led me to read and reread Toni Morrison, Alice Walker, and Maya Angelou, to rekindle friendships with African-American women whom I admire and trust and to pursue with new conviction an active role in addressing student and faculty needs that I had assumed in my years as an administrator at the college.

The economic history course that I revised is a general liberal arts course that has recently become a required course within the paralegal and human services or social work programs at the college, out of the recognition that students need to understand the economic system inside which they live and work.[1] Most of the students who enroll in the course are Black, and I had earlier included in the course an African-American history focus. I now revised the course to be more interdisciplinary, bringing in materials from sociology, anthropology and psychology. I also made it less Eurocentric, including more material on the economic status of women from developing countries and emphasizing the links between the development of private property and the status of women.

When I began teaching the revised course, I was quickly reminded that the students play a large role in the methodology we employ. In the first semester, when I introduced the focus on women, all eight of the students were female: two white Americans, five African-Americans, and one Black Jamaican. All were enthusiastic about the focus on women, but I had to make sure that they understood that our study of society's attempts to solve the problems of scarcity would emphasize not only "woman," but the differences among women in race, gender, ethnicity, and class. In addition, I had to make sure that both the students and I avoided overgeneralizing about the behavior, roles, or status of males in the various societies we studied and that we put into perspective the personal negative attitudes towards men that may have surfaced.

The second semester, all of the sixteen students, except one from Trinidad, were African-American, and seven were male students. When introducing the focus on women, I explained more extensively why this was the focus: I am an African-American woman who has a particular interest in the role, status, and education of African-American women in our society, and I strongly believe that the history and education of all women of color may be crucial to the survival and success of many, if not all, societies—something I would not have said a decade earlier. The response was guarded interest by the males and more open enthusiasm by the females. As the semester progressed, this male guardedness was shown when one man questioned the validity of using a text written by a woman that cited other resources by women (although there were also sources written by men cited in the text). I told the student I would bring to class other sources written by men that supported the premise for our focus, but I also discussed the question of whose history is to be considered "true." Our final consensus was that before arriving at conclusions we had to take into account both the weight of the evidence and the values that researchers may both derive from and impose upon their materials. Although male resistance to the focus on women is generally lighter than I had anticipated, I do not avoid conflict, as I might have in earlier years. Rather, I encourage students to find evidence to support their points of view, especially if these disagree with mine. And I have scheduled several discussion sessions in which students and I will directly address the issue that so greatly concerns them, that of African-American male-female relationships. In this way, I hope that the class will encourage both male and female students to find their individual and their collective voices.

All in all, the project led me to investigate current research on African-American women—who and what is being studied, and who and what is not. I have found that the research on African-American women in higher education focuses on those who are in predominantly

Black institutions or predominantly white four-year colleges and universities. There is little information on Black women in the community colleges. However, since they are often older, working women, and frequently single heads of households, Black women in community colleges frequently do not fit the four-year college student norm, nor, therefore, the predictors of success that much of the research examines. Participating in the project thus helped me find not only my personal voice, but an area of research for my professional voice as well.

NOTE

1. Since the Towson State University/Maryland Community Colleges Curriculum Integration Project, this economic history course has been replaced by an economic principles course (because the history course does not transfer for credit as an economics course). The economic history course was also used as the basis for creating an Economic History with Computers course for a National Science Foundation grant, 1993–1995.

Barbara Bourne Murray *participated in the Towson State University/ Maryland Community Colleges Curriculum Integration Project as the project coordinator for Baltimore City Community College. She is currently completing her dissertation entitled* Selected Variables for the Success of African-American Students Who Transfer from Two-Year to Four-Year Public Institutions of Higher Education in Maryland, *Morgan State University. Her current focus is on instructional technology.*

Revisioning Business Ethics

E. Michelle Rabouin

Introduction

My work is an extension of the ideas of my colleagues regarding the integration of feminist pedagogy into the core curriculum at the Community College of Denver. I built on our collective discoveries and insights about curriculum revision to define, rethink and rework the Business Ethics curriculum, an area not "naturally" hospitable or inclined to feminist integration.

Business Ethics is a core course required of all students receiving the AAS (Associate in Applied Science) degree in Business Administration at the Community College of Denver. Currently the class is approved for transfer throughout the state community college system. It is generally also an approved elective for the transfer pre-business AGS (Associate in General Studies) degree. The basic reading and writing requirements of this course have been established by the Community College of Denver Academic Standards, and the content influenced by requirements of the American Assembly of Collegiate Schools of Business (AACSB). AACSB, an accrediting body for business schools in the United States, has sent a strong message to the deans of business schools that ethics should be part of the business curriculum.

At the Community College of Denver, this course is taken after a sequence of core curriculum courses which include the introductory courses, English 121, Speech 115, and Sociology 101. These courses have also been revisioned to include feminist pedagogy, so Business Ethics builds on the integration concepts introduced in those core courses.

Deconstruction

Participating in the project, my first task was to examine the goals and pedagogical framework of the current course, and then to ask myself a few pertinent questions. First, what is the supposed goal of teaching business ethics? Although it obviously arises from both an academic and public mandate, the supposed goal is not always clear from the face of most syllabi. In recent years, the media's concern with ethical conduct has particularly centered on the issue of ethics in business and business education. In answer to this concern, business curricula aimed to inculcate business students and business people with a more ethical framework with which to make decisions.

As academe responded to this concern, some rather loose definitions of what should be taught emerged: ethics as the morality or principles of right and wrong behavior; ethics as the discipline of determining and then solving a problem around organizational moral duty and obligation in situations where there is a risk of potential harm to an individual or group; and business ethics as the process of studying morality within profit-making organizations, with the aim of developing reasonable moral standards and decision-making frameworks.

Interestingly enough, when I began to review moral psychology literature, I discovered empirical evidence that traditional business education pedagogy does not, as currently constructed, foster moral or ethical development, in contrast to other college educational experiences. More unexpected was the research that suggested that these courses seem also not to develop human value systems needed for successful guidance of organizational behavior into the twenty-first century. Why not?

The focus of business ethics generally, and at CCD in particular, has been student understanding of "ethical issues." The curriculum is designed to teach very generalized moral principals based on male-centered, status-quo oriented paradigms. Thus Business Ethics, like other business courses, has often been accused of being taught in an "orthodox-single-set," homogeneously focused manner, only recently adding the lens of contemporary public issues. While the course, of necessity, considers social, ethical and public policy dimensions, the pedagogical focus is on the cognitive domain, with minimal consideration of the affective domain, and often without empirical ties. It would seem that the goal of integrating ethics into the business curriculum to develop "ethics" as a strategic decision variable rather than to facilitate students' development of moral agency or ethical decision making.

Issues of race, ethnicity, gender, and class are currently discussed, if at all, as discrete "employment issues." Discussion of sexism, racism, and other factors of diversity are isolated from the actual framework of analysis itself, and business ethics does not even touch on alternative ways of knowing, analyzing, and problem solving. The current model suffers from limitations which are generated by pedagogy and content. Thus, the Business Ethics class does not provide analytical tools which assist students in approaching hard ethical issues from a holistic framework—or in developing their ethical growth.

I began to wonder if there weren't ways in which faculty could do better, and how that might be connected to the integration of feminist pedagogy.

Reconstruction

It occurred to me that most ethical questions could be reenvisioned as incidents of collision, of potential conflict between organizations and their stakeholders; the human desire to avoid conflict and its irreducible presence; the economic imperative and the necessity for moral agency in an increasingly complex world. The inability to balance these conflicts successfully in the business setting results in less than optimal and ethical organizational decisions because options are not fully generated nor considered and because the enterprise fails to conceive rightly of its responsibility to use its power in the world.

If the goal is to enhance ethical development which might lead to improved critical thinking and analytical skills, I began to feel that the course requires not only integration of previously excluded viewpoints, but *complete* revisioning. What I proposed as a useful process, therefore, is a blend of moral theory with a conscious, experientially connected examination of factual blindness versus factual analysis, and the inclusion of affective as well as cognitive analysis as tools for dealing with the very human aversion to conflict.

The fundamental question then becomes to what extent would feminist pedagogy and scholarship, in all its diversity, help advance such a curricular goal? That soon became framed as: Where are the women in ethics, in business ethics? Why are they missing? More questions tumbled out: Is there a difference between men's and women's moral choices and analysis? Does the current literature reflect this difference if there is one? In what ways would adding feminist ethics move the basic content and pedagogy of the class in the direction I envision?

As I perused the literature, it became clear to me that feminist ethics, a field of study which has only come into existence in a meaningful way in the last twenty years, and which includes interdisciplinary work by philosophers, psychologists, theologians, and others, could be a meaningful basis upon which to construct a course. By integrating feminist scholarship I could build on the relationship between stages of moral development and moral action, and focus on more fully human frameworks of morality, and on ethical frameworks which consciously consider the affective and cognitive domains. If organizational participants become more familiar with tools to resolve conflict more effectively by generating the most inclusive range of options, their decision making might become more responsible. It might also be more ethical. Certainly, it could generate richer and more confident conflict resolution.

When students are equipped to make decisions with a full range of options, they have the freedom to expand their strategic decision-making skills in meaningful ways. When students have respect for the proper use of empathy, they begin to appreciate power as a theory of community. With the inclusion of authenticity and mutuality, the definition of business ethics expands beyond "social responsibility" to include models of interrelationships which can be critically analyzed for their potential enhancement of human life and the facilitation of personal growth.

Tall order. Where to begin?

The Beginning: Fashioning a Hypothesis

If the desired result is to enhance moral growth by introducing new paradigms of conflict resolution, one way to accomplish this is to purposely create cognitive dissonance about ethical reasoning. When an individual becomes aware that her reasoning about resolving ethical conflict is inadequate, that awareness may lead to a search for new ways of thinking about moral issues. This search can generate intellectual growth and form a natural rationale for thinking about alternative theories. If facilitated carefully, and with malice aforethought, this could lead to the construction of new frameworks for working out conflict ethically, and for ethical decision making.

Perceptual discordance is reportedly most powerfully stimulated by aging and experience. At some point, however, the aging process will not stimulate further moral growth in the absence of disequilibrium from some another source. One such source is education. When educating students about the marketplace, one must combat their natural aversion to conflict and take advantage of their curiosity and awe of entrepreneurial fortitude by encouraging them to practice operating outside their comfort zones. The trick then is to introduce cognitive dissonance in a safe environment, while at the same time introducing alternative and perhaps blended frameworks through which to analyze and ultimately harmonize the conflict. Thus diversity becomes an intervention technique which can directly promote dise-quilibrium and the ethical growth that flows from it.

To accomplish this, I found it necessary to turn the course upside down. Rather than beginning with ethics and business organizations, I decided to begin the class with ethics in terms of self, identity, and autonomy. I would begin with self, not in the classical abstract, but in a way that grants connection of the self with the world. I would infuse teleological and deontological theories of ethical analysis with recordings of experiences. I would use experiences not only of males or classical ethicists, but also the experiences of diverse women who have pondered the meaning of ethical behavior. The most powerful way of introducing and facilitating such intervention is to interweave diverse feminist scholarship with more classical theories, as well as new theories postulated by men who have examined ethical behavior in unbiased ways.

Next I looked at the issue of consciously examining factual analy-sis versus factual blindness. My goal was to introduce female ways of knowing and problem solving, thereby expanding the range of voices, as well as focus, from relentlessly public to those considered private by organizational participants and stakeholders. This in turn result-ed in consciously examining concepts of dualism, power, and empa-thy, which lead back to legitimizing and teaching theories of justice and models of caring. It also meant being careful about incorporat-ing into the course content learning strategies, speakers, and multi-visual tools which are learner-centered and which actively model empathetic, affective, and cognitive styles of learning.

My joyful discovery was that this effort at integration could be enhanced by using an interdisciplinary approach, fusing feminist scholarship from psychology, sociology, theology, and literature, as well as economic and business organizational theory.

Anticipated Results

I understand that what I teach has political as well as "power" impli-cations. Therefore, I have had to examine my own biases and be explicit about what I think the goal of teaching Business Ethics should be. It has evolved throughout the process, somewhat in step with feminist phase theory. At first I merely wanted to introduce excluded viewpoints. But, as I began to consider the possibility of developing the risk-taking instincts of business students by encourag-ing their discovery of power and responsibility as ethical change agents, I became fascinated by how students might move toward decision making that elevates human potential and performance. And at that point I knew that inclusion of excluded viewpoints was not enough.

Here is one representation of the process I now visualize:

ETHICAL CONCEPTUALIZATION:

MORAL GROWTH

↑

RATIONAL ⟶ COGNITIVE DISSONANCE ⟵ AFFECTIVE
COGNITIVE ⟶ AVERSION

PRECOGNITIVE
IMPULSIVENESS
FACTUAL BLINDNESS
ETHICAL THEORY
EPISTEMOLOGY
GOOD vs. EVIL
MORAL EXTENSION
MORAL REASONING

I was helped in transforming Business Ethics by the process of trying to identify the appropriate body of knowledge required to do so. I was excited by the diverse body of feminist ethics and moral psychology readings that touched on philosophy and ethical precepts. The presence of such works has been growing over the last twenty years. My research also unearthed integration materials in undergraduate science, mathematics, and technology, which addressed some of the issues of student and faculty resistance, as well as suggestions about teaching methodology. More ideas were forthcoming as I joined the Women's Studies List on the Internet, as well as the Business Ethics and Feminist Journal discussion groups.

Building on previous integration efforts from first-year core courses in other courses, Business Ethics now could integrate feminist theories and pedagogies which include the diversity of women in terms of race, ethnicity, class and sexual preferences. This integration would thereby expand the topic of Business Ethics to include issues of power, gender, and cultural and theoretical conceptualizations, both with regard to morality and ethical constructs of analysis. My belief is that this work will produce a more holistic curricula for Business Ethics. When defined as the study of how humans grow in their capacity and ability to resolve moral conflicts, this course might enhance students' moral analysis, and thus their ability to act ethically when faced with moral conflicts in the future. My hope is that revisioning Business Ethics as a learning process that uses both cognitive and affective processes, and which considers a diversity of moral reasoning and ways of knowing, will enhance moral growth.

What a concept. (And a powerful thought.)

See "Resources: Course Syllabi" for a syllabus and "Resources: Bibliographies" for a select bibliography.

E. Michelle Rabouin *participated in the Community College of Denver's curriculum development project "The Integration of Women's Studies and Feminist Pedagogy into the Core Curriculum."*

Changing Introductory College Mathematics

Chiu-Min Lai

Introductory College Mathematics is the prerequisite course for middle-level mathematics courses at Essex County College. In addition, it is either a required or recommended course for most of the degree programs at the college. Since a large number of students take this course, the math department offers about fifteen sections each semester. Each instructor is expected to cover the same course topics and all students take the same departmental final. The course is transferable to four-year institutions and prepares students to take the Rutgers Math Proficiency Examination. Any changes in the course curriculum requires at least a department-wide effort.

Therefore, for the initial phase in revising this syllabus, I only made changes in the process of teaching and learning, not in the curriculum. My goals were to reduce the amount of class time used for lectures (although there are merits to lectures) and to spend more time in discussion, group work, and writing. To introduce activities which required group work and writing, I included examples from the field of ethnomathematics. Besides providing another dimension of mathematics, reading and discussing case studies from ethnomathematics also help students become more aware of their own ways of doing mathematics.

Ethnomathematics is the study of mathematical ideas of cultures. D'Ambrosio describes ethnomathematics as "the mathematics which is practiced among identifiable cultural groups, such as national-tribal societies, labor groups, children of a certain age bracket, professional classes, and so on." Fashch's description is different: "Ethnoma-the-matics means working hard to understand the logic of other peoples, of other ways of thinking." Gerdes calls "mathematics . . . the union of all ethnomathematics." Frankenstein and Powell suggest incorporating the results from ethnomathematical research into the curriculum as a teaching technique to empower non-traditional college students.[1]

The following case study provides material for a student group activity focusing on ethnomathematics: Many western anthropologists have claimed that the cultures they have studied are "childlike" and "primitive." Yet Marcia Ascher, a mathematician, and Robert Ascher, an anthropologist, argue that "there is not one instance of a study or a restudy that upon close examination supports the myth of the childlike primitive." They go on to quote other anthropologists and conclude that "cultural differences in cognition reside more in the situations to which particular cognitive processes are applied than in the existence of a process in one cultural group and its absence in another."[2] A clear example of the kind of distortion or racist misunderstanding that has occurred involves a frequently repeated anecdote in mathematics history books. It tells of an exchange between an African sheep herder and someone who is variously described as an explorer, trader, or anthropologist. It is intended to show that the herder cannot comprehend the simple arithmetic fact that $2 + 2 = 4$. It describes how the herder agrees to accept two sticks of tobacco for one sheep, but becomes confused and upset when given a total of four sticks of tobacco after a second sheep is selected.

Students can be asked to think of another interpretation of the sheep herder's confusion: Actually, the problem is not that the herder doesn't understand addition, but that the scientist or trader doesn't understand that sheep are not standardized mathematical units. The shepherd's confusion could be attributed to the trader's assumption that he could pay an equal amount for a second, different sheep.[3] In the process of realizing that there is a logic to the shepherd's reasoning, students may learn to respect their own reasoning. In other words, reflecting on and discussing other people's mathematical methods and concepts may motivate students to reflect on their own methods of conceptualizing mathematics and thus allow them to become more aware of their own reasoning process. Once a student's thinking process becomes visible then I, as the instructor, will know the starting point of teaching.

Group Activities

Examples from the ethnomathematics field provide new opportunities for students to interact with each other and talk mathematics. Encouraging group work is one way to facilitate this interaction. Since students are more accustomed to working in isolation than working in a group, they need a structure within that group work:

The group's task, each individual's responsibility within the group, a breakdown of the task into smaller steps with suggested time limits, and other guidance all need to be specified.

How the groups are formed depends on the circumstances. Sometimes groups work better when students form their own groups and sometimes they work better when the teacher assigns groups. Although I want to encourage culturally and gender-mixed groups, I have had students who, because of their low self-confidence in mathematics, want to work with a group in which they feel safe. Usually a safe group contains classmates from the same gender and/or culture.

Writing Activities

When I first started teaching part-time a few years ago, I learned how to be a better teacher through my students' writings about their feelings, confusions, realizations, and accomplishments in the area of mathematics. Since I always responded to each writing, the activities also provided another means to communicate and establish rapport on an individual level. When I began teaching full-time, I began using writing less and less in my classes mainly because of time constraints. I also had less need to use writing as a means to understand my students. Fortunately, participating in a faculty development project reminded me of the value of writing in mathematics. I have since begun to reintegrate writing activities into my class, but this time with the emphasis on facilitating the students' learning process.

The activities now include informal writing assignments instead of term papers. I allow the class time for freewriting (especially during the early part of the semester) and assign brief writing activities (as suggested by Joan Countryman[4]) such as: Describe what we did in class yesterday; explain what went wrong on problem three in the test; or, discuss the most difficult homework problem. Writing assignments also ask students to discuss or explore a concept in a group and then individually to summarize their ideas.

MATH 100: INTRODUCTORY COLLEGE MATHEMATICS

The curriculum has not been revised and will remain as is. What has changed is *how* the actual classes are structured. The amount of class time used for lectures has been reduced and been replaced by the following:

1. Group activities/projects where students are:
   - Learning from and explaining to each other.

- Exploring and discovering concepts.
- Learning to use the calculator.

2. Activities which allow students to investigate and construct concepts:

- Solve a quadratic equation using various methods to discover personal preference and the merits of each method.

- Juxtapose problems involving fractional equations and those dealing with addition/subtraction of fractional expressions so that students can compare and explore the similarities and differences of these two types of problems.

- Use calculator and construct right triangles to learn radicals.

3. Writing Activities:

- Discuss/explore a problem, first within a group, and then write individual responses.

- Compare, describe, justify, or explain a concept, method, etc.

- Discuss/review mistakes on a homework assignment or test.

4. Ethnomathematics. Readings from ethnomathematics research are used:

- To demonstrate the diversity in mathematics knowledge;

- To motivate students to be more aware of their mathematical reasoning;

- For writing and group activities.

NOTES

1. Frankenstein, M. and Powell, A., "Empowering Non-Traditional College Students: The Dialectics of Society and Mathematics Education," Sixth International Congress on Mathematics Education, Budapest, Hungary, 1988.
2. Ascher, M. and Ascher, R., "Ethnomathematics," *History of Science*, 24 (1986).
3. Ascher, M. and Ascher, R., "Ethnomathematics," *History of Science*, 24 (1986): 125–144.
4. Countryman, J., *Writing to Learn Mathematics*, Portsmouth, NH: Heinemann, 1992.

Chiu-Min Lai *participated in the Ford Foundation Curriculum Main-streaming and Teaching Initiative project at Essex County College (NJ) in 1994.*

Integrating Scholarship on Women into Physics

Lalitha Dorai

When I was a student in 1970, I was asked to write on the topic "Women in Physical Sciences" for a History of Science course. Being a physics major, I accordingly chose to write about women in physics. Yet I found that information was available on only one woman in the field—Marie Curie—and I had to I ask myself whether she could really be the only woman of importance in physics. Fortunately, since the 1970s, considerable research has been done in the area of women in science and one can now find information, including biographical tools for further research, on specific women scientists.

Regardless of the abundance of information on women scientists, however, the myth that there are hardly any women physicists or engineers remains firmly entrenched in the minds of the public and of practicing scientists alike. This stereotyping itself delivers a mixed message. To a few young women it signals opportunities for achieving distinction, but to a great majority of people it suggests that there is indeed something about physics or engineering that is unsuitable for women, or that women really are not somehow well enough equipped to be physicists or engineers. Without arguing the merits of the case either way, it must be stressed that there are in fact many women physicists and engineers working in the United States today. The National Science Foundation reported that in 1990 22.4 percent of those working in science and engineering were women; this represents a marked increase from 1980, when women represented only 13.3 percent of this workforce.[1]

Particularly at advanced professional levels, the sciences attract far greater numbers of women than one might expect. Furthermore, women scientists do work that is significant and of lasting importance. Their numbers have increased dramatically during the last two decades largely as a result of equal opportunity laws that made the exclusion or differential treatment of women from any aspect of education and work illegal. Despite these gains, however, the belief that science and women are somehow incompatible persists, and women scientists remain less visible than their achievements warrant.

Educating scientists is an expensive undertaking even at the undergraduate level. Given that anything other than a uniform price per student would be politically unwise and an administrative nightmare, coeducational institutions long ago must have seen the advantage of steering women into the less expensive departments, thus enabling them to subsidize the education of men in the sciences. Indeed in "Making Affirmative Action Work in Higher Education," the Carnegie Commission on Higher Education observed just this phenomenon in at least two traditionally all-male institutions, Williams and Princeton, when they became coeducational.[2] Historically, most, if not all, coeducational colleges and universities restricted women's access to science departments either by simple fiat, by requiring substantially higher qualifications for women, or by "ingenious" regulations such as one at Cornell University that allotted only a few females each year to the more expensive departments. Many women's colleges, however, could not afford to offer any real science at all. Conversely, those women's colleges wealthy enough to do so found their women students quite amazingly interested in science.

For example, a century ago, when Wellesley College was newly established, nearly 40 percent of its graduating classes majored in just two fields: chemistry and mathematics.[3] Why then does the myth of women's scarcity among scientists persist even among women themselves? For one thing, traditions die hard in education because they are so easily transmitted by both precept and example.

Male scientists who learned their science in an environment devoid of women in professional roles, but peopled with female secretaries and research assistants, have also internalized the notion that women are not real scientists but good helpers. When the time came for them to run the departments and make the decisions about whom to admit and whom to hire, they tended to shape their environment in the image of the one they knew.[4] Women who aspire to careers in science, on the other hand, also see that same environment but from an outside perspective, and the message most of them receive is that this environment is unfriendly. Successful women scientists are the product of such a skewed system. Most of these women, however, simply relied on sheer ability and dedication to transcend the limitations that a bigoted policy tried to impose. Clearly, some escaped its influence by staying in women's colleges for most of their careers, and others by working in industry where the yardstick of accomplishment is less who you are and more how much money you can make for the company.

These women enlarge our understanding of ourselves and give us reason to take pride in the heritage they leave to us. The proliferation of women's consciousness groups and women's studies programs in the past few decades has raised questions about women's participation in physics and engineering. Books on women in science and general biographical dictionaries provide a comprehensive picture of the achievements of women in the growth and development of these sciences. However, it is important to note that in almost all these sources there is only limited and inadequate information on the contributions of women of color to science.

Transforming the Faculty

Traditional pedagogical concerns of women's studies can easily be adapted to the science classroom.[5] They include:

1. Attention to language in order to avoid stereotyping applies to the science classroom and includes using non-sexist language when referring to scientists; that is, not referring to the scientist as "he" as well as avoiding stereotypical ascriptions of gender to natural phenomena, namely references to nature as female.

2. Rather than referring to scientists simply by their last names, the inclusion of full names assists in undermining the stereotype that all scientists are male, i.e., "the work of Lisa Meitner and Otto Hahn."

3. As in any other classroom, sexist comments such as jokes that refer to physical or sexual characteristics are inappropriate.

4. A female-friendly science atmosphere will also be enhanced in the science classroom if the science faculty become sensitive to possible behavioral differences in the ways they treat female and male students. It is typical for professors to address the male students more frequently and to interrupt female students more often, and to give more positive reinforcement to male students in terms of eye contact and nodding. Since much of this behavior is unconscious, awareness is the first step to changing it.

Teaching Methodology

Integrating the diversity of women into the physics and engineering curriculum was very challenging for me for many reasons. First of all, I had only just started learning about women scientists through recent exposure to feminist scholarship. Furthermore, the lack of information on women of color in science contributed additional obstacles. I also found that curriculum integration is a long-term process. After reading all the literature that is available (and there is very little of it on physics and engineering), I find that even those who have been at it for a while are still learning how to integrate material into their courses and are fine-tuning how they conduct a classroom. Most of the literature that is available is meant for faculty in universities. Methods that work for universities do not necessarily work for two-year community colleges. In community colleges the number of female students taking physics and engineering courses is very few. I needed to be reasonable in setting and distinguishing between my long- and short-term goals. My long-term goal is to totally restructure courses in physics and engineering. But thus far I have begun restructuring simply by incorporating material on women into two lectures and developing one assignment in the first semester. The next time I teach the course I will develop two more lectures, and so on. The only realistic way for me to truly restructure a course is to allow time to be a factor.

Curriculum Transformation

According to Elizabeth Higginbotham of Memphis State University, successful transforming of a curriculum involves three overlapping steps.[6] The first step is to gain information about the scholarship on women. The second step is to decide how to teach this new material. This process typically involves changing the way in which instructors teach their disciplines. The final step includes addressing classroom dynamics to ensure a safe, supportive learning atmosphere for all the students.

To take the first of these steps within the classroom, I assign the following readings about women physicists/engineers: *Nobel Prize Women in Science,* by Sharon Bertsch McGrayne; *Women in Science (Antiquity through the 19th Century)* by Marilyn Bailey Ogilvie; *Women in Chemistry and Physics,* by Louise S. Grinstein, Rose K. Rose, and Mariam H. Rafailovich; *A Hand Up: Women Mentoring Women in Science,* by Deborah C. Fort; and *Blacks in Science and Medicine,* by Vivian Sammons.

Additionally I give students writing assignments based on these reading materials. Class discussions illustrate not only an understanding of the outstanding qualities of mind and character displayed by women scientists, but the great variety of backgrounds and educational milieus that aided these women, the strengths and weaknesses they developed, and the scope of the research they undertook. We discuss such issues as, for example, why only nine women have won Nobel Prizes in Science when more than three hundred men have done so. Students learn about the enormous obstacles many women have faced just to be in the profession. Confined to basement laboratories and attic offices, sneaking behind furniture to attend science lectures—women scientists have encountered relentless discrimination in universities both as students seeking a scientific education and as researchers who wish to make their career in scientific study and discovery.

We also discuss how, in the United States, women often worked in universities without pay as volunteers as late as 1950. Science was supposed to be tough, rigorous and rational; women were supposed to be soft, weak, and irrational. As a consequence, women scientists were by definition "unnatural beings." Sandra Harding concludes that "women have been more systematically excluded from doing serious science than from performing any social activity except perhaps front-line warfare."[7] Two factors, however, have contributed to women scientist's accomplishments: their love for science itself and their passionate determination to succeed.

In class we discuss how many women have played critical roles in discoveries that ultimately won a Nobel Prize for someone else—namely, men. For example, Lisa Meitner (1878–1968), a nuclear physicist, worked in a basement laboratory. Formerly a carpentry shop, this lab was the only room in Berlin's chemistry institute that Meitner was permitted to enter. No females, except, of course, cleaning women, were allowed upstairs with men. Prohibited even from using a restroom in the chemistry building, Meitner had to use facilities in a hotel up the street. Despite these conditions, she deciphered the experiment of the century and explained that the atomic nucleus can split. For the project she initiated, Otto Hahn received the Nobel Prize.[8]

Hilde Proescholdt Mangold (1898–1924) executed the crucial experiments demonstrating the nature and location of the organizer, the chemicals that direct the embryonic development of different tissues and organs. Her doctoral thesis in biology won her advisor Hans Spelmann the Nobel Prize eleven years after her death.[9]

For thirty years Frieda Robscheit Robbins (1893–1973) was the research partner of George Hoyt Whipple. Although their joint work led to a cure for the deadly disease, pernicious anemia, it was Whipple alone who won a Nobel Prize for Medicine in 1934. "Whipple's experiments," the Nobel Committee observed, "were planned exceedingly well and carried out very accurately and consequently their results can lay claim to absolute reliability. Frieda Robscheit Robbins helped to plan and carried out those experiments." In fact, Robscheit Robbins was listed as the first author on Whipple's most important single paper—the report upon which his scientific reputation rested. Whipple cited twenty-three scientific papers in his Nobel address; Robscheit Robbins was the coauthor of ten. To his credit, Whipple shared his prize money with Robscheit Robbins and with two women technicians.[10]

In the early 1950s, an X-ray crystallographer named Rosalind Elsie Franklin (1920–1958) discovered nearly enough information about the structure of DNA to explain the molecular basis of heredity. However, James Watson and Francis Crick beat Franklin to the Nobel Prize—with her data which they used without her knowledge and without fully crediting her.[11]

Another group of women that I introduce are black women science professionals, who have cleared the hurdles of both racism and sexism. These hurdles have been made a little easier with a combination of the civil rights and the feminist movements. Black women have thus availed themselves of an opening door. These women in science may be less well known, but there is still enough information about them to stimulate and encourage black women who are climbing the ladder or are pondering which ladder to climb. I introduce students to Susan McKinney, the first black woman doctor in the United States, who graduated from the New York Medical College in 1870; Jeanne Craig Sinkford, who at Howard University in 1975 was appointed the first woman dental school dean in the United States; Dorothy Lavinia Brown, the first black women surgeon in the South, who in 1968 was elected to the Tennessee legislature; and Dr. Jane C. Wright, a surgeon and educator who succeeded her father as director of the Harlem Hospital Cancer Research Foundation and pioneered the use of chemotherapy on tumors.[12]

Classroom Applications

In the classroom I incorporate information from the search for women scientists and about the potential biasing effects of male dominance in my class. I include names of famous women scientists in discussions wherever possible. I also use first and last names of all experimenters in order to break the stereotype that all scientists are male. In selecting problems or examples for illustrations, I look to fields such as home economics and nursing, which are dominated by women, to see if they might serve as a source for material. I encourage students to uncover all biases and to explore similarities and differences in the critiques written by individuals based on class, race, and gender. For example, reading Kenneth Manning's *Black Apollo of Science: The Life of Ernest Everett Just* helps to sensitize students to the discrimination and alienation felt by African-American male scientists.[13]

In the laboratory I organize exercises that include female subjects, pointing out to students how this redresses the flaws in earlier experiments. In drawing theories and conclusions from the data, I encourage students to describe their results in precise gender-neutral language. I also invite students to question to what extent the required use of the passive voice in scientific writing reinforces notions of objectivity and distance between observer and object of study while simultaneously hiding biases such as gender, race, and class that might be more readily apparent if scientists wrote in the active voice. Finally, I provide the class with role models of practicing women scientists who have demonstrated that a successful career in science can be combined with a variety of lifestyle options. To do this I invite practicing women physicists and engineers as guest speakers in the classroom.

Approaches to Problem Solving

One area identified by Sue Rosser in *Female Friendly Science* as crucial to transforming the science classroom involves attention to female approaches to problem solving. Rosser argues that a study of the work of women scientists reveals differences in observation, hypothesis formulation, data collection, use of scientific information, and the development of theories and conclusions. She identifies seven observational differences in the practice of women scientists:

1. Inclusion of nontraditional observations such as interactions and relationships.

2. Devotion of more time to observation and collection of more observational data.

3. Viewing the personal experiences of women as valid scientific data.

4. A predilection to research leading to solutions of problems of social concern and avoidance of military research.

5. Acceptance of the scientific worthiness of areas traditionally deemed "feminine."

6. A recognition of the importance of gender in framing hypotheses.

7. Investigation of problems of global scope.

Rosser also notes that women scientists are more likely to use both qualitative and quantitative methods to apply interdisciplinary approaches to employ interactive methods and to develop theories that are relational, interdependent, and multicausal.[14] She concludes that a female-friendly classroom will be one that includes and fosters these types of methods and approaches in the teaching of science.

In trying to incorporate some of Sue Rosser's ideas in the classroom and laboratory, I demonstrate and encourage students to use interdisciplinary approaches to problem solving that combine qualitative and quantitative methods where appropriate. I discuss the practical uses of scientific discoveries to aid the students in placing science in its social context. To address sex-role socialization which might affect females who have had significantly fewer science experiences than males of comparable ages, I consider alternative structures for the laboratory. I expand the number of kinds of observation stages in the laboratory, understanding that girls and young women who lack hands-on experience with laboratory equipment are apt to feel apprehensive about using it to gather data.[15] I now incorporate and validate in class discussions and laboratory exercises personal experiences that women are likely to have had. This allows women students to feel more comfortable in an environment in which many phenomena may be quite unfamiliar.

Research conducted in 1969 by Matina Horner and Philip Shaver indicates that women learn more easily when cooperative rather than competitive pedagogical methods are used.[16] While male students may thrive on competing to see who can finish the problem first, female students often prefer and perform better in situations where everyone wins. By emphasizing cooperative methods in the class and laboratory, I hope to have made mathematics and science more attractive to the women students in my classroom. Also, in order to reduce the competition and fear of not finishing on time initiated by timed tests, I give examinations with no time limit, although they must be completed in one sitting.

Conclusion

Women's preparation for science remains poor. Teachers and textbooks still downplay the scientific accomplishments of women. As was my experience in 1970, Marie Curie remains the only woman scientist mentioned in many classes. Parents and teachers widely believe outdated statistics that purport to show girls as innately unable to learn mathematics as well as boys. That evidence is now known to be either inaccurate or nonexistent. More girls are now completing advanced algebra classes than boys, although fewer high school girls study calculus. In countries like France, where all college-preparatory students—male or female—are required to take mathematics and physics, the percentage of women scientists is higher than in the United States. In France, 35 percent of the physicists who earn advanced doctoral degrees are women. In comparison, a mere 7 percent of employed American physicists and astronomers are women. Only about 14 percent of all bachelor's degrees in engineering go to women in the United States and fewer women earned degrees in engineering in 1990 than in 1984.[16]

With the benefit of the released time that I got with this grant, I was able to do a lot of reading about women in science which I may not have done otherwise. I thus became more sensitive to building a two-way street between feminism and science in my classroom. I hope other faculty who read this will share the responsibility for learning or teaching about women's scholarship and so communicate to their students through their actions its importance to core subject matter of study. Approaches like the ones described here can revitalize our programs for everyone.

NOTES

1. The National Science Foundation. "Women, Minorities and Persons with Disabilities in Science and Engineering." *NSF* (November 1994): 333.
2. Grinstein, Louise S., Rose K. Rose, and Mariam H. Rafailovich. *Women in Chemistry and Physics.* Westport, CT: Greenwood Press, 1993.
3. Grinstein, et. al. *Women in Chemistry and Physics.*
4. Grinstein, et. al. *Women in Chemistry and Physics.*
5. Tuana, Nancy. "FORUM: Feminism and Science." *NWSA Journal* 5, no. 1 (Spring 1993): 56–64. Other useful sources include: Rosser, Sue. *Female-Friendly Science: Applying Women's Studies, Methods, and Theories to Attract Students.* New York: Pergamon Press, 1988; Kahle, Jane. *Women in Science: A Report from the Field.* Philadelphia: Falmer Press. 1985; Kahle, Jane. *Double Dilemma: Minorities and Women in Science and Education.* Lafayette, IN: Purdue University Pub., 1982
6. Higginbotham, Elizabeth. A FIPSE-funded publication from The Research Clearinghouse and Curriculum Integration Project, Center for Research on Women, Memphis State University.
7. Harding, Sandra. "FORUM: Feminism and Science." *NWSA Journal* 5, no. 1 (Spring 1993): 49–55.
8. "Discovery of Uranium Fission: Its Intricate History and Far Reaching Consequences." *Interdisciplinary Science Reviews* 15 (1990): 4.

9. McGrayne, Sharon Bertsch. *Nobel Prize Women in Science: Their Lives, Struggles, and Momentous Discoveries.* New York: Carol Publishing Group, 1992.
10. McGrayne. *Nobel Prize Women in Science.*
11. McGrayne. *Nobel Prize Women in Science.*
12. Sammons, Vivian Ovelton. *Blacks in Science and Medicine.* New York: Hemisphere Publishing Corp., 1989.
13. Manning, Kenneth. *Black Appollo of Science: The Life of Ernest Everett Just.* Oxford: Oxford University Press, 1983.
14. Rosser. *Female Friendly Science.* 38–50.
15. Daniel, Jane and William LeBold. *Women in Engineering.*
16. Rosser. *Female Friendly Science.*
17. McGrayne. *Nobel Prize Women in Science.*

Lalitha Dorai *participated in the engineering, physics, and physical science curriculum development project at Essex Community College, Maryland, where she is assistant professor of physics and engineering. She is actively involved with the recruitment and retention of women in engineering.*

A Note on Gender
and Computer Literacy

Ned M. Wilson

At Essex County College, the course in computer literacy has a grand title, Computers in Society. The broad scope suggested by this title, however, had to be abandoned because of the need to train students in the mundane skills of using a computer: introductory procedures, care of floppy disks, use of DOS, keyboarding, basic word processing and other application programs. The changes in curriculum that are described below add new focus to this list of basic skills, particularly on the issues hinted at in the original title: the importance of computers in society. Computer technology does shape, in important ways, the political and social structures of our society. In addition to knowing how to use computers, students need to understand how these tools create economic and social realities and how they themselves can participate in that process of creation. Closely related to this issue is that of the well-publicized "technology" gap created by economic inequalities and educational gaps.

Two questions posed in Marilyn R. Schuster and Susan R. Van Dyne's article, "Syllabus Redesign Guidelines," are suggestive: "What questions might be asked if gender, race, and class of the writer, artist, reader, and critic were taken into account?" And even more important, "How would this course change if part of the goal were explicitly to include the study of women's experience, and racial, ethnic, and class diversity?"[1] I ask students to consider what gender, race, and class have to do with the subject. I discuss the history of the development of the computer technology. Finally, I ask students to reflect on their own experiences related to computer technology and to gender, ethnic, and class diversity.

The issue of gender and the curriculum in the area of computer technology may focus around questions that ask the students to explore their personal histories. How have they experienced encouragement or discouragement, because of gender, in regard to learning or using the technology? Students are also asked to expand their understanding of the role of computers in society by considering that computer technology was created by the military, drawing from a long history of intellectual inquiry and interest in the issues of logic, mathematics, and the process of mechanical representations of the world. Since its creation, the explosion of computer technology has been fueled largely by the business community that the technology serves. So, what class and economic issues are related to computer technology? In a course in computer literacy, it is appropriate to address both of these questions since the "literacy" movement claims that, in order to participate fully in modern society, students must be able to use the technology.

The first issue raises the question of whether there are personal experiences that may in subtle or not so subtle ways hinder the acquisition of the knowledge and skills necessary to participate in the technological revolution. The second issue raises the problem of who created the technology and for what purpose. In addition, these questions raise others about whether students may avail themselves of the technology with or without accepting the values of business or military establishments. Perhaps by questioning these issues students will know what they are accepting or rejecting as they become computer literate.

The first writing I assign students helps them focus on their own personal experience by asking them to write, using a word processor, about their own "intellectual or technological" history in relation to gender. In this essay they might write about who has helped them, who has not, or who has been indifferent. Students can explore what their own feelings are and from where they think these feelings originate. This essay will become the first of a journal that students will be required to keep as they take the course.

The second question is addressed in the discussion of the history of the development of computer technology. This question focuses the discussion so that the history of technology is more than a summary of the rather impressive statistics about how fast, how large, how much and what type of memory computers have developed. Students use the resources of the Internet and the library to find out who uses computers, who created the technology, and for what purposes, and how this might impact them.

Finally, and appropriately, this course allows students to spend a large amount of time in computer labs. The instructor therefore is able to help students overcome any anxieties that may be associated with computer technology so that they can become comfortable in a variety of computer situations.

While the above changes are essential, other additions and revisions to the course plan are also important, and include the following:

1. A history of the development of computers in both their philosophical and social contexts will be introduced. Some of the issues that will be discussed are the philosophical roots of the efforts to mechanize reasoning and calculation; the nature of digital computers; the technical discoveries that made digital computers possible; the role of women in the process; and the role of the political bodies in the process.

2. The writing assignments outlined above will be incorporated into the course requirements.

3. A section on the use of computers to access data will be added. This section will emphasize both how those who have access to information have power and the importance of the democratic process so that all people have access to this feature of technology. For example, the Internet offers direct access to most federally elected officials and thus is an appropriate tool for making one's interests known to those political bodies. Internet accounts will be opened for students, and several class sessions will be devoted to getting students comfortable using this network. Another source of information accessible through computer technology is the library, and a session will be devoted to helping students acquire the skills necessary to find information available there.

NOTE

1. Schuster, Marilyn R., and Susan R. Van Dyne, Eds. "Syllabus Redesign Guidelines." In *Women's Place in the Academy: Transforming the Liberal Arts Curriculum*, 280. Totowa, NJ: Rowman and Allanheld, 1985.

Ned M. Wilson *participated in the Curriculum Mainstreaming and Teaching Initiative project at Essex County College in 1994 entitled "Incorporating the Study of Gender, Race, Class, Ethnicity, and Sexuality into the Curriculum." He is professor of computer science and humanities at Essex County College, Newark, New Jersey, and is currently designing and creating a lab for the development of instructional materials on CD-ROM.*

Concepts of Physical Science

Lalitha Dorai

Course Description

For the general interest of non-science majors, this course is structured to develop an understanding of the scientific method and its application to the real world of the student. Principles are drawn from basic physical science and extended to fundamental applications which relate to matter and energy in one's environment. Emphasis is on conceptual understanding.

General Course Objectives

1. To demonstrate the methods and procedures of physics as the basic science.

2. To present science as an inquiry process which uses conceptual thinking and theories.

3. To demonstrate the relevance of science to the student's own contemporary situation.

4. To enable a student to logically reject myths and superstitions.

5. To encourage open-mindedness in thought patterns.

6. To promote curiosity about physical reality.

7. To develop the habit of weighing evidence.

8. To demonstrate the interaction of humankind, science, and technology.

9. To develop a willingness to be convinced by evidence.

10. To present the principles of physics as a general education degree requirement.

11. To develop scientific literacy.

Required Reading

1. *Nobel Prize Women in Science,* by Sharon Bertch McGrayne.

2. *Women in Science (Antiquity through the 19th Century),* ed. Marilyn Ogilvie.

3. *Women in Chemistry and Physics,* ed. by Louise S. Grinstein and Miriam H. Rafalovich.

Biography Paper

Choose a woman physicist/engineer. Research her life. Write a 3–5 page paper describing the life of the person you have chosen and her contributions to physics/engineering. Prepare a one-page summary of your paper to use in a 2–5 minute presentation.

Action Paper

Develop a strategy for addressing the Eurocentrism and Androcentrism in physics/engineering. This can be a personal plan, a plan for increasing participation in physics/engineering by women, a physics/engineering curriculum, etc. Write a 3–5 page paper describing your action plan. Prepare a one-page summary of your paper to use in a five-minute presentation.

Methods of Instruction

1. Lecture.
2. Demonstration.
3. Recitation: Much emphasis is placed on student participation.

Methods of Evaluation

1. Tests.
2. Recitation.
3. Quizzes (at option of instructor).
4. Final examination.

Content Outline

Motion, Newton's Laws, Energy, Momentum, Rotational Motion, Atomic Nature, Solids, Liquids, Gasses, Plasma, Heat and Temperature, Change of State, Vibrations and Waves, Sound and Music, Electricity at Rest and in Motion, AC-DC, Magnetism.

Resources: Textbook; all physics equipment (optics, mechanics, heat, electronics, sound).

Lalitha Dorai participated in the engineering, physics, and physical science curriculum development project at Essex Community College, Maryland, where she is assistant professor of physics and engineering. She is actively involved with the recruitment and retention of women in engineering.

World Civilization

David A. Berry

The Ford-funded project on "Mainstreaming Gender Studies in the Curriculum" provided an important forum for faculty to apply central concepts, especially in gender integration, to their own courses. I found myself rethinking the ways in which I had constructed a match between students' interests and needs and the concerns of "the rigorous discipline" of narrative and analytical history. The study of history demands making sense out of the past (and hence ourselves and our present). The focus on gender integration—mainstreaming gender—provides an important avenue for achieving this goal.

First, then, I decided to include in a more definite and explicit way the history of women and, thereby, to examine critical issues of race, gender, and class. In the past I had distributed handouts on the history of women, and I had lectured and focused students' discussions on topics related to gender, race, class, family, and sexuality. Now I have made the readings a part of the syllabus. Moreover, I have made these issues and themes an integral part of the course. I have accomplished this through a systematic examination of women's experience, and racial, ethnic, and class diversity in the readings and lectures. Students' writing assignments will include these questions, issues, and themes, as will the journal writing entries. My aim will be to try to move students from phase one in Peggy McIntosh's model of "Interactive Phases of Curricular Re-Vision" to phase four, which stresses diversity and plurality and "honors particularity at the same time it identifies common denominators of experience."[1] This will entail efforts to move the discussion of women beyond the pitfalls of viewing women as exotic, as victims, or as anomalies. Rather, we will view women as central to an integrated human experience. The examination of the film, *The Return of Martin Guerre,* will be used as a "capstone" learning experience in the course because in it the historical and gender issues are so vividly portrayed.

Second, I plan to expand my use of narrative and self-assessment techniques in order to continue my focus on student learning as a primary pedagogical strategy in the course. The use of narrative cuts through the barriers between the "two cultures" in the academic world—the faculty in one sphere and the students in another; it provides fresh insight into what it means to teach and to learn. McIntosh's notion of inclusion operates on a number of levels— epistemological, disciplinary, pedagogical, social, psychological— and narrative is an excellent way to focus on and integrate those levels. This is central to the discipline of history, and to the teaching and learning processes in the classroom. My study and application of the Perry[2] and Belenky, Clinchy, Goldberger, and Tarule models[3] helped me to become familiar with differences in intellectual capacity and developmental stages of students: Students perceive all experience in different ways. Students deeply appreciate being asked to tell their stories about their learning experiences in the classroom. As they learn about themselves as learners, their historical understanding is deepened and enriched. They can also generalize to apply their new insights about themselves in other courses and in other aspects of their lives. Gender, race, and class are critical lenses which can be used to illuminate the process of student learning. The use of narrative will help students make multiple connections.

Finally, I learned years ago that students learn best in communities; small-group strategies will be used to assist students to grapple with the issues of race, class, and gender. I want my students to "own" the history they study, to re-vision and re-create the past in the same way in which they "own" and re-vision themselves as learners. In this way students become their own historians.

COURSE SYLLABUS

In this course we will study four major historical periods in depth. The four periods are: the ancient Greeks, especially fifth century Athens; classical China; traditional West Africa; and early modern Europe (to the seventeenth century). We will devote approximately three weeks to the social, economic, political, and intellectual aspects of each historical period. Special attention will be paid to gender issues.

This course is part of the general education curriculum which is designed to educate a knowledgeable and thoughtful person who wants to comprehend the world s/he lives in. Knowledge of history is important because the world we live in is the result of historical developments. Therefore we will examine institutions and ideas as the outgrowth of historical processes and not as "eternal truths" or "natural facts." We will attempt to impart a history-minded treatment of the course material.

We know that a student cannot be expected to be familiar with "all" of history. That is why we have selected four major "moments" for study. These "moments" will be placed into the broad sweep of human history with bridge lectures. As we study these "moments" we will emphasize analytic thought and historical understanding, utilizing extensive reading and writing. We are going to build on current trends of historical scholarship, stressing interpretation and synthesis. The use of the computer will assist us in data analysis and in writing papers.

Student learning goals are as follows:

1. To receive an introduction to the nature of historical studies, including the use of evidence, the problems of periodization, causation, explanation, and the use and abuse of value judgments.
2. To understand four "moments" or periods in world history.
3. To become familiar with the types of thinking and understanding that can be gained through the study of history.
4. To understand historical context so that central works in world civilization can be read in their historical significance.
5. To become familiar with major historical issues of gender, class, and race.
6. To use the computer for word processing.
7. To become familiar with the historical component of the general education curriculum.

Required Texts

Plato, *Trial and Death of Socrates* (New York: Dover, 1992).
Arthur Waley, tr., *The Analects of Confucius* (New York: Vintage, 1989).
Eugene F. Rice, *The Foundations of Early Modern Europe, 1460–1559,* Second Edition. (New York: Norton, 1993).
Niccolo Machiavelli, *The Prince* (New York: Norton Critical Edition, 1992).
Chinua Achebe, *Things Fall Apart* (New York: Ballantine, 1994).

Additional readings will be photocopied and placed on reserve in the library. Key works are: Marjorie Shostak, *Nisa: The Life and Words of a !Kung Woman* (New York: Vintage, 1982); Iris Berger, *Religion and Resistance: East African Kingdoms in the Precolonial Period* (Tervuren, Belgium: Musée Royal de l'Afrique Centrale, 1981); Leila Ahmed, *Women and Gender in Islam* (New Haven, CT: Yale University Press, 1993); Bonnie S. Anderson and Judith P. Zinsser, *A History of Their Own, Vol. I* (New York: HarperCollins, 1989).

Journal

Each student is required to keep a journal in which four full pages are to be written for each week in the course. For the first two pages of each week's journal writing the content of the writing will be focused on the readings for the course, or on a lecture or discussion subject, or on topics in history generally. The content of the third and fourth pages must focus on your experience in the course as a learner. Additional handouts will describe this component of the journal.

Papers

Each student will write three analytical and/or comparative reaction papers to the primary texts assigned. Each paper must be word processed. Standard footnote or endnote form must be used. Paper topics will be assigned.

Oral Report

Each student will be required to make one five-minute oral report. Topics will be assigned from Rice, The Foundations of Early Modern Europe.

Examinations

There will be a midterm and a final examination.

Weekly Reading Assignments

1. Selections from M. Shostak, *Nisa: The Life and Words of a !Kung Woman,* Chap. 11, "Women and Men"; Genesis; Egyptian sources.

2. Plato, *Trial and Death of Socrates,* pp. 55–115; women in 5th-century Athens.

3. Plato, pp. 1–54; "The Cave."

4. Confucius, *The Analects,* Books I–IX.

5. Confucius, Introduction, pp. 13–16, 27–33, 83–122, Books X–XX; selections from J. Spence—gender relations and family in China.

6. Selections from Lao Tzu and Han Fei Tzu.

7. Medieval Europe and N. Africa handouts on reserve; Rice, *The Foundations of Early Modern Europe,* Chap. 1; Ahmed, *Women and Gender in Islam.*

8. Rice, Chaps. 2–3.

9. Rice, Chap. 4 (95–106); begin Machiavelli, *The Prince.*

10. Finish *The Prince;* Anderson and Zinsser, *A History of Their Own,* Part VI, Chap. 6, Part VIII, Chaps. 1–2 (on reserve).

11. Rice, Chaps. 5–6.

12. Achebe, *Things Fall Apart,* Chaps. 1–6.

13. Achebe, Chaps. 7–12.

14. Finish Achebe; Berger, *Religion and Resistance: African Kingdoms in the Precolonial Period* (on reserve).

15. Review.

16. Final Examination.

NOTES

1. Peggy McIntosh. "Interactive Phases of Curricular Re-Vision." Paper. Drew University, New Jersey.
2. Perry, William G. *Forms of Intellectual and Ethical Development in College Years.* New York: Holt, Rinehart and Winston, 1970.
3. Belenky, Mary Field, Blythe McVicker Clinchy, Nancy Rule Goldberger, and Jill Mattuck Tarule. *Women's Ways of Knowing.* New York: Basic Books, 1986.

David A. Berry, professor of history at Essex County College, Newark, New Jersey, participated in the Curriculum Mainstreaming and Teaching Initiative project at Essex County College in 1994 entitled "Incorporating the Study of Gender, Race, Class, Ethnicity, and Sexuality into the Curriculum." In addition to teaching World Civilization, David Berry is currently directing a FIPSE project, "Coordinated Curriculum and Learning Communities Across Institutions," in partnership with Rutgers-Newark, the New Jersey Institute of Technology, Malcolm X Shabazz High School and Central High School. He is executive director of the Community Colleges Humanities Association.

Introduction to Microeconomics

Kostis Papadantonakis

Looking back at what I have accomplished since being a part of the Ford Foundation Curriculum Inclusion Project, I am happy to report that each of my initial objectives has been met and, in the crucial area of instructional results, exceeded.[1] Although the work I have been doing will ultimately affect all our economics courses, I initially chose to revise Introduction to Microeconomics so as to include gender issues with particular emphasis on minority women. The topics covered in the fourteen-week course were rearranged and redefined to allow for the inclusion of two weeks' worth of lectures and discussion on new material as well as substantial revisions in the material contained in four other weeks of the course. I also replaced three shorter papers with one long research paper which, for many of my students, became the focus of an investigation into gender, race, and class.

The new material consisted of the household as an economic unit, and the household as a focus for understanding poverty and welfare reform issues. In addition, I made significant modifications to the course by including feminist perspectives in the opening critique of economic rationality. This critique is frequently part of an introductory discussion of microeconomics as the study of economic choice. It is also included in subsequent discussion of consumer behavior and the ethics of consumerism. I also shifted in emphasis during the week dedicated to the distribution of income and wealth, when focus on the relationships among gender, race, and class became the springboard for considering the particular predicaments of minority women in U.S. society. This was accomplished not only through the examination of statistical evidence, but also by debating the role of racism in the perception of inequality as more of a "family values" consequence and less of a class and gender issue in our society. Conveniently, this emphasis served to interest a majority of the students in writing their term papers on the intersections of gender and race in the reproduction of inequality. Finally, during the last week, the class debated healthcare reform as a battleground for the de-linking of gender issues from class- and race-driven politics.

Complementing this was an extensive enrichment of our library holdings. These new books and reprints served as a starting source for many of the students' papers, and I believe will serve a similar purpose in many other economics courses, as well as women's studies classes, including the course I have produced jointly with Linda Zeidman, Women in the Economy.

The work of this past semester has shown that it is possible to redefine the scope of the traditional introductory microeconomics course so as to include issues of gender and race and, in so doing, to address the particular issues of their intersections without in the least diminishing its effectiveness as a component course in a business and economics curriculum. I am certain that similar progress can be made in other economics courses.

Perhaps the most significant change, both personal and professional, for me was the loosening of the distinction between the personal and the academic in my teaching style. As a man and as a white-skinned person, I had often found it convenient to lecture and invite discussion on issues of gender and race by emphasizing my cross-solidarity, so to speak, with the "Other"—white women and persons of color. Such cross-solidarity, after all, had paved the way for white women in my predominantly white classroom and other white men in my coeducational environment to consider the ramifications of their own gender and race privileges in the political economy of our society. While I still believe that such is the case, I have now begun to come to grips with the need to stimulate my "Other" students beyond the facile appeals of cross-solidarity, toward critical thinking of the challenges facing them in the same context of political economy. Motivated by the many examples set in the presentations of my colleagues in the curriculum transformation seminar, I have resolved to address this problem by sharing with my students some of my personal experiences which, it so happens, place me on the other side of the solidarity divides I mentioned here.

A digression is necessary at this point. On one level, I am referring, of course, to my experiences as a "minority" not because I am an immigrant in this country (for, on that score, I have hitherto fared exceptionally well, having escaped the ghettoization of many immigrants, thanks to my entry and assimilation into the North American academe, beginning as a Fulbright student in the Ivy League), but rather because, before coming here (and since then, both in political activism and in personal links) I was a Greek in the new Europe, where Southerners and Easterners are looked down on as "Turks." The dilemmas of all such "Turks" who can enjoy the luxury of any

172 *Women's Studies Quarterly 1996: 3 & 4*

choice in the matter resemble those of the Asian, Hispanic, and African-American bourgeoisie: to assimilate on the basis of class privilege (as much as one can—and of course, one can never fully do so) or to openly resist assimilation at the risk of diluting the class consciousness of those who lack the luxury of choice. Until now, these matters have been easier for me to approach in abstract, theoretical discussions. Thanks to my exposure to the "feminist classroom" (as one of my colleagues put it), I am in the process of discovering how unnecessarily limiting this past reluctance to include the personal in the academic has been.

The second level on which all this applies has to do with my evolving experience as a primary reproductive worker—a direct consequence of the transformation of my family life from one of equal partnership with my wife in housework and parenting to the many adjustments made necessary because of the chronic and progressive multiple sclerosis from which she suffers.[2] Again, what is possible here, as I have been discovering in my new classroom approach, is that I may lead the way in opening up discussion on gender issues, not only by addressing them as a matter of cross-solidarity but also by inviting my students to join me in contemplating the challenges (and joys) of being on the other side of the divide between masculine and feminine roles in productive and reproductive divisions of labor.

Participating in the project's seminar has helped me in significant and perhaps unanticipated ways. As a consequence, I find my work as a teacher both more exciting and more effective. And I also see new ways in which to participate in other aspects of my professional work. I have been experiencing this as a college activist in the development of a successful women's studies program and in the development of cultural diversity in every aspect of our educational institution. And I am also reaping some benefits in this context as a low-intensity, high-aspiration scholar with a renewed interest in the study of the political economy of the household, an endeavor which I hope to pursue with or without further grant support.

As part of the work initiated under this grant, I plan to produce a number of specialized bibliographies for use in different aspects of the introductory economics courses. Ideally, I would like to work with my colleagues in the discipline to develop bibliographical modules by topic, so that our students will find it easier to research term-paper assignments. Topics will include the feminization of poverty; health-care as a gender issue; the role of the welfare state in gender and race divisions; minority women in the professions; the political economy of the household; the political economy of the African-American communities in Baltimore; and, race and gender in educational and class mobility. In addition, I will be developing student-oriented research bibliographies for the Women in the Economy course, as well as other courses in the discipline (for example, a bibliography on gender and ethnicity issues for my honors seminar on Post-Communist Europe next fall semester.)

By the end of the project, I had found and read a good deal more on the political economy of the minority household and the intersection of race and sex as an area of economic accomplishment as well as crisis. I was able to have in place a usable cluster of readings for both instructors and students, as well as modules of presentations on economic analysis (e.g., women as catalysts in the economic development of minority communities; the economics of the female-headed minority household; minority women in the professions) and policy making (e.g., welfare reform; healthcare; affirmative action). Finally, I had acquired the desire to continue this work over the summer and beyond, as an integral component of my ongoing, long-term interest in conducting scholarly work on the political economy of gender.

SYLLABUS AND SUPPLEMENTARY READINGS: INTRODUCTION TO MICROECONOMICS

Course Objectives

This course is the second of the standard two-semester sequence in introductory economics. As such, it is transferable to any undergraduate curriculum. Economics 202 approaches the market economy as the environment in which consumers, workers, investors and other resource owners operate. It examines the behavior and performance of business firms in alternative market structures, ranging from idealized competition to monopoly. In covering this subject matter, students will gain an understanding of the historic evolution and current problems of the U.S. economy cast in the context of the changing conditions of international competition, including the challenges emanating from the rapidly changing regions of Europe and East Asia. Likewise, students will improve their understanding of the problems facing the underdeveloped and newly industrializing economics of the Third World. This class requires a college-level background in mathematics and will introduce students to the use of quantitative information and its analysis through algebra and graphs. In addition, this particular class places emphasis on the development of critical reading and writing skills.

Reading Reviews

A special feature of this course is the use of *Annual Editions: Microeconomics,* an anthology of recent articles on a broad range of microeconomic topics from a wide variety of sources and points of view. As a means of helping focus student comprehension and of facilitating both preparation for classroom discussion and eventual review for examination, students are required to prepare a brief set of notes on the items assigned from this anthology (marked on the syllabus with an asterisk). The recommended format for these notes is the article review form included on the page following the index at the end of *Annual Editions* (p. 244).

Term Paper

In addition to the reading reviews, one longer essay is required in this class (minimum length: five double-spaced pages). The topic for this paper should fall, broadly speaking, within the general area of poverty and welfare reform in the United States. As a starting point, all students are expected to read Stephen Rose's pamphlet, *Social Stratification in the United States,* as well as all the other readings assigned for the eighth week. Beyond those, material for the paper should be sought not only in your assigned readings but also in the library and elsewhere (e.g., the *Wall Street Journal* and other business/economics periodical publications). You are also encouraged to talk with the instructor, who may be able to provide additional guidance and feedback on your choice of topic and suggest particular approaches in your research and argumentation.

Textbooks

William Boyes and Michael Melvin, *Microeconomics.* Second edition. Boston: Houghton Mifflin, 1994.

Don Cole, ed., *Annual Editions, Microeconomics.* Second edition. Guilford, CT: The Dushkin Publishing Group, 1993.

Stephen J. Rose, *Social Stratification in the United States.* New York: The New Press, 1992.

Class Schedule

Week 1: Microeconomics: The Study of Economic Choice
Boyes and Melvin, Ch. 1 (including appendix to p. 28), Ch. 2 and 23.
    "The Behavior of Households and Firms," *Annual Editions,* pp. 4–5.*

Steven E. Rhoads, "Kind Hearts and Opportunity Costs," *Annual Editions,* pp. 6–12.
Diane Cunningham, "An Economic Case for Funding AIDS Research," *Annual Editions,* p. 172.

Week 2: Public Choice: The Government Sector
Boyes and Melvin, Ch. 5 (pp. 118–120) and 22.
Dan M. Becliter, "Congested Parks: A Pricing Dilemma," *Annual Editions,* pp. 174–79.*
Joel Popkin, "Four Myths About the U.S. Mail," *Annual Editions,* p. 180.*
Cheryl O. Ronk, "The Growing Interest in Privatization," *Annual Editions,* pp. 185–87.*
Anthony A. Parker, "Choosing Sides on School Choices," *Annual Editions,* pp. 227–29.*

Week 3: Private Choices: Business Behavior
Boyes and Melvin, Ch. 3, 4.
Thomas A. Hemphill, "Marketer's New Motto: It's Keen to Be Green," *Annual Editions,* pp. 12–17.*
Business Week, "King Customer," *Annual Editions,* pp. 18–21.*
Jeffrey Denny, "King of the Road," *Annual Editions,* pp. 22–27.*

Week 4: Private Choices: Consumer Behavior
Boyes and Melvin, Ch. 6 (including appendix) and 7.
Jeffrey Zack, "The Hullabaloo Over Boycott Ballyhoo," *Annual Editions,* pp. 28–37.*
Timothy Tregarthen, "American Consumers Get Milked . . . Again," *Annual Editions,* pp. 94–95.*
John Holusha, "Pricing Garbage to Reduce Waste," *Annual Editions,* p. 173.*

Week 5: Private Choices: Labor Behavior
Boyes and Melvin, Ch. 16, 17.
"Labor Markets and Unions," *Annual Editions,* pp. 96–97.*
Gus Tyler, "Laboring to Counterbalance Concentrated Capital," *Annual Editions,* pp. 106–13.*
Kevin P. Phillips, "Reagan's America: A Capital Offense," *Annual Editions,* pp. 190–94.*
Herbert Stein, "The Middle Class Blues," *Annual Editions,* pp. 195–99.*

David M. Cutler and Lawrence F. Katz, "Untouched by the Rising Tide," *Annual Editions,* pp. 200–204.*

Week 6: The Household as an Economic Unit
Boyes and Melvin, Ch. 19 (to p. 490).
Juliet B. Schor, "Workers of the World, Unwind," *Annual Editions,* pp. 140–47.*

Week 7: Social Choices: The Distribution of Income and Wealth
Boyes and Melvin, Ch. 15, 18.
Rose, *Social Stratification in the United States,* pp. 3–14, 25–35.
Peter Passell, "Women's Work: The Pay Paradox," *Annual Editions,* p. 218.*
Randy Albelda, "Earning Disabilities: Job Market Undermines Education Payoff for Many," *Annual Editions,* pp. 219–22.*

Week 8: Focus on the Household: Poverty and Welfare Reform
Boyes and Melvin, Ch. 20.
Rose, *Social Stratification in the United States,* pp. 15–24.
"Economic Justice and Income Distribution," *Annual Editions,* pp. 188–89.*
Timothy M. Smeeding, "Why the U.S. Antipoverty System Doesn't Work Very Well," *Annual Editions,* pp. 205–211.*
Sheila B. Kamerman, "Starting Right: What We Owe to Children Under Three," *Annual Editions,* pp. 212–17.
Gary Burtless, "When Work Doesn't Work: Employment Programs for Welfare Recipients," *Annual Editions,* pp. 223–26.*
John J. Dilulio, Jr., "There But for Fortune," *Annual Editions,* pp. 230–36.*

Week 9: The Business Firm as an Economic Unit
Boyes and Melvin, Ch. 8, 9 and Appendix to Ch. 1 (pp. 27–31).
"Market Structures in the American Economy," *Annual Editions,* pp. 46–47.*
The Economist, "Costing the Factory of the Future," *Annual Editions,* pp. 35–36.*
Liz Roman Gallese, "The Strange World of Business Forecasters," *Annual Editions,* pp. 37–40.*
Alan S. Blinder, "Pay, Participation, and Productivity," *Annual Editions,* pp. 125–30.*

David I. Levine and Laura D'Andrea Tyson, "No Voice for Workers," *Annual Editions*, pp. 122–24.*

Week 10: Market Competition: The Free Enterprise Ideal
Boyes and Melvin, Ch. 10.
Margaret M. Blair, "Who's in Charge Here?" *Annual Editions*, pp. 41–45.
Thomas B. Mechlin, "Food Lion: Cut-Rate Prices, Cut-Throat Practices," *Annual Editions*, pp. 70–72.*
Martin Kenney and Richard Florida, "How Japanese Industry Is Rebuilding the Rust Belt," *Annual Editions*, pp. 73–81.*

Week 11: Global Competition: The Free Trade Ideal
Boyes and Melvin, Ch. 24, 25.
J. Ørstrom Moller, "The Competitiveness of U.S. Industry: A View From the Outside," *Annual Editions*, pp. 59–65.*
Thomas Karier, "Unions: Cause or Victim of U.S. Trade Deficit?" *Annual Editions*, pp. 114–21.*
Robert Weissman, "The Plant Closing Epidemic," *Annual Editions*, pp. 131–33.*

Week 12: Big Business: Models and Case-Study
Boyes and Melvin, Ch. 11, 12,13.
Walter Adams and James W. Brock, "1980s Gigantomania Follies," *Annual Editions*, pp. 48–52.*
Business Week, "The Stateless Corporation," *Annual Editions*, pp. 66–69.*

Week 13: Big Government: Tamer or Prop?
Boyes and Melvin, Ch. 15.
Mark S. Kahan, "Confessions of An Airline Deregulator," *Annual Editions*, pp. 150–56.*
Thomas Gale Moore, "Unfinished Business in Motor Carrier Deregulation," *Annual Editions*, pp. 157–65.*
Jonathan Brown, "Risk, Regulation, and Responsibility: Reforming the Banks," *Annual Editions*, pp. 166–71.*

Week 14: Societal Choice Revisited: Health and the Environment
Boyes and Melvin, Ch. 19 (pp. 490–509) and 21.
"Market Failures and Public Microeconomics," *Annual Editions*, pp. 4–5.

Samuel Bowles, "What Markets Can—and Cannot—Do." *Annual Editions,* pp. 53–58.*

Doug Bandow, "Doctors Operate to Cut Out Competition," *Annual Editions,* pp. 89–93.

Alain C. Enthoven, "A Cure for Health Costs," *Annual Editions,* pp. 237–40.

Supplemental Readings for Term Paper Research

Books on Reserve

Amott, Teresa. *Caught in the Crisis: Women in the US Economy Today.* New York: Monthly Review Press, 1993.

Amott, Teresa, and Julie A. Matthaei. *Race, Gender, and Work: A Multicultural History of Women in the United States.* Boston: South End Press, 1991.

Axinn, June, and Mark J. Stern. *Dependency and Poverty: Old Problems in a New World.* New York: Free Press, 1988.

Bergmann, Barbara R. *The Economic Resurgence of Women.* New York: Basic Books, 1988.

Blau, Francine D. and Marianne A. Ferber. *The Economics of Women, Men, and Work,* Second Edition. Englewood Cliffs, NJ: Prentice Hall, 1992.

Brown, Clair, and Joseph A. Pechman, eds. *Gender in the Workplace.* Washington: The Brookings Institution, 1987.

Collins, Jane L., and Martha Gimenez, eds. *Work Without Wages: Domestic Labor and Self-Employment within Capitalism.* Albany, NY: SUNY Press, 1990.

Cook, Alice H., Val R. Lorwin, and Arlene Kaplan Daniels. *The Most Difficult Revolution: Women and Trade Unions.* Ithaca, NY: Cornell University Press, 1992.

Davis, Angela Y. *Women, Race, and Class.* New York: Vintage Books, 1983.

Edsall, Thomas Byrne and Mary D. Edsall. *Chain Reaction: The Impact of Race, Rights, and Taxes on American Politics.* New York: W.W. Norton and Co, 1991.

Feiner, Susan F., ed. *Race, & Gender in the American Economy.* Englewood Cliffs, NJ: Prentice Hall, 1994.

Friedman, Milton and Rose Friedman. *Free to Choose: A Personal Statement.* New York: Harcourt Brace Jovanovich, 1980.

Gilder, George. *Wealth and Poverty.* New York: Basic Books, 1991.

Gordon, Linda, ed. *Women, the State, and Welfare.* Madison: The University of Wisconsin Press, 1991.

Hacker, Andrew. *Two Nations: Black and White, Separate, Hostile, Unequal.* New York: Charles Scribners Sons, 1992.

Jacobs, Jerry A. *Revolving Doors: Sex Segregation and Women's Careers.* Stanford, CA: Stanford University Press, 1989.

Kemp, Alice Abel. *Women's Work: Degraded and Devalued.* Englewood Cliffs, NJ: Prentice Hall, 1993.

Koziara, Karen et. al., eds. *Working Women: Past, Present, Future.* Washington: The Bureau of National Affairs, 1989.

Levy, Frank. *Dollars and Dreams: The Changing American Income Distribution.* New York: W. W. Norton & Co., 1988.

Miliband, Ralph. *Divided Societies: Class Struggle in Contemporary Capitalism.* Oxford: Clarendon Press, 1989.

Pechman, Joseph A., ed. *Fulfilling America's Promise: Social Policies for the 1990s.* Ithaca: Cornell University Press, 1992.

Phillips, Kevin. *Boiling Point: Democrats, Republicans, and the Decline of Middle-Class Prosperity.* New York: HarperCollins, 1994.

Reiter, Rayna R., ed. *Toward An Anthropology of Women.* New York: Monthly Review Press, 1975.

Rodgers, Harrell R., Jr. *Poor Women, Poor Families: The Economic Plight of America's Female-Headed Households.* Armonk, NY: M.E. Sharpe, 1990.

Rodgers-Rose, LaFrances, ed. *The Black Woman.* London: Sage Publications, 1980.

Thurow, Lester. *Generating Inequality: Mechanisms of Distribution in the U.S. Economy.* New York: Basic Books, 1975.

"Women in the U.S." Special issue of *Dollars & Sense,* issue no. 182 (December 1992).

Reprints on Reserve

Bergmann, Barbara R. "The Job of Housewife." In *The Economic Emergence of Women,* 199–226. New York: Basic Books, 1986.

Fulbright, Karen. "The Myth of Double Advantage: Black Female Managers." In *Slipping Through the Cracks: The Status of Black Women,* Ed. Margaret C. Simms and Julianne Malveaux, 33–45. New Brunswick: Transaction Books, 1987.

Mason, Beverly J. "Jamaican Working-Class Women: Producers and Reproducers." In *Slipping Through the Cracks: The Status of Black Women,* Ed. Margaret C. Simms and Julianne Malveaux, 259–75. New Brunswick: Transaction Book, 1987.

Nelson, Barbara J. "The Origins of the Two-Channel Welfare State: Workmen's Compensation and Mothers' Aid." In *Women, the State, and Welfare*, Ed. Linda Gordon, 123–51. Madison: The University of Wisconsin Press, 1990.

Pearce, Diana. "Welfare Is Not for Women: Why the War on Poverty Cannot Conquer the Feminization of Poverty." In *Women, the State, and Welfare*. Ed. Linda Gordon, 265–79. Madison: The University of Wisconsin Press, 1990.

See "Resources: Bibliographies" in this issue for an annotated bibliography, "Selected Annotated Bibliography for Economists and Other Social Scientists."

NOTES

1. I'd like to thank Linda Zeidman, my colleague and the department head; her advice and cooperation were instrumental in the revision and implementation of this course.

2. I use the term primary reproductive worker here because it is the preferred term in political economy to describe the direct production of use-values, such as one's own housework and child care, as part of the process of reproduction of labor value.

Kostis Papadantonakis *teaches economics at Essex Community College, Maryland, where he was part of the faculty team on "Integrating Minority Women into the Curriculum," a project supported by the Ford Foundation in 1993–1994. His work includes publications on the political economy of dependance and is currently focused on the relationship of class, race, and gender in history and in contemporary capitalist societies.*

Business Ethics: A Core Course

E. Michelle Rabouin

Required Texts

Beauchamp, Tom L. and Norman E. Bowie. *Ethical Theory and Business,* 4th ed. Englewood Cliffs, NJ: Prentice Hall, 1992.

Newton, Lisa H. and Maureen Ford, eds. *Taking Sides: Clashing Views on Controversial Issues in Business Ethics and Society,* 3rd ed. Guilford, CT: Dushkin Publishing Group, Inc., 1994.

Rabouin, Michelle, ed. *Ethical Business: Multiple Perspectives.* Carlsbad, CA: Southwestern Press, 1994.

Introduction

This course is designed to teach students how to holistically and critically solve complex ethical issues by modeling diverse analytical frameworks and methodologies. Students will critically compare the current value systems and cultural beliefs of organizations against the ethical standards needed for the twenty-first century. They will also examine their own roles as future change agents by the way in which they solve ethical problems and are able to make strategic, yet ethical, decisions. The goal is to enable students to construct models of ethical reasoning that are contextual, being grounded in experience, and that grant the connected nature of all organizational stakeholders. Course work is designed to facilitate student analysis and resolution of select, ethical issues which have arisen or might arise in typical U.S. business organizations.

The scope of the course is interdisciplinary, drawing on canons from philosophy, psychology and organizational behavior. In this course students will study and build on theories which encompass classical, modern, postmodern and feminist ethical viewpoints. This course usually meets for fifteen weeks and carries three semester hours of credit with three hours per week of lecture and classroom activities.

Transferability of credit will depend upon the institution to which the student desires to transfer. However, the subject matter covered in this course is generally consistent with that which might be covered in an introductory ethics course, where the context is fully human business organizations.

Course Activities and Design

There will be required reading in assigned texts and supplemental readings. Each topic will be presented by lecturers, class discussions, films, timely case studies, etc. Role playing, oral presentations and guest speakers will be utilized when considered appropriate. Activities are designed to create a climate in which participatory learning is facilitated and supported.

Prerequisites, Knowledge, and Skills

Good reading and writing skills are recommended. Reading Level 4, Writing level 4, Study Skills level 3 or REA 05 and Math level 3 are required. Additional prerequisites include completion of eighteen semester hours of college level course work including the following specific related courses: BUS 115, ENG 121, and ECO 201. MAN 226 is a course co-requisite for business majors.

Evaluation

Evaluation procedures will be discussed during the first class meeting.

Course Outline

This course outline is not necessarily a statement of the sequence in which the topics will be presented.

1. Autonomy and Ethics

1. Self Identity
2. Selfhood and Social Expression
3. Moral Development: Valuing Self and Others
4. Moral Agency: Identity as Power

2. Ethical Analysis and Strategic Decision Making

1. Ethical Theories: Justice, Rights, Caring, and Utilitarianism
2. Moral Reasoning and Ethical Analysis
3. Fact Finding and Factual Blindness
4. Empathy and Problem Solving

3. Society and Business

1. Self and Social Transformations
2. Business and Social Transformations
3. Stakeholder Concepts
4. Defining Business Ethics

4. Contextual Ethics: Internal Stakeholders

1. Employees
   - Discrimination and Equality: Sexism, Racism, Homophobia
   - Privacy
   - Reproductive Technology, Family, and Quality of Life
2. Owner Stakeholders
3. Corporate Governance

5. Contextual Ethics: External Stakeholders

1. Business Competitors as Stakeholders
2. Government and Regulation
3. Consumers as Stakeholders
   - Ethical Issues of Products
   - Ethical Issues of Services and Health Care
   - Ethical Issues of Marketing
4. Environmental Issues
5. Business and Global Public Policy

6. Challenges for Future Strategic Decision Making

1. Future conflict resolution between organizations and their stakeholders
2. Strategic management processes for analyzing major ethical challenges
3. Proper use and construction of social audits
4. Future organizational structures

Instructional Goals and Expected Outcomes

1. Autonomy and Ethics

Instructional Goal: The student will gain an understanding that ethics begins with the individual, and construct a picture of self that grants the connected nature of all humans. Upon successful completion of this unit, the student will be able to:

1. Define the ethical theory of autonomy and guides to personal ethical decision making.

2. Explain the relationship of self to "others."

3. Discuss mind/body, reason/emotion, culture/nature dichotomies and their limitations, and characterize general responses.

4. Identify ways in which concepts of identity constitute power.

2. Ethical Analysis and Strategic Decision Making

Instructional Goal: The student will be able to identify and define four major ethical theories. The student will recognize and be able to use a model of reasoning for strategic decision making that is contextual, and has rules-of-thumb grounded in experience. Upon successful completion of this unit, the student will be able to:

1. Define the theories of Justice, Rights, Caring and Teleology.

2. Construct an analytical framework within which to scrutinize ethical issues.

3. Understand and be able to define the different ethical and strategic levels at which organizational issues may be addressed, and the different ways of "knowing."

4. Use these different levels to address empathetic conflict resolution in strategic decision making.

3. Society, Business Organizations and Ethics

Instructional Goal: The student will gain an appreciation for the complex interactions among businesses, government, and the public using an ethical framework. Upon successful completion of this unit, the student will be able to:

1. Provide a perspective on the ethical and historical relationship of business, government and society.

2. Understand and describe major types of regulatory reform, their characteristics, and the rationale for and results of these attempts at social transformation.

3. Describe the "stakeholder" concept and relate it to ethical theories.

4. Formulate and justify a definition of Business Ethics.

4. Contextual Ethics: Internal Stakeholders

Instructional Goal: The student will gain an appreciation for the interaction between theory and practice and engage in explicit application of ethical conflict resolution processes. Upon successful completion of the unit, the student will be able to:

1. Understand and be able to formulate real-life illustrations of the different ethical theories using examples which concern internal stakeholders.

2. Analyze and resolve conflicts of discrimination and equity, with particular emphasis on sexism, racism, and homophobia in private life and in the organization.

3. Analyze and resolve conflicts of personal privacy in the organization.

4. Define and make decisions about conflicts which involve reproductive technology, family and/or quality of life for workers in the organization.

5. Define and strategically resolve issues of stakeholder interests which conflict with the self interest of corporate management.

5. Contextual Ethics: External Stakeholders

Instructional Goal: The student will be introduced to external issues of organizations. The student will identify and define major issues using four ethical theories. The student will recognize and be able to use a model of reasoning for strategic decision making appropriate to the external concerns of an organization. Upon successful completion of this unit, the student will be able to:

1. Examine the competitive impact on organizations when they attempt to resolve issues such as bioethics, health care, property rights, and technological development from each of the four ethical viewpoints.

2. Define consumers as stakeholders and construct a model of consumers' rights and responsibilities using an ethical framework.

3. Describe and construct an appropriate ethical model that could be used to resolve ethical issues which arise when producing and marketing products.

- Examine regulatory issues through the lens of environmental issues which create ethical issues for business.
- Examine corporate philanthropy and social responsibility using an ethical framework.

4. Describe an appropriate ethical model for resolving ethical issues that arise within the health care and other service industries.

5. Describe multinational and global ethical issues and prescribe resolutions using an ethical framework.

6. Challenges for Future Ethical Strategic Decision Making

Instructional Goal: The student will construct personal models of ethical conflict resolution for the future which move the individual and the organization toward ethical performance—ultimately facilitating maximum human potential. Upon successful completion of this unit, the student will be able to:

1. Describe issues that will be the most important to organizational members over the next five years and prescribe resolutions.

2. Define and describe a six-step strategic management process for dealing with conflict between organizations and their stakeholders.

3. Understand the proper use and construction of social audits and their relationship to strategic planning and decision making.

4. Describe tools and processes for moving beyond current organizational structures for ethical resolution of organizational conflicts.

E. Michelle Rabouin participated in the Community College of Denver's curriculum development project "The Integration of Women's Studies and Feminist Pedagogy into the Core Curriculum."

Women Writers:
Multicultural Perspectives

Diane Lebow

If you live long enough as a feminist professor and organizer, some things change for the better. After teaching for 33 years, 28 years of those in a conservative college district, I find myself increasingly delighted when college students actually open their minds and learn and when resistant faculty and administrators reduce their hostility—and perhaps even initiate feminist and ethnic-inclusive projects. In this college district in the 1970s, when I developed one of the first community college women's studies and reentry programs in the nation, faculty and administrators found me a dangerous radical and referred to the new program as "Diane's rear entry program." I was denied a sabbatical for three years on the basis of what was known as my "political activity" until I finally called in the troops—the American Federation of Teachers, the American Civil Liberties Union, et al.—and threatened a lawsuit.

During the semester in which we actually implemented the Curriculum Mainstreaming and Teaching Initiative project and on-going seminars, many older faculty and administrators did not participate. However, I am heartened as I become aware almost on a daily basis that the positive influences from the program are far greater than I had even dared to anticipate. One thing I learned, but too often forget during my many years as a feminist, union activist, and organizer, is that it really is often darkest before the dawn. People often are most antagonistic just as they are reevaluating their views. Conception and gestation take many forms.

At Cañada College, for the first time in its twenty-eight year history, a faculty committee selected a pro-feminist person—and the first woman—to be its president. Had Marie Rosenwasser been on campus two years prior, the project would actually have received support from administrators, and more faculty might have been encouraged to participate. In contrast, our former president did his best to discourage implementation of the Ford-funded project, his major comment being: "By getting this grant, Diane, all you're doing is giving me more work." Another positive development is that the three-campus college district has recently elected two women as board members, both much stronger advocates of educational needs and new ideas than most previous members have been since the district began in 1922. In fact, only two other women had been elected to the board during the previous thirty years. Finally, after years of conflict and controversy, a second child-care center is being built in the district.

Faculty on all three campuses are continuing to develop new courses and reconstruct old courses in order to be more inclusive of gender, race, and class issues. New courses in women's literature are now established at the two campuses where such courses did not exist before. Additional courses in Latino, Asian-American, and African-American literature and culture now exist or are being developed. Perhaps most heartening, as I walk through the bookstores on each of the three campuses, is the sight of works by women included to a much larger extent among the required texts. My eyes almost misted over when I saw that one of our most feminist-bashing female professors is now including Virginia Woolf and Sandra Cisneros in her course!

Among my students, I am finding a resurgence of interest in feminist materials and ideas. Women Writers: Multicultural Perspectives, a course which I have taught in various incarnations over the past twenty-five years, is filled to overflowing with enthusiastic and hard-working students. This is truly one of those courses where repeatedly students call, write, or return to visit and say: "That course changed my life."

SYLLABUS FOR WOMEN WRITERS: MULTICULTURAL PERSPECTIVES

Reading List

Spider Woman's Granddaughters: Traditional Tales and Contemporary Writing by Native American Women, ed. Paula Gunn Allen. New York: Fawcett Columbine, 1989.

Home to Stay: Asian American Women's Fiction, eds. Sylvia Watanabe and Carol Bruchac. Greenfield, NY: Greenfield Review Press, 1990.

The Bluest Eye, Toni Morrison. New York: Plume, 1994.

Cuentos: Stories by Latinas, eds. Alma Gómez et al. Brooklyn, NY: Kitchen Table: Women of Color Press, 1983.

Course Requirements

1. Read assignments prior to class, take notes, and come prepared to participate fully in the discussion. There will be unannounced quizzes.

2. Reading Notes: In a notebook, write notes as well as your reactions to the reading, using the following list as a guide. Bring these notes to class each day and use them to focus your class discussion. I will collect these notebooks and evaluate them several times during the semester. They will be a major instrument for me to judge the amount of consideration you have given to the reading. These notes should be brief but clear. Include as appropriate:

- Brief plot summary or outline.
- List of main characters (fiction) with descriptive adjectives and page references.
- Statement of theme (main idea) in a complete sentence with your explanation. How do you know what the theme is?
- Major symbols in the work and what they symbolize.
- Brief notes on author (at least note ethnicity).

3. Each Friday you will hand in one page of writing on the week's reading assignment. Typed papers preferred. Sometimes a specific assignment will be made for this page. If no assignment is made, this page should be based on the reading of that week and contain one of the following:

- Secrets of women's lives or a particular ethnic perspective revealed in this piece that a male or Anglo writer would not likely have presented. Or:
- Your reaction to some aspect of the work that particularly interested, amused, startled, or distressed you. Avoid generic words like "boring," "liked," "disliked." Or:
- A dialectical journal: Make two columns. In the left column, copy two or three quotations from the work(s) under discussion that week that you consider particularly significant. In the right column, discuss why you consider the quotes central or important to the work.

4. Two to three short papers.

5. Final Exam.

Course Outline

Week 1: Introduction to Women's Studies and Women Writers

- How have race, class, and gender affected people's lives? Interview a parent, friend, younger person, stranger. Include specific examples.

- Watch television with the sound off. "Surf" the channels. Jot down notes on number of men, women, non-whites depicted. Make notes on who looks self-confident and in charge. What models does television give us about female and male identity?
- Definitions of issues to be discussed: 1) Gender—sexual identity, 2) Race—a group of persons related by common descent, blood, or heredity; a distinctive combination of physical traits are transmitted in descent, 3) Class—social stratum sharing basic economic, political, or cultural characteristics.

Three topics we will be considering are:

1. What is *literature?* Why and how can we read and discuss it? Is it an opening up to more of life? Whose life?

2. Why talk about *women writers?* What are some special issues in relation to them?

- Reproduction; access to education; time; privacy; publishing and audience.
- Rambo is universal; what happens between people while they are preparing a meal together is not.
- Attitudes toward women: "other," dirty, less intelligent, dangerous, etc. (List others.)

3. Why consider cultures other than European (i.e. white; generally English speaking) and upper middle class?

- What are some different issues within those cultures? What issues are especially different for women?
- Native-American and African-American oral traditions; people buy books about white males; translation issues.

Week 2: Overview of Women Writers

- Reading: Virginia Woolf: Selections from *A Room of One's Own:* Shakespeare's sister, and Alice Walker's essay "In Search of our Mother's Gardens."
- Eileen Atkins' video, *A Room of One's Own.*

Week 3: Introduction to Native-American History and Writers

- Zuni flute music
- Film on Hopi (Tellens: Museum of Northern Arizona)
- Reading: Introduction to *Spider Woman's Granddaughters.*
- "Rethinking Matriliny among the Hopi," Diane Lebow (in *Women in Search of Utopia,* Schocken, 1984), on reserve.

• "A Woman's Fight," Pretty Shield; "A Warrior's Daughter," Zitkala-Sa; "Oshkikwe's Baby," Delian Oshogay: What have you learned about the oral tradition from these stories? about Native-American culture?

• "American Horse," Louise Erdrich: Explain Erdrich's use of symbolism: butterfly, car, chocolate. Give examples of sensory imagery. Explain how the author uses traditional Michif elements in this contemporary story.

• "The Warrior Maiden," "The Woman Who Fell from the Sky," "As It Was in the Beginning," E. Pauline Johnson: Explain how this story illustrates aspects of early contact between European-Americans and Natives. Discuss how the point of view contributes to the effectiveness of this story.

Week 4: Native-American Women Writers—Early Traditions

• "The Clearing in the Valley," Soge Track: What place do ritual and magic hold in this story?

• "Blue Bird's Offering," Ella Cara Deloria: Rewrite this story in a contemporary setting.

• "The Warriors," Anna Lee Walters; "The Beginning and the End of the World," Okanogan Traditional: Explain the various meanings of "warriors."

• "Coyote Kills Owl Woman," Okanogan Traditional; "The Story of Green-blanket Feet," Humishima: How many comparisons can you find between these two stories, one coming out of oral tradition and the other a "told on the page story"?

Week 5: Native-American Women Writers—Clash of Cultures

• "Grace," Vickie L. Sears: Retell this story from the point of view of Grace; then of the county worker.

• "Whirlwind Man Steals Yellow Woman," Laguna Pueblo Traditional; "Yellow Woman," Leslie Marmon Silko: Connect the modern version of Yellow Woman to the traditional versions.

• "The Power of Horses," Elizabeth Cook-Lynn: Explain the conclusion.

• "An American in New York, " LeAnne Howe: What is written on the base of the Statue of Liberty? Discuss it from a Native-American perspective.

Week 6: Introduction to Asian-American History and Writers

- Native-American paper due.

Introduction to Asian-American History and Writers
- Film: Maxine Hong Kingston. *Talking Story* (San Francisco: KQED, Crosscurrent Media, 1990).
- Reading: Poetry and background on Asian-American literature and culture (handout).
- Texts: *Home to Stay: Asian American Women's Fiction*, eds. Sylvia Watanabe and Carol Bruchac. Passage from *Chinamen*, Maxine Hong Kingston: How is this a "talk story"? Describe "ocean people."

Week 7: Asian-American Women's Fiction—Living in Two Worlds

- "1895: The Honeymoon Hotel," Marie Hara: What are some of the positive aspects of such an arranged marriage from various perspectives: that of the woman, the man, family?
- "Grandmother's Letters," Meena Alexander: Explain the development of each section of this story.
- "Changes," Marnie Mueller: What changes occur to each character in this story of an American internment camp for Japanese-Americans?
- "On the Other Side of the War," Elizabeth Gordon: How many similarities and differences between Vietnamese and American customs and people can you find?

Week 8: Asian-American Women Writers

- "The White Umbrella," Gish Jen: What does the umbrella symbolize?
- "Brave We Are," Tahira Naqui: Discuss the word "hybrid" as central to the story.
- "Family Dinner," Tina Koyama: Why is the story divided into different sections? Explain the final statement of the story.

Week 9: Asian-American Women Writers

- Video: *Neighborhoods of San Francisco: Chinatown* (PBS)
- "Double Face," Amy Tan: This piece is an excerpt from a long autobiographical novel. What fictional techniques in this selection pull it together as a work of art in itself? Explain the title. How many references to faces can you find?

• "Doors," Chitra Divakaruni: Explain the contribution to the whole story by each of the five sections. Analyze the symbolism of the title. Explain the conclusion.

Week 10: Asian-American Women Writers

• "And the Soul Shall Dance," Wakako Yamauchi: From whose point of view is the story told? What does this perspective add to the story? Tell the story from other points of view. Explain Yamauchi's statement, "My stories are permeated with this landscape of longing."

• "Professor Nakashima and Tomiko the Cat," Rosanna Yamagiwa Alfaro: Find examples of humor in this story. In what respects can the professor's messing up the house be seen as parallel to the cat's destructive behavior as well as the wife's? Analyze this story from a feminist perspective: What did you perhaps overlook?

• "Visiting Places," Arun Mukherjee: List examples of racism, sexism, and class conflict in this story.

"Wilshire Bus," Hisaye Yamamoto: Is this story only about racism or also sexism? Explain.

Week 11: Introduction to African-American History and Writers

• Asian-American paper due.
• Video: Toni Morrison.

Weeks 11–14: The Bluest Eye by Toni Morrison

• Reading: *The Bluest Eye,* Toni Morrison.

Study Guide Question. Read the novel through one time. Then as you read it a second time, write your answers to these questions.

Opening Section:

1. Read the *Dick and Jane* primer from the point of view of a little African-American girl. What do you notice?

2. Explain the passage, "There is really nothing more to say—except why. But since why is difficult to handle, one must take refuge in how." Relate this statement to the reasons for writing a novel.

Autumn:

1. Identify all the characters who are introduced. Give page numbers for two to three key passages that help to clarify this character. Select two or three words of your own to describe them.

2. List the main events that happen.

3. What is the symbolism of the Shirley Temple cup? Who was Shirley Temple?

4. Part 2 of this section is like a poem. What is its theme?

5. What is the possible symbolism of the name "Breedlove"? Is there irony here? (Define "irony.")

6. Give examples of what Pecola's world consists of.

7. What is the point of view of each section? What does Morrison accomplish by switching the point of view?

Winter:

1. Page 61: Read this opening paragraph closely. Explain the passage, "Wolf killer turned hawk fighter." Who was "Vulcan"?

2. Compare Claudia's home and family to the Breedloves'.

3. Why, on page 62, is Maureen Peal described as "a high-yellow dream child with long brown hair"? Explain the students' attitude toward her. Why is Claudia jealous?

4. Explain the discussion on pages 71–72 concerning naked men. Why is this passage significant to the rest of the novel?

5. Explain how Morrison uses the weather and the girls' actions on page 80 to demonstrate their emotions concerning what has just happened.

6. How does introducing Geraldine and her son, Junior, broaden our view of African-American families? How many types of families have you met so far in this novel?

7. Page 83: What does Morrison mean by "funkiness"?

8. Why does Junior kill his mother's cat?

9. Page 93: Again explain how Morrison used a description of nature and the weather to make the reader aware of the character's feelings.

Spring:

1. Page 98: Spring is usually thought of as a season of love and happiness. In this world, how is spring depicted?

2. Page 101: What do the girls mean by "ruined"? What is their remedy?

3. Describe the house where Pecola's mother works. Why does the little white girl call her "Polly"? Why does Pecola's mother act in such a hostile manner toward her own daughter? Does it feel different to read a novel in which there are so few white characters? How do you react to this scene?

4. The second section of "Spring" tells the story of the meeting of Pauline Williams and Cholly Breedlove and the development of their lives together. Outline the stages. Why are parts of this section written in italics? What outside forces cause each character to change?

5. Page 114: In what ways does Pauline confuse religious imagery with romance? What makes her particularly vulnerable to Cholly's advances?

6. Pages 132–158: Describe Cholly's birth, childhood, and first sexual experience. What elements of his life so far help to explain the type of man he becomes? What do you think about the portrayal of the white men? Is it believable? Who is Cholly's father and how does their meeting go?

7. Explain the passage, "The pieces of Cholly's life could become coherent only in the head of a musician."

8. Pages 161–163: What happens here? Morrison approaches this scene in an usual way. How and why?

9. Who is Soaphead Church and what does he do for Pecola?

Summer:

1. What is the change in point of view here? What does this accomplish?

2. What is "Moira"?

3. When did you hear about these seeds before? Does the prologue now make sense?

4. Page 190: What reference here also brings us back to the opening scenes of the novel?

5. Page 191: How are Claudia's and Frieda's reactions different from other people's? What is Morrison doing here?

6. Pages 193–204: Whose voice/s is/are this/these? Explain.

7. What happens to Pecola? What is a scapegoat? What are some scapegoats in society today? How can Morrison say Cholly loved Pecola?

8. Pages 205–206: Explain the lines: "We rearranged lies and called it truth."

9. Page 206: "Too late" for what? Explain. Is it still too late today? Relate these lines to today's world. Has anything changed? Are they better? worse? Be specific.

10. How many symbols and metaphors can you find throughout the book? List them with page references and your explanation of what they mean and their relevance for the novel as a whole.

- Essay due on *The Bluest Eye.*

Week 15: Introduction to Latina History and Writers

- Begin *Cuentos,* ed. Alma Gómez et al.

- Discuss bilingual tradition.
- Reading: Handout of history and poetry.
- "Doña Marciana García," Rocky Gámez: Discuss the irony in this story. Compare to "A Worn Path," Eudora Welty.
- "Snapshots," Helena María Viramontes: This is a story of dying and generational conflicts. Explain. Compare to "Tell Me a Riddle," Tillie Olsen.
- "The March," Lake Sagaris: Explain how the author's style emphasizes the horror of the reality. Discuss race, class, and gender in this story.
- "Hunger's Scent," Cenen: Discuss human dignity and survival as possible contradictory forces in life.

Week 16: Latina Fiction—Growing Up

- "Childhood," Carolina María de Jesus: Do you think this young girl is strange in desiring to be a man?
- "El Sueño Perdido," Alma M. Gómez: Discuss dreams and reality in these people's lives.
- "Growing," Helena María Viramontes: How does humor balance the somberness in this story?
- "Teenage Zombie," Amina Susan Ali: Which conflicts in this story are a result of race and of gender? Under what circumstances could the narrator have continued her friendship with Jim?

Week 17: Latina Fiction—Compromise and Survival

- "Amanda," Roberta Fernández: Is Amanda a witch? What does this mean?
- "We Woman Suffer More than Men," Cicera Fernández de Oliveira: Discuss the effect of anger in this story.
- "El Paisano is a Bird of Good Omen," Gloria Anzaldúa: What is odd about this marriage?
- Review of Semester, Final Exam

Essay Assignments

Essay #1: Native-American Writers

Select one of the following topics and write a 2–4 page typed, well-constructed and documented essay. Refer to page numbers in the text using parentheses following each quotation or reference to the story.

1. Write a 2–4 page, well-constructed and documented essay, using

at least four of the pieces read in *Spider Woman's Granddaughters*. Discuss one theme that you see carried throughout these selections that in some way is significant to Native-American values, ideas, or way of life. Some suggestions:

- Techniques of survival.
- Attitudes toward female and male roles, especially as they contrast with those of our dominant culture: thematic discussion.
- Relation between oral and written traditions: literary analysis.
- Attitude toward nature: thematic discussion.
- Nature imagery or nature symbolism: a discussion of literary technique.

2. The attitude of many white Americans toward Native American groups is that they are dying or extinct cultures that would be better off either exterminated or assimilated. Ronald Reagan expressed this view when he said: "We were wrong to let the Indians stay separate; we should have insisted that they come and join us." What do you think about the "Native-American problem"? Relate your answer to materials we have read in our text, referring specifically to at least four works read.

3. Research a specific topic relevant to Native-American women writers and present it either orally to the class or in written form. If you choose to make an oral presentation, hand in a written outline or notes as well. Some suggestions:

- Biography of a Native-American woman writer.
- Native-American poetry, short stories, or a novel we have not discussed in class.
- Spider Woman tales or Yellow Woman tales: Research other materials and information beyond our text.

Look at *Readers' Guide to Periodical Literature* (in the library) and other reference books for recent articles on Native women/women writers/ issues affecting Native women.

If you have another idea, please clear it with me before you begin.

Essay #2: Asian-American Writers

Write a 2–4 page typed essay using standard essay form with thesis in introduction, topic sentences and well developed paragraphs, sufficient specific examples to support each generalization you make, and correct mechanics and sentence structure. Indicate page numbers in parenthesis following direct quotations or specific references [e.g. (42)]. Double space, use 1-inch margins. Give your essay a title.

Assigned readings: Kingston, 2; Tan, 126; Hara, 8; Divakaruni, 146; Alexander, 20; Alfaro, 194; Gordon, 48; Mukherjee, 204;

Jen, 52; Yamamoto, 216; Koyama, 80; Yamauchi, 165; Naquvi, 72; Watanabe, 310.

Select one of the following choices and write a well constructed essay. Realize that these are broad topics and you need to carefully limit your thesis before you begin.

1. Select one theme that you find significant and recurring in the Asian-American women's fiction we have read. Explain this theme and illustrate how it is presented in similar or contrasting forms in several (at least four) of the stories. Here are some suggestions to help you get started:

- The Asian-American women's fiction we have read can be analyzed on a variety of levels, among them: 1) a depiction of Asian-American culture, specific problems, and history; 2) a reflection of women's roles and status (recall the introductory lectures); 3) a universal interpretation of life. (Of course, these categories overlap and intertwine). Or,

2. Discuss the styles and literary techniques used in several (at least four) of these stories. Consider the various elements of fiction. Do you find any similar patterns that you might say characterize Asian-American women's fiction? Some differences?

Essay #3: **The Bluest Eye,** *Toni Morrison*

2–4 typed, double-spaced pages (approx. 600–1,000 words). Choose one of the following topics:

1. What does the juxtaposition of third- and first-person narrative accomplish in *The Bluest Eye*?

2. *The Bluest Eye* is divided into four sections, each referring to a season. Discuss what particular ideas unify each section.

3. What is the theme of this novel? Explain your interpretation, using several key passages from the novel as support.

4. What aspects of black culture has this novel made you more aware of? Refer specifically to the novel as you answer, using quotations and references. Think about the sexism, racism, and classism of our culture.

Final Exam

This paper should be approximately 750–1,000 words in length (approx. 3–4 typed pages). If you miss the exam, you will receive an automatic F as your exam grade. This is an open book essay that requires you to read and assimilate the material covered throughout the semester; this includes the assigned readings, lectures, and discussions.

Review your reading notebooks, Friday papers, and class notes as you prepare your material and ideas. Remember to have fun as you realize how much you've learned. You may write on either 1 or 2:

1. Imagine that the following six people are sitting around a table having dinner. They discuss at least three of the following topics: parents, men, marriage, work, children, animals, Euro-Americans (i.e., "White" people). Write their dialogue. You can also include stage directions as necessary. Your paper will be evaluated on the depth of your comprehension of each character in the context of their respective work and how well you use the various characters to demonstrate your understanding of the themes and issues covered this semester regarding race, gender, and class. Think of each character as speaking out of his or her specific ethnicity.

- Claudia or Cholly, *The Bluest Eye,* Toni Morrison
- Mrs. Jong, "Double Face," pp. 126–39, Amy Tan
- Albertine American Horse, "American Horse," pp. 48–61, Louise Erdrich
- Angie, "Teenage Zombie," pp. 82–87, Amina Susan Ali
- Esperanza, "Doña Marciana García," pp. 7–15, Rocky Gámez
- Andrea, "El Paisano Is a Bird of Good Omen," pp. 153–75, Gloria Anzaldúa

2. Choose one of the following topics and develop it in a well-constructed essay, with a thesis as well as careful structure and support. Your thesis should include some analysis concerning the similarities as well as the differences of the material read. Include in your discussion at least two examples and references to each of the readings in Native-American, Latina, and Asian-American literature.

- A common theme in the literature of Third World women is the conflict of opposing values or ways of life. This may take the form of racial tension (e.g., white versus black); the individual caught between two worlds; or traditions versus a changing world. Discuss how the conflict is resolved. What is communicated by that resolution?

- Kinship is another common theme in the literature of Third World women. Kinship connects the individual to her history and illuminates the values and traditions by which she lives. Discuss this idea and illustrate it from the material read.

- The mother-child relationship is significant as a universal as well as an ethnic-specific theme. Discuss.
- The relationships of men and women, traditional and changing patterns, and conflicts play a significant role in clarifying some of the similarities and differences of one culture and another. Discuss.
- Humor is both universal and culture specific. Discuss the use of different types of humor throughout these works.

Diane Lebow, Ph.D., Professor of English and Women's Studies at Cañada College, San Mateo Community College District, wrote and was Project Director for the curriculum transformation project, "Mainstreaming the New Gender and Multicultural Research into the Community College Curriculum," 1994. Dr. Lebow was involved in the founding of NWSA, developed one of the first Women's Studies degree programs and reentry programs at the community college level in the early 1970s, has written Selfhood in Freefall: Novels by Black and White American Women, *"rethinking Matriliny Among the Hopi" (ed. Rohrlick,* Women in Search of Utopia*), has lived and taught in Europe for many years, and is currently completing a picaresque work of adventures, living, and traveling solo in many parts of the world.*

The Integration of Women's Studies and Feminist Pedagogy into the Core Curriculum

An Annotated Bibliography

Barbara Bollmann, Judith McManus, E. Michelle Rabouin, and Peggy Valdez-Fergason, Community College of Denver

Articles

Acosta-Belén, Edna, Christine E. Bose, and Barbara Sjostrom. "An Interdisciplinary Guide for Research and Curriculum on Puerto Rican Women." In *Women of Color and the Multicultural Curriculum: Transforming the College Classroom.*, Ed. Liza Fiol-Matta and Mariam K. Chamberlain, 343–86. New York: The Feminist Press, 1994. A complete faculty development guide for studying and teaching about Puerto Rican women.

Anderson, Margaret L. "Changing the Curriculum in Higher Education." *Signs* 12, no. 2 (1987): 222–54. Describes the process of building an inclusive curriculum and provides information to assess the "climate for change" in specific disciplines.

Banks, James A. "Integrating the Curriculum with Ethnic Content: Approaches and Guidelines." In *Multicultural Education: Issues and Perspectives.* Ed. J. A. Banks and C. A. Banks, 189–207. Boston: Allyn and Bacon, 1989. Explains the negative effects of the "mainstream-centric" curriculum on both mainstream and ethnic minority students. Provides four approaches to integrating ethnic content into the curriculum.

Banks, James A. "Multicultural Education: Characteristics and Goals." In *Multicultural Education: Issues and Perspectives.* Ed. J. A. Banks and C. A. Banks, 2–26. Boston: Allyn and Bacon, 1989. Describes multicultural education as containing three components: an idea or concept, an educational reform movement, and a process. Argues that all students should experience equality in education.

Bennett, Christine L. "Cultural Diversity in the United States: The Conflicting Themes of Assimilation and Pluralism." In *Comprehensive Multicultural Education: Issues and Perspectives.* Ed. Christine L. Bennett, 85–125. Boston: Allyn and Bacon, 1990. Provides historical sketches of some of the major ethnic groups in the United States.

Collins, Patricia Hill. "On Our Own Terms—Self-Defined Standpoints and Curriculum Transformation. *NWSA Journal,* no. 3 (1991): 367–81. Explains how feminist theorists use phase-theory models to describe approaches to transforming the curriculum. Suggests black feminist thought as an example of "subjugated knowledge" to be considered in curriculum transformation.

Collins, Patricia Hill. "Toward a New Vision: Race, Class and Gender as Categories of Analysis and Connection." Keynote address. Memphis: Center for Research on Women, 1989. Argues for rethinking race, class, and gender as categories for analysis to create new categories of connection.

Fiol-Matta, Liza. "Litmus Tests for Curriculum Transformation." *Women's Studies Quarterly* 21, nos. 3–4 (1993): 161–63. A useful list of questions to consider when revising a course or syllabus.

Frankenberg, Ruth. "White Women, Racism and Anti-Racism: A Women's Studies Course Exploring Racism and Privilege." *Women's Studies Quarterly* 1, no. 2 (1990): 145–53. Describes the course "White Women, Racism and Anti-Racism" taught at the University of California at Santa Cruz. Syllabus provided.

Gilett-Karam, Rosemary, and John E. Roueche. *Underrepresentation and the Question of Diversity: Woman and Minorities in the Community College.* Washington, DC: The Community College Press, 1991. Discusses the underrepresentation of women and minorities teachers and administrators in the community colleges.

Goodstein, Lynn, and Laverne Bryant. "A Minor of Our Own: A Case for an Academic Program in Women of Color." *Women's Studies Quarterly* 1, no. 2 (1990): 39–45. Examines the need for a woman of color minor as well as the inclusion of women of color in the general curriculum.

Higginbotham, Elizabeth. "Designing an Inclusive Curriculum— Bringing All Women into the Core." *Women's Studies Quarterly* 18, (1990): 7–23. Describes three interrelated tasks needed to successfully transform the curriculum: (1) to gain information about the diversity of the female experience, (2) to find new ways of teaching the material to move typically marginal groups into the curriculum, and (3) to create a supportive classroom environment for all students.

Lehrman, Karen. "Off Course." *Mother Jones* (1993 September/ October): 45–68. Argues that women's studies programs should broaden their "narrow politics" to include multiple women's perspectives and should not treat woman as "an ensemble of victimized identities."

Levine, Arthur, and Jeanette Cureton. "The Quiet Revolution: Eleven Facts about Multiculturalism." *Change* (1992 January/February): 25–35. Provides multicultural curriculum data from a study of 196 colleges and universities. Concludes that the level of multicultural activity indicates that the academy has shifted its thinking about multiculturalism and the curriculum.

Linkugal, Wil A. "The Rhetoric of American Feminism: A Social Movement Course—a Symposium of Selected Approaches to the Teaching of Public Address." *Speech Teacher* 23. no. 2 (1974 March): 121–30. Includes a philosophical framework and implementation details for a public speaking course.

McNaron, Toni. "Making Life More Livable for Gays and Lesbians on Campus." *Educational Record* (1991 Winter): 19–22. Describes what is and is not being done to make campus life more responsive to lesbian and gay students in higher education institutions.

Paige-Pointer, Barbara, and Gale Schoreder Auletta. "Restructuring the Curriculum: Barriers and Bridges." *Women's Studies Quarterly* 18 (1990): 86–94. Describes a project at California State University called "Mainstreaming Cross-Cultural Perspectives into the Curriculum." This project allowed faculty to integrate materials about men and women of color into general education courses.

Reinharz, Shulamit. "Teaching the History of Women in Sociology: or Dorothy Swaine Thomas, Wasn't She the Woman Married to William I?" *American Sociologist* 20 (1989 Spring): 87–94. Describes an undergraduate research seminar that examines how sexism has biased the history of women in sociology. Explains how the author engaged students in asking new questions and reading standard sociological materials in critical ways while working toward a less biased understanding of the history of sociology.

Schuster, Marilyn R., and Susan R. Van Dyne. "Syllabus Redesign Guidelines." In *Women's Place in the Academy.* Ed. Marilyn R. Schuster and Susan Van Dyne. New York: Rowman and Allanheld, 1989. Provides guidelines for redesigning courses in humanities, social science, and science. Looks at four components: goal, content, organization, and method.

Schweickart, Patrocinio. "The Challenge of Diversity." *ADE Bulletin* (1988 Winter): 21–26. Claims that undergraduate curricula shows a tension between the commitment to diversity and a commitment to coherence. It argues that the issues of "minority" students, including blacks and homosexuals, allow for a coherent exploration of different lifestyles and perspectives.

Shrewsbury, Carolyn M. "What is Feminist Pedagogy?" *Women's Studies Quarterly* 15, nos. 3–4 (1987 Winter/Fall): 6–13. Defines three concepts—empowerment, community, and leadership—which are central to feminist pedagogy.

Thomas, Douglas. "Rethinking Pedagogy in Public Speaking and American Public Address—a Feminist Alternative." *Women's Studies in Communication* 14 (1991): 42–56. Critiques the traditional study of rhetoric including standards of eloquence, leadership, and effective speaking. Douglas suggests that faculty provide classes as forums where students analyze traditional speaking styles; explore issues of gender, race, and class stratification; and focus on styles of speech geared to change.

Twombly, Susan B. "New Directions for Studying Women in Higher Education: Lessons from Feminist Phase Theory." *Initiatives* 54, no. 1 (1991 Spring): 9–17. Describes how feminist phase theory can be used to reexamine our thinking and direct our research and practice so that difference is integrated into the fabric of higher education.

Vinton, Linda. "Women's Content in Social Work Curricula: Separate but Equal?" *AFFILIA* 71, 74–89 (1992). Analyzes the debate concerning whether women's issues should be taught in separate courses or throughout the social work curriculum.

Zaremba, Stacey Beth. "The Teaching of Psychology with a Gender-Balanced Curriculum." *Teaching of Psychology: Ideas and Innovations, Proceedings of the Sixth Annual Conference on Undergraduate Teaching of Psychology* (Paper presented, 1992 March). Examines the theory that traditional psychological theories are designed in large part to explain the behavior of white males viewing female behavior as deviant or deficient, or ignoring it altogether. The paper suggests an alternative approach. Specifically, it advocates spending class sessions on sexism and discussion of the stages of the research process in which such biases can have an effect. The paper makes the case that integrating women's issues into psychology courses is the first step towards fully integrating diversity into the psychology.

Books

Andersen, Margaret L., and Patricia Hill Collins, eds. *Race, Class, and Gender: An Anthology.* Belmont, CA: Wadsworth, 1992. A useful collection of readings—some academic, others personal essays—which addresses the range of intersections of the categories in its title.

Antler, Joyce, and Kari Knopp, eds. *Changing Education: Women as Radicals and Conservators.* Albany, NY: State University of New York Press, 1990.

Anzaldúa, Gloria. *Making Face, Making Soul/Haciendo Caras: Creative and Critical Perspectives by Women of Color.* San Francisco: Aunt Lute, 1990. An important and illuminating anthology of readings which includes poetry, short fictional narrative, personal essays, and political critiques. Anzaldúa's introduction addresses exclusions in the curriculum.

Butler, Johnnella E., and John C. Walter, eds. *Transforming the Curriculum: Ethnic Studies and Women's Studies.* Albany, New York: State University of New York Press, 1991. This book provides a collection of nineteen essays that discuss curricular change in higher education regarding ethnic and women's studies and presents the theoretical and practical bases for accomplishing this restyling.

Culley, Margo, and Catherine Portugues, eds. *Gendered Subjects: The Dynamics of Feminist Teaching.* Boston: Routledge and Kegan Paul, 1985. Issues of pedagogy, classroom dynamics, content and syllabi revision, personal transformation and identity, departmental and institutional concerns are considered through the lens of feminism.

De la Torre, Adela de la, and Beatriz M. Pesquera, eds. *Building With Our Hands: New Directions in Chicana Studies.* Berkeley: University of California Press, 1993. An important compilation of materials on Chicanas in the United States and the growing field of Chicana Studies.

DuBois, Ellen Carol, and Vicki L. Ruiz, eds. *Unequal Sisters: A Multicultural Reader in U.S. Women's History.* New York: Routledge, 1994. A comprehensive collection of resources naming and placing the "missing" voices and experiences of women in the history curriculum.

Faludi, Susan. *Backlash: The Undeclared War Against American Women.* New York: Crown, 1991. Highly readable and still pertinent analysis of media, politics, and the status of women in the 1980s.

Farnham, Christie, ed. *The Impact of Feminist Research in the Academy.* Bloomington, IN: Indiana University Press, 1987. The cumulative effect on this body of scholarship is to pose paradigm shifts for the disciplines.

Fiol-Matta, Liza, and Mariam K. Chamberlain, eds. *Women of Color and the Multicultural Curriculum: Transforming the College Classroom.* New York: The Feminist Press, 1994. A useful volume of syllabi for both faculty development workshops and undergraduate courses culled from the Ford Foundation-sponsored curriculum transformation initiative, Mainstreaming Minority Women's Studies Program.

Friedman, Ellen G., Wendy K. Kolmar, Charley B. Flint, and Paula Rothenberg, eds. *Creating an Inclusive College Curriculum: A Teaching Source Book from the New Jersey Project.* New York: Teachers College Press, 1996. A collection of resources for curriculum transformation across the disciplines.

Hawisher, Gail E., and Anna O. Soter, eds. *On Literacy and Its Teaching: Issues in English Education.* Albany, NY: State University of New York Press, 1990. This book examines such issues as the interconnectedness of the study of language, literature, and composition; curriculum problems in language instruction in teaching education; the relationship between our traditional notions of literature study and our emerging view of literacy in the contemporary information age; and the ways in which current theory and research can be translated into innovative designs for the teaching of written composition.

Hilary, Ann Phoenix, and Jackie Stacey. *Working Out: New Directions for Women's Studies.* London: The Faimer Press, 1992. This book assesses the developments within women's studies and points to some of the crucial questions and key debates. Some of the issues discussed are sexuality, paid work, the development process, equal opportunities legislation, lesbian history, women's writing, and the whiteness of feminism.

Hull, Gloria T., Patricia Bell Scott, and Barbara Smith, eds. *All the Women Are White, All the Men Are Black, But Some of Us Are Brave: Black Women's Studies.* New York: The Feminist Press, 1982. This groundbreaking volume on black women's studies addresses the historical development of feminism in African-American contexts.

Humm, Maggie. *The Dictionary of Feminist Theory.* Columbus, Ohio: Ohio State University Press, 1990. Presents a collection of both feminist theories and theorists.

Knowles, Marjorie Fine, ed. *Cases and Materials on Women and the Law for GS 200: Introduction to Women's Studies.* New York: Feminist Press, 1973. This classroom material document contains cases and materials used in an undergraduate course, "Women and the Law," and is divided to cover women and the Constitution of the United States, including the Equal Rights Amendment, the Supreme Court abortion decisions and contemporary legal status of women including employment, education and criminal law. Fifteen cases highlight the issues concerning women and the law.

Kramarae, Cheris, and Dale Spender, eds. *The Knowledge Explosion: Generations of Feminist Scholarship.* New York: Teachers College Press, 1992. This anthology of articles is divided into two sections: disciplines and debates. The articles celebrate the achievements of women's studies, its ways of knowing, and its challenges.

Lips, Hilary M. *Women, Men, and Power.* Mayfield, CA: Mayfield Press, 1992. This book explores the inequality of personal, collective, and institutional power that exists between women and men. It analyzes gender power relations in the context of family, sexuality, the workplace, and politics. Topics include cultural images of power, power motives, strategies of interpersonal influence, feelings of effectiveness and control, and stable power structures of dominance.

McCullough, Rita L., ed. *Sources: An Annotated Bibliography of Women's Issues.* Manchester, CT: Knowledge, Ideas, and Trends, 1991. Examines a variety of sources, mostly from small and alternative presses, grouped according to topic.

McIntosh, Peggy, comp. *Directory of Projects: Transforming the Liberal Arts Curriculum through Incorporation of New Scholarship on Women.* New York: Andrew W. Mellon Foundation, 1985. This directory lists and describes projects at colleges and universities that are designed to integrate the work of feminist scholars into the higher education curriculum. It is designed to provide a support system among the coordinators of these programs by informing them of each other's existence and progress. Sixty institutions are covered in the directory.

Minnich, Elizabeth. *Transforming Knowledge.* Philadelphia: Temple University Press, 1990. A lucid analysis of the errors in thinking which underlie universalizing and essentialist notions of knowledge and how this impacts the curriculum.

Mohanty, Chandra Talpade, Ann Russo, and Lourdes Torres, eds. *Third World Women and the Politics of Feminism.* Bloomington, IN: University of Indiana Press, 1991. An interdisciplinary anthology exploring women of color feminisms in global contexts.

O'Malley, Susan Gushee, Robert C. Rosen, and Leonard A. Vogt, eds. *Politics of Education: Essays from Radical Teacher.* Albany, NY: State University of New York, 1990. Thirty of the best essays from *Radical Teacher.* The journal is devoted to feminist and socialist approaches to teaching and showing teachers how to democratize the classroom and empower students.

Pagano, Jo Anne. *Exiles and Communities: Teaching in the Patriarchal Wilderness.* Albany, NY: State University of New York, 1990. This is a meditation on the profession of teaching from the perspective of

a woman whose intellectual identity as teacher and writer is insep-
arable from her whole life as a woman. She brings the methods
and insights of feminist literacy criticism to bear on a reading of
her own educational practice in order to reach a transformed
understanding of the educational enterprise.

Sapiro, Virginia. *Women in American Society: an Introduction to Women's
Studies.* Third Edition. Mayfield, CA: Mayfield Press, 1994. This
text offers an integrated, interdisciplinary approach to women's
studies which incorporates findings and insights from the social
sciences, education, history, and law. Highlights of the third edition include an expanded consideration of the bases of oppression, increased coverage of cognitive-developmental theory and
gender and moral development in individuals, expanded discussions of sexually transmitted diseases, PMS, women in the military,
and women and poverty.

Schuster, Marilyn R., and Susan Van Dyne, eds. *Women's Place in the
Academy: Transforming the Liberal Arts Curriculum.* New Jersey:
Rowman & Allanfeld, 1985. The report discusses the integration of
the recent scholarship of women and minorities into the undergraduate curriculum in eighteen articles. Attention is directed to
case studies, theoretical issues, models for institutional change,
and faculty development, syllabus redesign guidelines, and a bibliography arranged by academic fields.

Spanier, Bonnie, Alexander Bloom, and Darlene Boroviak, eds. *Toward
a Balanced Curriculum: a Sourcebook for Initiating Gender Integration
Projects.* Cambridge: Schenkman, 1984. The resulting "product" of
the Wheaton Conference, this book addresses women's studies
issues, including taking women and gender seriously, models for
changing the curriculum, strategies for integrating the classroom,
locating resources, assessment methodologies, and models for
transforming courses.

Spelman, Elizabeth V. *Inessential Woman: Problems of Exclusion in Feminist
Thought.* Boston: Beacon, 1990. An important critique of ethno-
centricism in women's studies and feminism.

Stineman, Esther. *Basic Reference and Periodical Resources to Support
Women's Studies: a Recommended List.* Madison, Wisconsin: Wisconsin
University Center System, 1978. This annotated bibliography for
undergraduate libraries lists 67 reference sources on women's
issues and 13 periodicals for a core collection to support women's
studies. The works listed were chosen as a representative sampling
for ready reference or as the initial step for in-depth research on
women and women's issues.

Tierney, Helen, ed. *Women's Studies Encyclopedia*. Westport, CT: Greenwood Press, 1989, 1990, 1991. Presents encyclopedic information according to disciplines in three volumes: "Sciences" (vol. I); "Art, Literature, and Music" (vol. II); and "Women's History, Religion, and Philosophy" (vol. III).

Walters, Marianne, Betty Carter, Peggy Papp, and Olga Silverstein. *The Invisible Web: Gender Patterns in Family Relationships*. New York: The Guilford Press, 1991. These women family therapists have taken a critical look at some of the theoretical assumptions of family therapy, particularly as these assumptions influenced their roles as women working with families. The book redefines family and family-related concepts, explores family relationships, family transitions, and single women through the life course.

Weiler, Kathleen. *Women Teaching for Change: Gender, Class and Power*. Boston: Bergin and Garvey, 1987. This book explores the complexity of being a feminist teacher in a public school setting.

Wetzel, Jodi, Margo Linn Espenlaub, Mony A. Hagen, Annette Bennington McEhiney, and Carmen Braun Williams. *Women's Studies: Thinking Women*. Iowa: Kendall/Hunt, 1992. Grounded in the past twenty years of feminist scholarship, this book is designed to cross disciplines and to use materials and methods in interdisciplinary ways. The perspective is multicultural, multiethnic, interdisciplinary, and includes contributors who are located at various places throughout the life course. Designed to be used in introductory courses, the book includes information on the shaping of gender, women's health and well being, patriarchal institutions, women's creativity and spirituality, and the future of feminism.

Wood, Julia T. *Gendered Lives: Communication, Gender, and Culture*. Belmont, CA: Wadsworth Publishing Company, 1994. "[This book uses] relevant work from a range of disciplines to examine the construction of gender and the theory and practice of language. Accessible and carefully organized, [the book] continues and expands the discussions about communication, gender, and culture, encouraging readers to become critical actors in questioning and re-making our relationships, our institutions, and ourselves," says Cheris Kramarae.

Videotapes

American Association of University Woman, producer. *Shortchanging Girls, Shortchanging America*. Washington D.C.: AAUW, 1991. Presentation of the AAUW Educational Equity Roundtable, held January

9, 1991 in Washington D.C., which stressed promotion of self-esteem in female students in math and science.

Bikel, Ofra, producer/writer. *Clarence Thomas and Anita Hill: Private Pain.* Alexandria: PBS Video, 1992. Discusses the Thomas confirmation hearings, the charges of sexual harassment by Anita Hill, and the reactions of Afro-Americans.

Arcana, Judith, producer. *Arab Women.* Washington D.C.: Moonforce Media, 1992. Panel discusses images, stereotypes, and the reality of Arab women and their lives.

Attie, Barbara, Nora Monroe, producers. *Skin and Ink.* New York: Women Make Movies, 1990. Tattoo artists and collectors show their tattoos and discuss tattoos as an art form, motives to get tattooed, and the responses their tattoos elicit from others.

Blumenthal, Lyn, producer. *Art Is Stranger Than Fiction.* New York: Video Data Bank, 1987. Seven short videotapes comprise worlds made up of fantasy, illusion, fact, and speculation. Focuses on what women believe.

Blumenthal, Lyn, producer. *We Are Not Sugar and Spice.* New York: Video Data Bank, 1987. A collection of short videorecordings and films representing alternative views of family and relationships, primarily from women's points of view.

Bonvicini, Joan, producer. *Do It Better: Women's Basketball.* Eugene, OR: ESPN Home Videos, 1990. Instructional video about the fundamentals of basketball.

Boothe, Claire, author. *The Women.* Culver City: Columbia Tristar Video, 1989. Based on the play by Boothe, this 1939 film focuses on relationships between various women.

Briggs, Pamela, producer. *Funny Ladies: A Portrait of Women Cartoonists.* Washington D.C.: Pamela Briggs, 1991. History of women cartoonists and a close look at such comic strips as *Brenda Starr, Cathy, Sylvia,* and *Ernie Pook's Comeek.*

Brockway, Merrill, producer. *Phil Donahue Examines the Human Animal.* Princeton: Films For the Humanities, 1986. Explores human relationships in respect to love and sexuality.

Camacho, Mark, producer. *Women's Gold.* Denver: Video Engagements, 1989. Tells the stories of prominent women in Colorado's first hundred years. These women are depicted on the wall-hanging entitled *Women's Gold,* which hangs in the state capitol.

Coberg, Thaddeus, producer/director. *Dorothy Brooten.* St. Louis: Sigma Theta Tau International, 1992. This program profiles Dorothy Brooten, who is a renowned authority on low-birthweight infants and their families, and whose current work includes identifying families at risk and analyzing the benefits of sending clinical nurse specialists into the homes of women delivering low birthweight infants.

Cuevas, María, director. *Adelante Mujeres!* Windsor, CA: The National Women's Project, 1992. Documents the five-century history of Mexican-American/Chicana women, emphasizing major themes, organization, and personalities.

Dash, Julie, producer. *Illusions.* New York: Women Make Movies, 1983. This narrative film follows the lives of two black women who struggle to make it in Hollywood during WWII.

Degiuli, Sandra, editor. *Becoming a Woman in Okrika.* New York: Film-makers Library, 1991. Five females undergo a traditional rite of passage which was once a necessary prelude to marriage in Okrika, Nigeria.

Ferrero, Pat, producer. *Hearts and Hands.* San Francisco: Ferrero Films, 1988. Uses diaries, letters, photographs, and quilts to tell the story of nineteenth-century women in the Unites States.

Garey, Diane, producer. *Sentimental Women Need Not Apply.* Los Angeles: Direct Cinema Ltd., 1988. Traces the evolution of professional nursing, chronicles the ways in which nurses relate to the society they serve, and examines the areas of hospital, military, and mental health which have shaped and been shaped by nursing.

Gillooly, Jane, producer. *I Said, So Sorry, So What.* Boston, MA: Fanlight Productions, 1990. Conversations with JoAnne Petrus, a 28 year-old recovering drug addict and prison inmate with AIDS, at the Massachusetts Correctional Institute at Framingham.

Harrison, Amy, producer. *Guerillas in Our Midst.* New York: Women Make Movies, 1992. Gallery owners comment on the actions of a group of anonymous women artists who call themselves the Guerilla Girls. Also interviewed are members of the Guerilla Girls, who, dressed in gorilla masks, work to promote greater representation of women and minority artists in art exhibitions.

Hausman, Michael, producer. *Heartland.* Wilderness Women Productions, 1985. Examines the hardships that pioneers faced at the turn of the century in the Rocky Mountains.

Hedley, Philip, producer. *Classical Comedy: Aristophanes.* Princeton: Films for the Humanities and Sciences, 1988. Discusses the concept of humor in two plays, *Women in Power* and *The Braggart Warrior.*

Jhally, Sut, writer. *Dreamworld.* Northampton, MA: Foundation for Media Education, 1990. A controversial video which shows the impact that sex and violence and objectification of women in media have on society and culture in our everyday life.

Jones-Eddy, Julie, producer. *Women of Northwest Colorado*. Denver, 1984. Women reminisce about their work, home remedies, art and crafts, and their difficult and challenging lives in early Colorado.

Kilbourne, Jean, producer. *Still Killing Us Softly*. Cambridge: Cambridge Documentary Films, 1987. Discusses the manner in which women are portrayed by advertising and the effects that this has on women and their images of themselves.

Lane, Jenai, producer. *Warning: The Media May Be Hazardous To Your Health*. Santa Cruz: Media Watch, 1990. Exposes the dangers of media models that glamorize violence, fear, and hatred between the sexes. Based on the slide show by Ann Simonton.

Moir, Ann, author. *Brain Sex*. Canada: Baker and Taylor Videos, 1993. This three-part series explores scientific studies that indicate men and women do not have identical brain structures and that these biological differences may account for the differences in male and female behavior.

National League for Nursing, producer. *Sarah Weddington*. New York: National League for Nursing, 1991. Lecture emphasizes that some women are born leaders.

Nearhood, Janet, producer. *On The Frontline*. Lincoln, NE: Nebraska ETV Network, 1991. The women who served in Vietnam as nurses and entertainers discuss their experiences in the war.

Perry, Michael, producer. *The Public, The Journalists, and the Social Scientist*. Hollywood: Melrose Productions, 1990. Discusses the need for a gender movement in which men and women share the risks of rejection and sexual responsibility. Explains how the lack of this shared responsibility in relationships is a causal factor in sexual harassment, acquaintance rape, learned helplessness, and other problems.

Read, Donna, director. *The Burning Times*. Los Angeles: Direct Cinema Ltd., 1990. Discusses legends and misconceptions regarding the term "witch". Also examines church- and state-sanctioned torture and killing of women during witch-burning times.

Read, Donna, director. *Full Circle*. Santa Monica: National Film Board of Canada, 1993. Discusses environmental issues in relation to women and spirituality.

Read, Donna, director. *Goddess Remembered*. Los Angeles: Direct Cinema Ltd., 1990. Describes and discusses early goddess-worshiping cultures and the current women's spirituality movement.

Ruthsdotter, Mary, producer. *Women in American Life*. Santa Rosa: National Women's History Project, 1989. This five-part series documents the contributions of women in America from the Civil War through the 1950s.

Scott, Cynthia, writer/director. *Strangers In Good Company*. Burbank: Buena Vista Home Video, 1991. Seven elderly women and their bus driver band together to survive when their bus breaks down. As the women draw closer, the women begin to share stories from their past.

Selinger, Janice, producer. *AIDS: The Women Speak Out*. Princeton, N.J.: Films for the Humanities and Sciences, 1990. Tells the stories of women intimately involved with AIDS.

Shepard, Bill, producer. *A Room of One's Own*. New York: Arthur Cantor Films, 1980. Virginia Woolf's piece emphasizes the need for women to declare their independence, talent, and freedom to control their own destinies.

University of California at Santa Cruz, producer. *Going Out of Our Minds*. Santa Cruz: University of California, 1988. Sonia Johnson speaks about the need for an internal spiritual revolution of women changing their feelings about themselves and transforming their lives to stop being the economic base enabling patriarchy.

Van Falkenburg, Carole, producer. *Wild Women Don't Get the Blues*. San Francisco: California Newsreel, 1989. The story of many pioneer blues women from early in the century. The videotape covers Ma Rainey, Ethel Waters, Alberta Hunter and others.

Vecchione, Judith, producer. *Americas*. Boston: WGBH, 1992. Tape 5 discusses the changing role of women in Latin America.

Walton, Pam, producer. *Out in Suburbia*. New York: Filmmakers Library, 1990. Eleven lesbians discuss their lives, including marriage, motherhood, discrimination, stereotypes, and female roles.

Wheelock, Martha, director. *One Fine Day*. Patterson, NY: Ishtar Films, 1984. A five-minute montage of American women from the eighteenth century to the present day.

WNET, producer. *Sexual Harassment From 9 to 5*. Princeton: Educational Broadcasting Corporation, 1986. Discusses the changing laws regarding sexual harassment in the workplace and how companies are responding to and complying with new laws.

WNET, producer. *A World of Ideas*. New York: WNET, 1989. Forty-two videotapes of interviews conducted by Bill Moyers. Moyers interviews many women, such as Louise Erdrich, Sara Lightfoot, Barbara Tuchman, and others, about American life today.

Barbara Bollmann, Ph.D., dean of the Division of Health and Human Services, was project director for the Community College of Denver's curriculum development project "The Integration of Women's Studies and Feminist

Pedagogy into the Core Curriculum." She has also authored How to Start a Gerontology Project in a Community College, Introduction to Sociology: A Multicultural Reader, *and* Sociology.

Judith McManus *participated in the Community College of Denver's curriculum development project "The Integration of Women's Studies and Feminist Pedagogy into the Core Curriculum."*

E. Michelle Rabouin *participated in the Community College of Denver's curriculum development project "The Integration of Women's Studies and Feminist Pedagogy into the Core Curriculum."*

Peggy Valdez-Fergason *is professor of English and director of the La Familia Scholars Program at the Community College of Denver. Her current work focuses on the retention of first-generation college students through the integration of learning communities and diversity into the community college core curriculum.*

National Center for Curriculum Transformation: Resources on Women

Sara Coulter, Elaine Hedges, Beth Vanfossen, Towson State University

The National Center for Curriculum Transformation Resources on Women was formed to meet the needs of educators involved in addressing curriculum change in regard to women and gender in secondary and post-secondary education in the United States. Project Directors Sara Coulter, Elaine Hedges, and Beth Vanfossen designed the Center to serve as a source of information on the resources developed by diverse projects over fifteen years of focused curriculum transformation work. The Center also creates and publishes manuals, quick-reference materials, and directories to facilitate the organization and implementation of curriculum transformation activities.

Two teams of experts, the National Committee of Curriculum Consultants and a national network of consulting scholars, aid the Center in developing materials and identifying needs and resources. The former, a working committee which, in addition to offering ongoing input throughout the year, meets annually as a group, is made up of longtime curriculum transformation and women's studies specialists Edna Acosta-Belén, Margaret Andersen, Rose M. Brewer, Johnnella Butler, Bonnie Thornton Dill, Liza Fiol-Matta, Myrna Goldenberg, Beverly Guy-Sheftall, Dorothy Helly, Joan Korenman, Peggy McIntosh, Elizabeth Minnich, Janice Monk, Deborah Rosenfelt, Sue Rosser, Paula Rothenberg, Karen Rowe, Betty Schmitz, Bonnie Spanier, Emily Style, Phyllis Weisbard, and Rhonda Williams. The consulting scholars, who have written essays for the Center in discipline-specific knowledge areas, are noted scholars in their fields. They include: Louise Lamphere, University of New Mexico (Anthropology); Linnea Dietrich, Miami University and Diane Smith Hurd, Art Academy of Cincinnati (Art); Bonnie Spanier, State University of New York, Albany (Biology); Susan Wolfson, Princeton University (British Literature); Lynne Worsham, University of Wisconsin, Milwaukee (Composition); Madeline Grumet, Brooklyn College, City University of New York (Education); Julie Nelson, Brandeis University (Economics); Sylvia Schafer and Merry Wiesner Hanks, University of Wisconsin, Madison (European History); Janice Monk, University of Arizona (Geography); J. Michele Edwards, Macalester College (Music); Andrea Nye, University of Wisconsin (Philosophy); Virginia Sapiro, University of Wisconsin (Political Science); Nancy Russo, Arizona State University (Psychology); Jacqueline Johnson and Barbara Risman, North Carolina State University (Sociology); and Nancy Hewitt, Duke University (U.S. History).

While the information provided by the Center is useful to anyone doing curriculum transformation, it is especially important to institutions and faculty without extensive resources to initiate and support initiatives from scratch. Connecting with the national activity in curriculum transformation will help give them context, as well as the basic resources, through which to sustain and extend their own interest and involve their institutions. While the Center aims to include the issues of women and gender in general education as well as multicultural curriculum reform in colleges and universities, schools and teachers in secondary education will also gain enhanced access to the resources generated by higher education and other projects in secondary education.

Publications on Curriculum Transformation

The following are some of the publications available from the National Center for Curriculum Transformation Resources on Women. These consist of directories, manuals, and essays covering the primary information needed to do curriculum transformation, and have been designed to be brief, user-friendly, and cross-referenced to each other. For a complete list of publications and prices, and to place orders, please contact the Center at the Institute for Teaching and Research on Women, Towson State University, Baltimore, MD 21252; phone: (410) 830-2334; fax: (410) 830-3469; e-mail: e7w8cct@toe. towson.edu; URL: http://WWW.towson.edu.ncctrw.

Basic Information

Directory of Curriculum Transformation Projects and Activities. This directory provides brief descriptions of over 200 curriculum transformation projects or activities from 1976 to the present. These projects
have focused on changing courses in higher and secondary education to reflect the new scholarship on women that has emerged from
women's studies, black studies, and ethnic studies. Each description
includes the name of the project, the name of the project director,
and the name, address, phone numbers, and e-mail address, if available, of the current contact person. There is a brief description of
the project, its outcome, the amounts and sources of funding, and
any publications of or about the project that provide fuller information. The projects are listed in the text alphabetically by name of
institution where they occurred or from which they were organized,
and in appendices by date, state, kind of educational institution, and
amount of funding. The directory's introduction discusses consortial
projects—including a list of participating institutions—and describes
the work of centers that have been particularly active in curriculum
transformation. The *Directory* is intended to help educators review
the amount and kinds of work that have been occurring in curriculum transformation on women and to encourage them to consult
project publications (see also *Catalog of Resources*) and contact project
directors for more information about those of particular interest and
relevance to their needs.

Catalog of Curriculum Transformation Resources. This catalog lists materials developed by curriculum transformation projects and national
organizations that are available either free or for sale. These include
proposals, reports, bibliographies, workshop descriptions and reading
lists, revised syllabi, classroom materials, participant essays, newsletters, and other products of curriculum transformation activities, especially from those projects listed in the *Directory*. These resources
provide valuable information, models, and examples for educators
leading and participating in curriculum transformation activities.

Introductory Bibliography for Curriculum Transformation. This bibliography
provides lists of references for beginning curriculum transformation
on women, especially for those organizing projects and activities for
faculty and teachers. It does not attempt to be comprehensive but

rather to simplify the process of selection by offering an "introduction" that will lead you to other sources.

Advice on Conducting Projects and Activities

Getting Started: Planning and Organizing Curriculum Transformation Work. This manual describes the major stages and components of curriculum transformation projects as they have developed since about 1980 and is essentially a distillation of the experience of previous and current projects. Using information acquired from both published and unpublished materials and from formal interviews and informal conversations with directors and participants in several hundred curriculum transformation projects nationwide, this manual summarizes what has been done in the past, what is currently being done, and what has worked well or is currently working well.

Written by Elaine Hedges, whose long experience in women's studies and curriculum transformation projects informs this synthesis, *Getting Started* is designed to help faculty and administrators initiate, plan, and conduct faculty development and curriculum projects whose purpose is to incorporate the content and perspectives of women's studies and race/ethnic studies scholarship into their courses.

Using the Internet for Curriculum Transformation. This manual gives clear, step-by-step instructions on how to use e-mail, how to find e-mail addresses, and how to access e-mail discussion lists relevant to curriculum transformation. It explains Telnet, FTP, Gopher, World Wide Web, and how to access and use them. It discusses online information about women on e-mail lists and World Wide Web sites. Written by Joan Korenman, who has accumulated much experience through running the Women's Studies Listserv, this manual answers the questions of beginners and of advanced Internet users on how to access and take advantage of the information related to curriculum transformation available on the Internet. Identifying the best sources of information on women for curriculum transformation on the Internet enables educators to save time and find valuable material. Updates to this manual will be available on the National Center Web page (http://www.towson.edu/ncctrw).

Funding for Curriculum Transformation Projects and Activities. This manual provides basic information on how to pursue funding for curriculum transformation from a variety of funding sources—from budgets within educational institutions, from state and federal agencies, from private foundations, from corporations, and from local groups and individuals. It takes the reader through the process of grant funding—from initial development of an idea to the submission of a proposal and its outcome, whether positive or negative. Appendices provide sample pages of sources of information, such as *The Federal Register* and tax forms, with instructions on how to read them to obtain the relevant information.

Written by Jolie Susan and Sara Coulter, who have learned the process through personal experience, this manual is intended to assist educators who are frequently expected to secure their own funding for projects and lack experience in applying for grants. The manual provides an overview of the process, basic information and models, and advice from others experienced in fund raising.

Evaluating Curriculum Transformation Projects. This manual outlines several types and forms of evaluation designs which could be used in evaluating curriculum transformation projects. It briefly traces the history of the development of traditional evaluation research methods, presents the pros and cons of different types, and suggests adaptations which could be useful for curriculum transformation. It lists pragmatic steps in planning an evaluation, such as developing goals, designing what concepts are to be measured, and scheduling the different components of the evaluation. An appendix includes sample instruments for simple as well as more complex evaluations, such as a simple checklist to be given to participants in a seminar, pre- and post-project questionnaires to be given to students or project participants, a checklist of steps and outline of procedures for doing a syllabus examination, and information about observing classrooms. References for additional reading are provided.

Evaluating Curriculum Transformation Projects is written by Beth Vanfossen whose background in the teaching of research methods as well as practical experience in conducting evaluation research informs the manual's advice. Evaluation is an increasingly important component of curriculum transformation work on which project directors and others often need assistance.

Analysis and Discussion

Discipline Analysis Essays. Under the general editorship of Elaine Hedges, the National Center has requested scholars in selected academic disciplines to write brief essays summarizing the impact of the new scholarship on women on their discipline. These essays identify and explain the issues to be confronted as faculty in these disciplines revise their courses to include the information and perspectives provided by this scholarship. Disciplines include: anthropology, art, biology, British literature, composition, education, economics, European history, geography, music, philosophy, political science, psychology, and sociology, and U.S. history.

CUNY Panels: Rethinking the Disciplines. Panels of scholars in seven disciplines address questions about the impact on their discipline of the scholarship on gender, race, ethnicity, and class. The panels were developed under the leadership of Dorothy Helly as part of the Seminar on Scholarship and the Curriculum: The Study of Gender, Race, Ethnicity, and Class within The CUNY Academy for the Humanities and Sciences. Disciplines and panel participants include: Anthropology (Louise Lamphere, University of New Mexico); Biology (Bonnie Spanier, SUNY-Albany; Sue V. Rosser, University of Florida; Joseph N. Musio, Kingsborough Community College, CUNY; and Edward B. Tucker, Baruch College, CUNY); Education (Madeline Grumet, Brooklyn College, CUNY); History (Carol Ruth Berkin, Baruch College, CUNY; Martha C. Howell, Columbia University; Altagracia Ortiz, John Jay College, CUNY; and, Judith Zinsser, Miami University); Literature (Joan E. Hartman, College of Staten Island, CUNY; Daisy Cocco de Filippis, York College, CUNY; Steven F. Kruger, Queens College, CUNY; Sally O'Driscoll, Fairfield University; Amy Ling, University of Wisconsin, Madison; and Barbara J. Webb, Hunter College, CUNY); Psychology (Nancy Russo, Arizona State University); and Sociology (Margaret L. Anderson, University of Delaware; Rose M. Brewer, University of Minnesota; Natalie J. Sokoloff, John Jay College, CUNY; Julia Wrigley, Graduate Center, CUNY; and, Gloria Bonilla-Santiago, Rutgers University).

Essays on Selected Topics and Issues

As educators define and confront the issues raised by the scholarship on women and the reexamination of the curriculum that it requires, new insights are achieved on the construction of knowledge, on interdisciplinary relationships and gaps, and on cooperation and conflict among colleagues. These essays, written by educators with much experience in diverse kinds of curriculum transformation work, are brief discussions of some of these issues. Titles will be added in response to interest and the evolution of curriculum transformation work. Essays and authors include: *Necessary Turbulence* (Deborah Rosenfelt, University of Maryland, College Park); *Interdisciplinary Intersections* (Dorothy Helly, Hunter College, CUNY); *International Perspectives* (Janice Monk, University of Arizona); *Commonality and Difference* (Rhonda Williams, University of Maryland, College Park); *Gender, Race, Nationality, and Science* (Rhonda Williams, University of Maryland, College Park).

Elaine Hedges *was codirector of a four-year, FIPSE-funded curriculum transformation project at Towson State University, 1983–1987, and a two-year FIPSE community college project, 1988–1990, which involved five institutions from the Baltimore-Washington D.C. area. She is currently a codirector of the National Center for Curriculum Transformation Resources on Women at Towson State University.*

Sara Coulter, *a professor of English at Towson State University, has codirected two curriculum transformation projects, one at Towson State University and one with five community colleges in the Baltimore and Washington DC area. She is currently codirector of the National Center for Curriculum Transformation Resources on Women located at the Institute for Teaching and Research on Women at Towson State University.*

Beth Vanfossen, *director of the Institute for Teaching and Research on Women at Towson State University, was director of the Curriculum Integration Project at SUNY—Brockport, codirector of the SUNY Women's Studies Council's Curriculum Transformation Project, and currently is codirector of the National Center for Curriculum Transformation Resources on Women. Her research interests concentrate on social and gender inequality in education and work, as represented by numerous journal articles as well as a book,* The Structure of Inequality.

Minority Women and the Dance Curriculum

An Annotated Bibliography

Carole M. Cascio

Texts

Adair, Christy. *Women and Dance: Sylphs and Sirens.* New York: New York University Press, 1992. Recording history from the point of view of gender, the author argues that dance is important in shaping our ideas about ourselves and is thus an arena for feminist practice. The book focuses on the consequences for female dancers of the development of Western dance technique in a patriarchal society. The author shows how women's dance works challenge traditional images of women in dance and provide visions for future possibilities. African-American women are represented throughout the text.

Banner, Lois W. *American Beauty.* Chicago: University of Chicago Press, 1983. This work traces the social history of changing American definitions, perceptions, and standards of feminine beauty. The various trends are related to other social and cultural events as the author considers the history of dress, cosmetics, beauty contests, exercise and health reform, and magazine illustration among other topics. That beauty has been a source of power for women is expressed, but more importantly, the author reminds the reader that it has also been "the most divisive, and ultimately oppressive of all the aspects of women's culture." The text does not adequately consider women of color within the research.

Buonaventura, Wendy. *Serpent of the Veil: Women and Dance in the Arab World.* New York: Interlink Books, 1994. A discussion of the history of female solo dancing in the Middle East during the nineteenth and early twentieth centuries, this source is lavishly illustrated, communicating the color, sensuality, poetry, and passion of the subject. The author explains the origins of this ancient work and the way in which the sensual ease and bodily awareness of the women in the Arab world, the close nature of female relations and conscious union with others, is affirmed by the dance.

Chapkis, Wendy. *Beauty Secrets: Women and the Politics of Appearance.* Boston: South End Press, 1986. The links between appearance, sexuality, gender, racism, class, and economics shape externalized standards of beauty and lead to conformity to those ideas. Interviews with and photographs of a wide range of representative women who share their experiences allow women to identify with the content and insights contained here.

Dash, Julie, et al. *Daughters of the Dust: The Making of an African American Woman's Film.* New York: The New Press, 1992. This source describes the story of Dash's struggle to complete the first nationally distributed feature film by an African-American woman, which was praised by critics and called "a film of spellbinding visual beauty" by the *New York Times*. The film gives respectful attention to the iconography of black women (hair, cloth, jewelry, skin tones, body language). In addition to the script for the film, this book includes Dash's extended interview with bell hooks, which gives voice to the emotionally charged and historical issue of African culture and the tension between tradition and assimilation by Western culture.

Desmond, Jane. "Dancing Out the Difference: Cultural Imperialism and Ruth St. Denis's 'Radha' of 1906." *Signs: Journal of Women in Culture and Society* 17, no. 1 (1991): 28–49. A demonstration of how investigation of the human body moving in performance will open further development of current theories about perception, pleasure, and mapping of meaning onto the gendered body. An example of how any investigation of gender in dance must be linked to concurrent analysis of other markers of cultural otherness, such as race and class.

Edelman, Marian Wright. *The Measure of Our Success: A Letter to My Children and Yours.* New York: HarperCollins, 1993. Twenty-five lessons for life prepared for her sons. Edelman shares the wisdom from her African-American community, in which the children and needy were placed first, as that wisdom was passed down from her parents and other role models. She suggests that race and gender differences are "shadows", while character, self-discipline, determination, and service are the "genuine substance of life."

Emery, Lynn Fauley. *Black Dance in the United States: From 1619 to Today,* 2nd Edition. North Stratford, NH: Ayer, 1980. A comprehensive study of the dance forms of people of African origin in the United States. Based on extensive research, this source includes Emery's analysis of the place of dance as fundamental to African aesthetic expression and as basic to social cohesion, ritual observance, maintenance of tradition, preparation for war, and the expression of joy and grief and play. An historically accurate account of the nature and contributions of African Americans to the cultural development of the United States and of dance as an instrument of survival under depressing economic and social circumstances.

Ferris, Lesley. "Absent Bodies, Dancing Bodies, Broken Dishes: Feminist Theory, Postmodernism, and the Performing Arts." *Signs: Journal of Women in Culture and Society* 18, no. 1 (1992):162–72. A review of recently published texts which share an interest in the body—its significance as a receptacle for social and political transition and as an initiator of that change. The importance of an individual's construction of self-consciousness through improvisation by the language of one's movement is explored. Through acknowledgment of the materiality of the body, using dance as a reference point, this source suggests women's bodies as a potential site of feminist cultural politics.

French, Marilyn. *The War Against Women.* New York: Ballantine, 1993. Based on research, the author documents the economic, political, and physical suppression and abuse of women everywhere in the world. She argues that the attack on women is an intrinsic part of our culture, values, and ideology. This book provides numerous concrete examples which illustrate the author's ideas.

Gadon, Elinor. *The Once and Future Goddess.* San Francisco: Harper-SanFrancisco, 1989. A scholarly look at the study of religion and the history of women which contributes to understanding the key role of women and feminine images in prehistoric times, modern art, and life. The author provides analysis of images and symbols in their cultural context in order to grasp the way in which the power of the feminine came to be seen as threatening to the established social order. In reclaiming the Goddess she believes that the deeply ingrained "truth" which led to male dominance may be re-visioned and will lead to the learning of other patterns of behavior.

Gioseffi, Daniela, ed. *On Prejudice: A Global Perspective.* New York: Doubleday, 1993. This source introduces the reader to the fundamental character of prejudice in its many forms—from slavery to the Holocaust to apartheid to the ethnic wars in Europe and Africa today. In addition, the aesthetic, emotional, and subjective aspects of prejudice are explored through intercultural fiction and poetry. At the end of the book, voices of hope, reconciliation, and commonality are provided. This collection contains valuable appendix material, including bibliographies for further reading and a list of organizations dedicated to global understanding. This is a monumental work in size and quality.

Hanna, Judith Lynne. *Dance, Sex and Gender: Signs of Identity, Dominance, Defiance, and Desire.* Chicago: University of Chicago Press, 1988. By addressing the implications of dance for gender roles within a historical and cross-cultural context the author draws on semiotic and psychological theory as well as anthropological models. The author focuses on the ways dancers confirm and challenge social and cultural construction of gender through kinetic visual models presented by dancers. She also examines the response to these models by audiences and critics. Included are photographs of dance in many cultures and extensive information on dance traditions and innovations.

———. *To Dance Is Human: A Theory of Nonverbal Communication.* Chicago: University of Chicago Press, 1987. Hanna provides a theory of dance drawing on work in anthropology, semiotics, sociology, communications, folklore, political science, religion, and psychology, as well as the visual and performing arts. Her success is in making clear the extent to which dance is a multisensory and multidimensional behavior. Included are discussions about dance movement and the communication of sociocultural patterns, dance in religion, dance rites in political thought and action, and warrior dances—which are illustrated through the author's ethnographic studies of dance in Africa, Mexico, the Caribbean, and the United States.

Harris, Maxine. *Down from the Pedestal: Moving Beyond Idealized Images of Womanhood.* New York: Doubleday, 1995. An exploration of the ways in which identification with images—mythologized and honored by American culture—may win a woman love and approval, but which obscures individuality. Harris, a psychologist, suggests ways for women to seek "authentic existence."

hooks, bell. *Ain't I a Woman? Black Women and Feminism.* Boston: South End Press, 1981. A work of history and theory which examines the impact of sexism on black women, the historic devaluation of black womanhood, racism in the women's movement and in black women's involvement with feminism. hooks emphasizes that the feminist movement must take as its starting point race, class, and gender as facts of human existence.

———. *Black Looks: Race and Representation.* Boston: South End Press, 1992. In twelve essays the author looks into the personal and political consequences of contemporary representations of black women and men within our "white supremacist society." hooks admits that the essays are "acts of defiance" and that her interest is to "pierce the wall of denial consumers of images construct so as not to face the fact that politics of domination inform the way the majority of images we consume are constructed and marketed." Images in popular music, advertising, literature, television, historical narrative, and film are contexts for discussion.

Hsu, George. "Are Eating Disorders Becoming More Common in Blacks?" *International Journal of Eating Disorders* 6, no. 1 (January 1987): 113–24. Research intended to discover the reasons for the increase in anorexia nervosa among the African-American population which, until recently, was rare. Research supporting the idea that in the past, black adolescent females were usually thinner and less concerned about dieting and shape and had better self-image is offered to explain the differences in the incidence among white and black adolescents. The author speculates that "increasing affluence among some blacks, and thus access to traditional white middle-class values and the homogenizing of life style and priorities perhaps because of the media have finally penetrated the black culture" leads to increased body issues and eating disorders among youth.

Jaggar, Alison M., and Susan Bordo, eds. *Gender/Body/Knowledge: Feminist Reconstructions of Being and Knowing.* New Jersey: Rutgers University Press, 1987. An interdisciplinary collection of essays which share the conviction that modern western paradigms of knowledge are gender-biased. The contributors refute our philosophical upbringing through a range of contexts, including visual arts by women artists, feminist literary criticism, feminist research methods, and a feminist reading of science. The contributors are diverse in backgrounds, including socialist, lesbian and non-Western writers.

Moraga, Cherríe, and Gloria Anzaldúa, eds. *This Bridge Called My Back: Writings by Radical Women of Color.* New York: Kitchen Table Women of Color Press, 1984. An anthology of prose, poetry, personal narrative and analysis by African-American, Asian-American, Latina and Native American women which intends to reflect a definition of feminism by women of color in the United States. Reflected areas of concern include: the ways visibility/invisibility as women of color form radicalism; the effects of racism in the women's movement; the cultural, class and gender differences that divide women of color; and writing as a tool for self-preservation.

Schechner, Richard. "Movement Analysis, Movement and Performance, Gender and Culture." *TDR: The Drama Review* 32 (Winter 1988): 4. Articles in this issue are about dance, and specifically about movement as an expression of culture, gender, and a means to self-transformation. Methods of analysis are discussed as well as the role of movement in culture. This issue provides a wealth of current and pertinent sources for related topics.

Steinman, Louise. *The Knowing Body: Elements of Contemporary Performance and Dance.* Stonybrook, NY: North Atlantic, 1995. Expressing that a deep trust in the wisdom of the body is at the core of performance, the author provides revealing interviews with artists working on the cutting edge of contemporary dance and theater. She shows how understanding our bodies through performance can help us understand ourselves and serve as a means of transformation.

Suleiman, Susan, ed. *The Female Body in Western Culture.* Cambridge, MA: Harvard University Press, 1986. Twenty-three specially commissioned essays explore the representations of the female body through a wide range of subject matter, ranging from Genesis to Gertrude Stein and Angela Carter; from ancient Greek ritual to modern film and surrealist art. Questions about power and powerlessness as well as subjecthood and objectification are discussed. The author points the way to possibilities for the displacement of traditional male-female opposition through androgyny.

Wolf, Naomi. *The Beauty Myth: How Images of Women are Used Against Women.* New York: Doubleday, 1992. An account of how affluent Western women have become "enslaved" by definitions of beauty in their professions, how the culture alienates women from their bodies and sexuality, and the ways in which choices about appearance become obsessions. The author challenges women to change the way they think and feel about appearance and thus become consumers of ideas and products based on documented evidence, leading to considered and individual choices.

Video

Black Dance America: A Festival of Modern, Jazz, Tap and African Styles. Pennebaker and Associates, 1984. This is a riveting video which documents a four-day festival at the Brooklyn Academy of Music. While it provides a wide spectrum of dancers and companies and styles, it celebrates the evolution of black dance parodies of plantation quadrilles to ethnic forms to modern forms and themes.

Everybody Dance Now. Thirteen/WNET, 1991. A look at MTV as an expression of the status of dance in America. Calling dance the drama of the body, the video illustrates the ways in which MTV takes dance from the streets and combines it with other forms cre-

ated by young, innovative choreographers to express social commentary. The power of dance to reach people is explored.

Dancing. Thirteen/WNET and RM Arts, 1993. Raoul Trujillo, narrator. This series encompasses dance, culture, art, history, religion,
race, gender, and class, and is visually enchanting and provocative. It
is an eight-part set, which looks at dancing as religion, theater,
power, intoxication, and self-expression: "The Power of Dance"
considers the primal power of dance and its diversity as a thread
which connects all people. "The Lord of Dance" explores the
relationship between religion and dance as viewed by Christians,
Hindus, and the Yoruba of Nigeria. "The Dance at Court" illustrates the political function of dance in the contemporary courts
of Japan, Java, and Ghana. "Sex and Social Dance" provides social
dance history, from Astaire to dances of Polynesia, Morocco, rock
and roll, and the disco scene. "Dance as a Performing Art in the
Cultures of Russia and Kabuki in Japan" traces the meaning
behind the evolution of classical ballet. The fusion of African and
European forms, popular dance in North and South America is
given historical and contemporary contexts in "New Worlds, New
Forms." Individual dance artists of the twentieth century are fea-
tured in "The Individual and Tradition." This also documents the
Los Angeles festival of 1990, which brought together cultures of
the Pacific rim, each expressing its identity in dance.

*As chair of the dance department at Essex Community College in Baltimore,
Maryland,* **Carole M. Cascio** *developed these ideas and materials through her
participation in the Ford Foundation Grant to Integrate the Scholarship on
Minority Women into the Curriculum. Although she retired from teaching in
1996, she continues to explore the way in which diversity and pluralism can
be infused into the curriculum. She is also a member of the grant team of the
College in the American Commitments Project, sponsored by the Association of
American Colleges and Universities.*

Selected Business Ethics Bibliography

E. Michelle Rabouin

Resource Articles

Bunche, Charlotte. "A Global Perspective on Feminist Ethics and Diversity." In *Exploration in Feminist Ethics*. Amherst, MA: University of Massachusetts Press, 1989.

Gilligan, Carol. "In a Different Voice: Women's Conception of Morality." *Harvard Educational Review* 47 (1977): 481–517.

Nedelsky, Jennifer. "Reconceiving Autonomy: Source, Thoughts and Possibilities." *Yale Journal of Law and Feminism* 1 (1989 Spring): 1.

Noddings, Nel. "Feminist Fears in Ethics." *Journal of Social Philosophy* 21, no. 2 (1990 Fall): 25.

Nussbaum, Marnsible. "Finely Aware Literature and the Moral Imagination." *The Journal of Philosophy* 82 (1989): 516–29.

Nye, Andrea. *Feminist Theory and the Philosophies of Man*. New York: Routledge, Chapman and Hall, 1989.

Okin, Susan. "Reason and Feeling in Thinking about Justice." *Ethics* 99, no. 2 (1981): 22–49.

Rosaldo, Michelle Z. "Moral/Analytic Dilemmas Posed by the Intersection of Feminism and Social Science." In *Social Science as Moral Inquiry*. Ed. Norma Hann. New York: Columbia University Press, 1983.

Sedgwick, Sally S. "Can Kant's Ethics Survive the Feminist Critique?" *Pacific Philosophical Quarterly,* 71 no. 1 (1990 March): 60.

Toulmin, Steven. "How Medicine Saved the Life of Ethics." In *New Directions in Ethics: the Challenge of Applied Ethics*. New York: Routledge, Chapman and Hall, 1986.

Walker, Margaret Urban. "Moral Understandings: Alternative Epistemology for a Feminist Ethics." *Hypatia* 4, no. 2 (1989 Summer): 15.

Resource Books

Altieri, Charles. *Canons and Consequences: Reflections of the Ethical Force of Imaginative Ideals*. Evanston, IL: Northwestern University Press, 1990.

Browning Cole, Eve, and Susan Coultrap-McQuin, eds. *Explorations in Feminist Ethics.* Amherst, MA: University of Massachusetts Press, 1992.

Cannon, Katie G. *Black Womanist Ethics.* Atlanta, GA: Scholars Press, 1988.

Card, Claudia. *Feminist Ethics.* Lawrence, KS: University Press of Kansas, 1991.

Collins, Patricia Hill. *Toward a New Vision: Race, Class and Gender as Categories of Analysis and Connection.* Memphis, TN: Research Clearinghouse and Curriculum Integration Project, Center for Research on Women, Memphis State University, 1989.

Daly, Mary. *Gyn/Ecology: The Metaethics of Radical Feminism.* Boston, MA: Beacon, 1978.

DeMarco, Joseph, and Richard M. Fox, eds. *New Direction in Ethics: The Challenge of Applied Ethics.* New York: Routledge, Chapman and Hall, 1986.

Gardiner, L. *Can This Discipline Be Saved? Feminist Theory Challenges Mainstream Philosophy.* Wellesley College Working Paper Series #118, Wellesley, MA: Wellesley College Center for Research on Women, 1983.

Gatens, Moira. *Feminism and Philosophy: Perspectives on Difference and Equality.* Bloomington, IN: Indiana University Press, 1991.

Gergen, Mary McCanney. *Feminist Theory and the Structure of Knowledge.* New York, NY: New York University Press, 1989.

Gilligan, Carol. *In a Different Voice.* Cambridge, MA: Harvard University Press, 1982.

Hoagland, Sara Lucia. *Lesbian Ethics: Toward New Values.* Palo Alto, CA: Institute of Lesbian Studies, 1992.

hooks, bell. *Feminist Theory from Margin to Center.* Boston, MA: South End Press, 1984.

Lips, Hilary M. *Women, Men and Power.* Mayfield, CA: Mayfield Publishing Company, 1992.

Lloyd, Genevieve. *The Man of Reason: Male and Female in Western Philosophy.* Minneapolis, MN: University of Minnesota Press, 1984.

MacIntyre, Alasdair. *After Virtue.* South Bend, IN: University of Notre Dame Press, 1981.

MacKinnon, Catherine A. *Toward a Feminist Theory of the State.* Cambridge, MA: Harvard University Press, 1989.

Mahowald, Mary B., ed. *Philosophy of Woman: An Anthology of Classic and Current Concepts.* Indianapolis, IN: Hackett, 1983.

Mill, John Stuart. *The Subjection of Women.* Indianapolis, IN: Hackett Publishing Company, 1988.

Morrison, Toni, ed. *Race-ing Justice, Engendering Power: Essays on Anita Hill, Clarence Thomas and the Construction of Social Reality.* New York, NY: Pantheon Books, 1992.

Olesen, V., A. Clarke, and P. Anderson. *Teaching Materials on Women, Health and Healing.* San Francisco, CA: University of California Press, 1986.

Williams, Patricia J. *The Alchemy of Race and Rights.* Cambridge, MA: Harvard University Press, 1991.

Videos

Arledge, Elizabeth, producer. *Prescription for Profit.* Washington, DC: PBS, 1989. Considers economic, social and ethical questions involving drug research and marketing.

Bikel, Ofra, producer/writer. *Clarence Thomas and Anita Hill: Private Pain.* Alexandria, VA: PBS Video, 1992. Discusses the Thomas confirmation hearings, the charge of sexual harassment by Anita Hill, and the reactions of African Americans.

Dash, Julie, director. *Daughters of the Dust.* 1992. Dreamy leave-taking of a Gullah family from a Georgia island to start anew on the mainland in 1910. Centers on the conflict between the women's perceptions of their African heritage and its ways of sustaining and infusing them with knowing, and the perceived need to move into the future, perhaps combining old with new.

Jhally, Sut, writer. *Dreamworld.* North Hampton, MA: Foundation for Media Education, 1990. Controversial showing of the impact that sex and violence and objectification of women in media have on society and culture in our everyday lives.

Kilbourne, Jean, producer. *Still Killing Us Softly.* Cambridge: Cambridge Documentary Films, 1987. Discusses the manner in which women are portrayed by advertising and the effect this has on women and their images of themselves.

Read, Donna, director. *Full Circle.* Santa Monica, CA: National Film Board of Canada, 1993. Discusses environmental issues in relation to women and spirituality.

Working Solutions, producer. *Work vs. the Family.* Washington, DC: PBS, 1994. Discusses companies that are developing ways to help employees balance the demand of work and family. Included examples are of a health care products company with a 50 percent female work force offering on site day care, and a small mail order firm that creates a family-friendly environment.

Feminist Integration Articles

Aiken, Susan, Karen Anderson, Myra Dinnerstein, Judy N. Unsink, and Patricia MacCorquodale. "Trying Transformations: Curriculum Integration and the Problems of Resistance." *Signs* 12, no. 2 (1987): 2–7.

Banks, James A. "Multicultural Education: Characteristics and Goals." In *Multicultural Education: Issues and Perspectives*. Ed. J. A. Banks and C. A. Banks, 2–26. Boston, MA: Allyn and Bacon, 1989.

Collins, Patricia Hill. "On Our Own Terms—Self Defined Standpoints and Curriculum Transformation." *NWSA Journal* 3 (1991): 37–81.

McIntosh, Peggy. "Interactive Phases of Curriculum Revision." *Working Paper Series*. Wellesley, MA: Wellesley College, 1983.

Schuster, Marilyn R., and Susan R. Van Dyne. "Syllabus Redesign Guidelines." In *Women's Place in the Academy*. Ed. Marilyn R. Schuster and Susan R. Van Dyne. Lanham, MD: Rowman and Allanheld, 1989.

Feminist Integration Books

Aiken, Susan, Karen Anderson, Myra Dinnerstein, Judy N. Unsink, and Patricia MacCorquodale, eds. *Changing our Minds: Feminist Transformations of Knowledge*. Albany, NY: State University of New York Press, 1988.

Butler, Johnnella E., and John C. Walter, eds. *Transforming the Curriculum: Ethnic Studies and Women's Studies*. Albany, NY: State University of New York Press, 1991.

Franzosa, Susan D., and Karen A. Mazza. *Integrating Women's Studies into the Curriculum: An Annotated Bibliography*. Westport, CT: Greenwood Press, 1984.

Higginbotham, Elizabeth. *Integrating Women of Color into the Curriculum*. Working paper. Center for Research on Women, Memphis State University, 1988.

Minnich, Elizabeth, Jean O'Barr, and Rachel Rosenfeld, eds. *Reconstructing the Academy*. Chicago, IL: University of Chicago Press, 1988.

E. Michelle Rabouin participated in the Community College of Denver's curriculum development project "The Integration of Women's Studies and Feminist Pedagogy into the Core Curriculum."

Selected Annotated Bibliography for Economists and Other Social Scientists

Kostis Papadantonakis

Printed Matter

Amott, Teresa L. "Black Women and AFDC: Making Entitlement Out of Necessity." In *Women, the State, and Welfare.* Ed. Linda Gordon, 280–98. Madison: The University of Wisconsin Press, 1990. With subheadings such as "Why Black Women are Single Mothers" and "Welfare and the Single-Parent Black Family," this essay offers well-articulated perspectives on the political, historical, and systemic economic reasons for the present treatment of women of color by the welfare state.

Amott, Teresa, and Julie A. Matthaei. *Race, Gender, and Work: A Multicultural History of Women in the United States.* Boston: South End Press, 1991. While it is neither multicultural (in that it tends to pigeonhole each cultural group in isolation from the rest) nor quite an economic history, this volume does contain much documentation and some cogently (albeit glibly at times) stated perspectives on each of the six categories into which U.S. women are divided: American Indian, Chicana, European-American, African-American, Asian-American, and Puerto Rican. My students liked it more than I did.

Amott, Teresa. *Caught in the Crisis: Women in the U.S. Economy Today.* New York: Monthly Review Press, 1993. A very readable (140 pp) economic analysis and information book which I am currently considering as a required collateral assignment in Economics 201. Among its many strengths is a lucid connection of "The Crisis at Home" with the broader, macroeconomic crisis of the U.S. working class (which various other authors have described as the shrinking middle class or the crisis of de-industrialization).

Brown, Clair, and Joseph A. Pechman, eds. *Gender in the Workplace.* Washington, DC: The Brookings Institution, 1987. Well-documented and well-argued, this is a collection of specially commissioned essays which add up to a coherent overall argument: that gender differences are deliberately exploited as a means of cementing broader income and power inequalities in our society. I particularly liked Heidi Hartmann's "Internal Labor Markets and Gender: A Case Study of Promotion," and my students were impressed by the concluding piece (which I recommended to a number of them as part of their term-paper work) on "Sex-Based Employment Quotas in Sweden," by Charles Brown and Shirley Wilcher.

Brown, Susan S. "Love Unites Them and Hunger Separates Them: Poor Women in the Dominican Republic." In *Toward an Anthropology of Women*. Ed. Rayna R. Reiter, 322–32. New York: Monthly Review Press, 1975. An excellent introduction to the dynamics of the feminization of poverty. Referring to well-documented research findings, the author shows that it is the poverty generated by unemployment and underemployment, not lack of appropriate "family values," that causes rural and lower-class urban women to opt for transitory or multiple-partner, matrilocal relationships (wherein the woman or her maternal relatives remain responsible for the raising of children) as distinct from permanent, monogamous, patrilocal and patriarchal nuclear families. I have used this ten-page essay in my classes with great success: It is readable and non-rhetorical; and because it concerns a foreign situation, it makes it easier for a class of students from different racial backgrounds to address and debate an issue which is heavily charged with racial perceptions.

Davis, Angela. *Women, Race and Class*. New York: Vintage Books, 1983. Like anything Davis has written, this is hard-hitting, readable, subtly argued, and partisan all in one. I recommend the whole book (and so did many of my students) and would particularly cite it as a very genuine and serious attempt to confront the stark dilemmas which are often imposed upon working-class minorities by well-defined pressure to choose between the primacy of race and that of gender.

Fuentes, Annette, and Barbara Ehrenreich. *Women in the Global Factory*. Boston: South End Press, 1983. A short (64 pp.), well-documented union-organizing pamphlet, with a special section, "South of the Border, Down Mexico Way" (6 pp.). The whole booklet is worth considering as a supplement to the more academically written work by Ruiz (1987) and to the film, *Global Assembly Line*.

Gimenez, Martha E. "The Dialectics of Waged and Unwaged Work: Waged Work, Domestic Labor, and Household Survival in the United States." In *Work Without Wages: Comparative Studies of Domestic Labor and Self-Employment*. Ed. Jane L. Collins and Martha Gimenez,

25–45. Albany: SUNY Press, 1990. A lucid tightly written twenty-page treatise on the relationships of race, class, and gender in the U.S., in the context of a core-periphery, world-economy perspective. Important because it is not confined to the consideration of lower-strata women alone, but instead takes on the analysis of how "the 'liberation' of professional and career women and the ability of vast numbers of working women to work is predicated on the labor of other women, a large portion of which are immigrant and nonwhite women" (p. 42).

Glazer, Nona. "Servants to Capital: Unpaid Domestic Labor and Paid Work." In *Work Without Wages: Comparative Studies of Domestic Labor and Self-Employment.* Ed. Jane L. Collins and Martha Gimenez, 142–47. Albany: SUNY Press, 1990. After a well-written introduction to the relationship of waged and unwaged labor, the author examines the emergence of self-service in the retailing sector in an attempt "to locate some of the crucial causes and the consequences of the work transfer, that is, the elimination of certain elements of work from the jobs of paid workers, not by new technologies, but by how firms restructure the work process so that the buyer must do work once done by paid workers" (p. 147). Along with her insightful critique of the self-service economy, Glazer offers a well-articulated description of how production relations tend to capitalize on 'pre-existing' forms of subordination, such as gender-domination (and one could easily form analogies to race-relations), in order to further the managerial objectives of profit-making.

Gordon, Linda, ed. *Women, the State, and Welfare.* Madison: The University of Wisconsin Press, 1991. An excellent collection of essays, a number of which I have singled out for individual mention in this bibliography, not only because of their general value but also because of their readability. By the same token, some of the essays in this volume are worth reading but may be too hard for students. Nevertheless, I strongly recommend, in addition to the individually cited items, the essays by Gordon herself ("The New Feminist Scholarship on the Welfare State") and by Frances Fox Piven ("Ideology and the State: Women, Power, and the Welfare State"). Also noteworthy, albeit a bit rhetorical, is Diana Pierce's "Welfare Is Not for Women: Why the War on Poverty."

Kemp, Alice A. *Women's Work: Degraded and Devalued.* Englewood Cliffs, NJ: Prentice Hall, 1993. A well-planned, well-written textbook for a women-in-economics course, this work offers excellent reviews of literature, concise perspectives on the evolution of women's work (as it relates to the evolution of the U.S. economy) and somewhat less-inspired presentations on the family, the state, and (very superficially) women in the Third World.

Mink, Gwendolyn. "The Lady and the Tramp: Gender, Race, and the Origins of the American Welfare State." In *Women, the State, and Welfare*. Ed. Linda Gordon, 92–122. Madison: The University of Wisconsin Press, 1990. Obtusely written and strongly opinionated, this is nevertheless a very good historical account of the rise of the particular form of welfare state which is the flip side of the feminization of poverty in the U.S. By explaining how "woman-directed reform took dependent womanhood as its premise and made the state the key to managing and mitigating that dependence" (p. 105), Mink exposes the ideology of permitting "lesser races" [sic] to be integrated into American society on terms which have been devastating to the integrity of the household.

Navarro, Vicente. *Dangerous to Your Health: Capitalism in Healthcare*. New York: Monthly Review Press, 1993. This brief (115 pp.), informative, analytically militant book includes a somewhat loudly written, but certainly stimulating and readable, chapter on "Classism, Racism, and Sexism in the Health Sector." Should be required reading of all our Allied Health students!

Nelson, Barbara. "The Origins of the Two-Channel Welfare State." In *Women, the State, and Welfare*. Ed. Linda Gordon, 123–51. Madison: The University of Wisconsin Press, 1991. An excellent historical account of the formulation of welfare as either relief for men who were incapacitated on the job or as support for mothers who were left without men, this essay was a hit with my microeconomics students, who frequently cite it in their term papers, other written work, and class discussion.

Rodgers, Harrell R., Jr. *Poor Women, Poor Families: The Economic Plight of America's Female-Headed Households*. Revised Edition. Armonk, NY: M. E. Sharpe, 1990. Thoroughly documented, this is a must for any research bibliography on the feminization of poverty. To be sure, much of what is worth reading in this book are the numbers and the well-written explanations of what they mean. For analytical perspectives, other works such as Gordon or Amott's are recommended.

Ruiz, Vicki L., and Susan Tiano, eds. *Women of the U.S.-Mexico Border: Responses to Change*. Boston: Allen and Unwin, 1987. Ten essays, supplemented by an introductory and a concluding chapter, encompassing the same topic that is treated by Fuentes (1988) on this list, as well as the film, *Global Assembly Line*. Of particular interest as possible independent reading assignments are the following essays: "Women's Work and Unemployment in Northern Mexico," by Susan Tiano (21 pp. with statistics and extensive bibliographic references); "Female Mexican Immigrants in San Diego County," by Rosalia Solorzano-Torres (16 pp. with bibliography); and "By the Day or the Week: Mexicana Domestic Workers in El Paso," by Vicki L. Ruiz (15 pp. and bibliography).

Sacks, Karen. "Engels Revisited: Women, the Organization of Production, and Private Property." In *Toward an Anthropology of Women*. Ed. Rayna R. Reiter, 211–34. New York: Monthly Review Press, 1975. A brief, critical review of the thesis that patriarchy is socially constructed. While contesting the (crude version of the) Marxist identification of capitalism as the cause of the oppression of women, it upholds the (broadly speaking, likewise Marxist) view that economic relations tend to determine the social relations of genders. This reading may be useful as a supplement to a discussion of class and gender and, by extension, race.

Sokoloff, Natalie J. *Black Women and White Women in the Professions: Occupational Segregation by Race and Gender, 1960–1980.* New York: Routledge, 1992. Even though I knew of this book since it first came out, I started reading it after its author came to our seminar. It is an excellent piece of scholarship which, like Sokoloff's seminar presentation, combines a thorough coverage of convincing documentation with plainly stated, analytical argumentation showing that race matters in ways that do not merely parallel how gender matters (and vice versa). Also, a good down-to-earth perspective on the realities and limitations (as distinct from liberal rhetoric and conservative hysteria) of Affirmative Action.

Films (re-runs, of course!)

Biberman, Herbert, director. *Salt of the Earth.* Chicago, IL: Macmillan Films, 1953. 16 mm., black and white; 3 reels; 97 minutes. The classic on race, gender and class! A long-suppressed classic, feature-length film on the lives of Mexican Americans who are on strike against the mining company that employs them. Focuses on the treatment of foreign-born workers by U.S. industry, and on women as vital and necessary participants in the fight for a better life for all. The punch line, delivered by the Chicana heroine after her husband literally raises his fist to punch her (she stops him): "That would be the old way! I want to raise myself and along with me raise higher everybody who is suffering *above* me!"

Field, Connie, director. *The Life and Times of Rosie the Riveter.* Los
Angeles, CA: Direct Cinema Ltd., 1980. VHS in abbreviated version
(50 minutes); 16 mm. (60 minutes). Another classic which I couldn't
resist mentioning. Includes excellent analysis of the contrast
between the reality of women's binds when caught between productive and reproductive labor obligations, and the publicity
version of this reality, which blames it all on the nature of women.
Excellent coverage of race and class as part of the main story,
which is how women's role in the economy is managed (i.e., not in
the interests of women).

Gray, Lorraine, director. *The Global Assembly Line.* Hohocus, NJ: New
Day Films, 1988. VHS or 16 mm.; 58 minutes. Among its many virtues,
this is an excellent women's film. We routinely use it in our economics classes and would recommend it to any teacher in just
about any kind of women's studies class. The shape and impact of
the contemporary international division of labor is explored primarily through profiles of working women in Mexico, the
Philippines, and the United States. As an added bonus in relation
to NAFTA, the film includes a discussion of the Maquiladora program related to the broader issue of runaway industry, considering
its consequences on both sides of the U.S.-Mexican border.

Kostis Papadantonakis *teaches economics at Essex Community College, where
he was part of the faculty team on "Integrating Minority Women into the
Curriculum," a project supported by the Ford Foundation in 1993–1994. His
work includes publications on the political economy of dependance and is currently focused on the relationship of class, race, and gender in history and in
contemporary capitalist societies.*

Newsbriefs

CALLS FOR PAPERS

Signs: Journal of Women in Culture and Society seeks submissions for an issue on feminism and youth cultures, planned for publication in spring 1998. Defining "youth" as any person age thirteen to thirty, the editors welcome submissions based on independent or collaborative research conducted by, about, and/or within youth communities, as well as textual analyses (widely defined) of popular culture produced by youth from a wide range of racial, ethnic, religious, and national origins. Submit five copies of articles no later than 31 January 1997 to **Signs,** Feminism and Youth Cultures, Box 354345, University of Washington, Seattle, WA 98195-4345. Please observe the guidelines in the "Notice to Contributors" printed in the most recent issue of the journal.

Lesbian Short Fiction, an ongoing anthology of short stories with lesbian themes, announces its premiere issue, to be published in spring 1997. Editors seek manuscripts with significant lesbian content in all genres and of all lengths up to 10,000 words. Send a #10 SASE for guidelines before submitting manuscripts. One-year subscriptions are available for $36.00; make checks payable to Tantra Publishers. Address all inquiries to Jinx Beers, Editor, *LSF,* 6507 Franrivers Avenue, West Hills, CA 91307; phone: 818-704-7825.

Gender, Technology and Development, a new journal based at the **Asian Institute of Technology,** examines links between gender and technological development. The editors welcome submissions that identify, extend, or unify knowledge and awareness in the field of gender and technology. Entries comprised of or incorporating the following research will be considered: empirical, field-based, case studies, and gender theory. Three issues will be published annually in March, July, and November. Prospective contributors should write for manuscript guidelines before submitting a final draft. Address inquiries and submissions to The Editors, *Gender, Technology and*

Development, Asian Institute of Technology, P.O. Box 4, Klongluang, Pathumthani 12120, Thailand.

The **University of Coimbra, Portugal** has issued a call for papers for the **Third European Feminist Research Conference,** titled "**Women, Mobility, and Citizenship in Europe,**" to be held at the University from 8–12 July 1997. The conference aims to discuss the complexity of women's experience of spatial, social, and cultural mobility in Europe. Submit abstracts of approximately 250 words to the organizing committee by 31 January 1997. For more information, contact Centro de Estudos Sociais, Universidade de Coimbra, Apartado 3087, 3000 Coimbra, Portugal; phone: 351-39-26459; fax: 351-39-29076; e-mail: EUROFEM97@GEMINI.CI.UC.PT.

CONFERENCES

The **Fourth Southern Conference on Women's History,** 12–14 June 1997 at the **College of Charleston in South Carolina,** provides a forum for the delivery of presentations and exchange of ideas relating to all aspects of women's history. The conference seeks to reflect the diversity of women's experiences and to document the history of women from a wide variety of racial, class, and ethnic backgrounds. For further information, please contact Elizabeth R. Varon at 617-283-2608.

The **City University of New York Graduate School and University Center** will host "**Forms of Desire: The Seventh Annual Queer Graduate Studies Conference**" from 3–6 April 1997. Cosponsored by the Center for Lesbian and Gay Studies, the conference is intended to spark interest in diverse forms of sexuality in a broad range of disciplines, including: history, philosophy and literature; art, music, theater, film and performance; architecture and public space; psychology and identities; nations, politics, and public policy; classrooms and communities; and theory and practice. "**Forms of Desire**" will feature keynote speakers, workshops, roundtables, and over sixty student panels. Please submit 8–10 page papers, abstracts, or panel proposals by 20 December 1996. Address proposals and inquiries to The Center for Lesbian and Gay Studies, 33 W 42nd St. Room 404N, New York, NY 10036; e-mail: fodquny@aol.com; http//members. aol.com/fodquny.

The **Center for Women in Coalition** at the University of California, Riverside will host "**Frontline Feminisms: Women, War, and Resistance**" 16–18 January 1997. The conference aims to link feminist activist and grassroots organizers engaged in innovative feminist praxes with a gathering of scholars and policy-makers engaged in theorizing conflict and promoting cooperation. For more information contact Piya Chatterjee and Marguerite Waller, Department of Women's Studies, UC Riverside, Riverside, CA 92521; fax: 909-787-6386; e-mail: mwaller2ucracl.ucr.edu; piya@ucrac1.ucr.edu.

PUBLICATIONS AND RESOURCES

The **American Association of University Women Educational Foundation** announces the publication of its most recent research, *Girls in the Middle: Working to Succeed in School,* the final piece of the foundation's Positive School Climate Research Initiative, an effort focused on highlighting what public schools are doing to encourage girls' success and achievement. A twenty-seven minute video captures the experiences of five girls in three of the school sites. For information on ordering the report or video, contact the AAUW sales office at 1-800-225-9998.

The *Guide to Political Videos,* published biannually by *Pacifica Communications,* is the only comprehensive resource of current political videos and is intended to provide an accessible resource for a varied audience. Each issue features approximately 350 new listings covering the politics of environment, campaigns and elections, foreign policy, gay and lesbian issues, health care, the peace movement, and women's issues. For ordering information contact Pacifica Communications, PO Box 4426, Santa Barbara, CA 93140-4426; phone: 805-965-5873; e-mail: 72622.1103@compuserve.com.

Stop Female Genital Mutilation—Women Speak: Facts and Actions, based on *The Hosken Report: Genital/Sexual Mutilation of Females* by Fran Hosken, is a comprehensive report on female genital mutilation, which includes personal accounts by African women from a variety of countries where female genital mutilation is still practiced. Chapters on essential background information, medical facts, actions for change, and grassroots initiatives are also included. To order, send $15 to the **Women's International Network** (add $5.00 for overseas air mail shipment), 187 Grant St., Lexington, MA 02173.

Metis: A Feminist Journal of Transformative Wisdom is a new annual interdisciplinary journal devoted to feminist consciousness and theory. This journal encourages a language of passionate scholarship that blends critical analysis and well-crafted writing. Named after a Greek Goddess of Wisdom and mother of Athena, *Metis* remembers and calls forth a creative energy that integrates the wisdom of heart, body, and mind. For information and subscriptions contact Candice Chase, California Institute of Integral Studies, 9 Peter Yorke Way, San Francisco, CA 94109; phone: 415-674-5500 x 454; fax: 415-674-5555; e-mail: candicec@ciis.edu.

Responsive Database Services Inc. (RDS) announces the release of *Contemporary Women's Issues,* a CD-ROM product designed to provide access to global information related to women's issues including development, human rights, violence and exploitation, women in politics, the workplace, education, legal status, lifestyles, health, and reproductive rights. The annual subscription price is $600 for libraries and other organizations. Developing nations receive a 40% discount. For ordering information, call 800-313-2212; or write *Contemporary Women's Issues,* 23611 Chagrin Blvd., Suite 320, Beachwood, OH 44122; phone: 216-292-9620; fax: 216-292-9621.

Women's Environment and Development Organization (WEDO) announces the release of *Beyond Promises: Government in Motion One Year After the Beijing Women's Conference,* its one-year progress report on the implementation of the Platform for Action. The issue includes 53 responses to WEDO's survey of 51 countries and territories and two regional reports for the Caribbean and the Pacific Islands. *Beyond Promises* spotlights government actions (or inaction) relating to the Platform's 12 Critical Areas of Concern, including: economic justice, political participation, human rights, violence against women, sexual exploitation and health. To order your copy, please send a check or money order for U.S.; $5.00 (per copy) payable to WEDO, 355 Lexington Avenue, 3rd floor, New York, NY 10017-6606; phone: 212-973-0325; fax: 212-973-0335; e-mail: wedo@ igc.apc.org; WWW: http://www.wedo.org.

Where Have All the Smart Women Gone by Alica Rowe relays the stories of intelligent and accomplished women in our culture, demonstrating that women continue to face limited opportunity. To order a copy of the book, send $14.95, plus $3.00 for shipping and handling, to Hara Publishing, PO Box 19732, Seattle, WA 98109.

FELLOWSHIPS, AWARDS, AND GRANTS

The **Center for Feminist Research (CFR)** at the University of Southern California is now accepting applications for its **Affiliated Scholars Program.** Individuals who have demonstrated excellence as feminist scholars in any field are invited to pursue gender-related research projects in association with CFR. The program offers an opportunity to live and work in the Los Angeles area for a minimum of one academic semester, renewable for up to two years of study. For application information, write to the Director, Center for Feminist Research, University of Southern California, SOS Suite B-15, Los Angeles, CA 90089-0036; phone: 213-740-8132; fax: 213-740-5122.

The **Henry A. Murray Research Center of Radcliffe College** offers several annual awards and grants. The *Radcliffe Research Support Program* offers grants of up to $5,000 for post-doctorate research; the *Jeanne Humphrey Block Dissertation Award Program* offers a grant of $2,500 to a woman doctoral student studying sex and gender differences or a developmental issue of particular concern to girls or women; the *Henry A. Murray Dissertation Award Program* offers grants of $2,500 to doctoral students focusing on issues in human development or personality; and the *Visiting Scholars Program* offers office space and access to the facilities of Radcliffe College and Harvard University to scholars who wish to investigate issues of women and social change or the study of lives over time. For more information, contact the Henry A. Murray Research Center, 10 Garden Street, Cambridge, MA 02138; phone: 617-495-8140; fax: 617-496-3993.

The **Womanist Studies Consortium** at the University of Georgia is offering four fellowships for 1997–1998. *The Flexible Fellowship* offers $33,000 for one scholar; the *Single Parent Fellowship* offers $10,000 for one single-parent scholar; the *Summer Seminar Fellowship* offers $3,300 to six scholars to attend the month-long WSC Summer Seminar; the *Graduate Summer Internship* offers $2,000 to one out-of-state graduate student working in any field. For an application, write to Fellowship Applications, Womanist Studies Consortium, The University of Georgia, Institute for African-American Studies, 164 Psychology Building, Athens, GA 30602-3012; phone: 706-542-5197; fax: 706-542-3071; e-mail: womanist@uga.cc.uga.edu; www: http://parallel.park.uga.edu/~bmccask.

PROGRAMS

The **National Center on Women and Family Law Inc.** offers training and case consultation as well as resources on child support, child custody and visitation, and domestic violence. For further information please contact Nechama Masliansky, NCWFL Inc., 275 Seventh Avenue, Suite 1206, New York, NY 10001-6708; phone: 212-741-9480; e-mail: HN1193@handsnet.org.

The **Institute for Women's Policy Research** is a national network of individuals and organizations that conduct and use women-oriented research to ensure that the needs of women and their families are not left out of policy debates. To join the **IWPR Information Network,** please call 202-785-5100; or write IWPR, 1400 20th St. NW, Suite 104, Washington, DC 20036.

Norcroft: A Writing Retreat for Women provides women writers with a place to withdraw from the usual demands of life and write. The project is funded by Joan Dury and Harmony Writer's Fund as part of their ongoing commitment to providing more choices and opportunities for women and enabling social change. For an application, send your name and address on a postcard to Norcroft, 32 East First Street, #330 Duluth, MN 55802; phone: 218-727-5199.

VOLUNTEER WORK

Begun in 1987 at California State University at Humboldt, the **Graduation Pledge Alliance** is a pledge of social and environmental responsibility made by graduating college students. Students "pledge to investigate and take into account the social and environmental consequences of any job opportunity [they] consider," a commitment that, when honored by a group of individuals, can be a focal point for consciousness raising both on and off campus. Contact GPA at NJWollman@Manchester.edu for an explanatory brochure or for questions/comments; or write GPA, MC Box 152, Manchester College, North Manchester, IN 46962.

Project India is a short-term volunteer program offering the opportunity to serve, learn, and make significant contributions in India. Operated by Cross-Cultural Solutions, a non-profit organization whose goal is to empower the underprivileged and facilitate cross-cultural communication, Project India places people of all ages and backgrounds in the three-week volunteer position of their choice in one of a variety of fields. The program runs from September to April in New Delhi, India, and no skills or experience are required. CCS also offers a number of other programs abroad, including the **Saheli Program,** a three week women's issues program in India held biannually. For more information contact Cross-Cultural Solutions, 965 Stunt Rd., Calabasas, CA 91302; phone: 818-222-8300; e-mail: CCSmailbox@aol.com.

CALL FOR PAPERS

Women's Studies Quarterly

Teaching about Violence against Women
Edited by Mona Eliasson

The Spring/Summer 1999 issue of *Women's Studies Quarterly* will focus on the teaching of violence against women worldwide. The editor seeks submissions that explore feminist scholarship in this field and, more specifically, that provide broad insight to international approaches to teaching about violence against women. Papers may examine issues of gender, ethnicity, class, and differing perspectives on research and/or politics. Papers highlighting areas in which feminist scholarship has had a significant impact or subjects of controversy relating to the teaching of women and violence are of special interest.

Contributions should be 9–20 manuscript pages, typed double-spaced throughout, including notes, and are expected to be written in a language that is accessible to the nonspecialist. Please consult *The Chicago Manual of Style* for manuscript form.

Please send submissions by February 15, 1997, to Mona Eliasson, Uppsala University, Center for Research on Women, St Johnnesgatan 21, S-753 12 Uppsala, Sweden.

AJWS

Asian Journal of Women's Studies

Asian Center for Women's Studies
Ewha Womans University Press

AJWS is an interdisciplinary journal, publishing articles pertaining to women's issues in Asia from a feminist perspective. The journal offers articles with a theoretical focus, country reports providing valuable information on specific subject and countries, and booknotes containing more information on recent publication on women in Asia.

AJWS has two major objectives: to share information and scholarly ideas about women's issues in Asia which incorporates a variety of cultural historical entities with varying levels of socio-economic development, and to advance womenps studies in Asia by developing feminist theories to contribute to realizing societies where women and men are free from poverty, violence and from all sorts of abuse and where they can cooperate with each other in order to restore human dignity and upgrade the quality of living.

The first edition of the journal was published in 1995 in commemoration of opening the **Asian Center for Women's Studies** at Ewha Womans University in Seoul, Korea.

**AJWS is a forum
on women in Asia,
for women and men in Asia,
and by feminists all over the world.**

ORDER FORM

PLEASE,CHECK ☐ AND PRINT
IN BLOCK CAPITALS

Name ....
Position ....
Organization ....
Address ....
Country ....
Phone ....
Fax ....

☐ vol 1. 1995. $10
☐ vol 2. 1996. $10
☐ vol 3. 1997. $10

Handling Charge to outside Korea will be added, US $7.50 per order.

Total $ ....

☐ Payment by Check
   (made payable to Asian Center
   for Women's Studies)
☐ Payment by
   Money Order in US Dollars
☐ Payment into
   A/c No.308-04-477591,
   Chang Pilwha, Seodaemun Br.,
   Cho Hung Bank, Korea

**Asian Center for
Women's Studies**
Ewha Womans University
#11-1, Daehyun-dong,
Seodaemun-gu,
Seoul (120-750), Korea
Tel : (82-2) 360-2150
Fax : (82-2) 360-2577
E-Mail :
acwsewha@nownuri.nowcom.co.kr

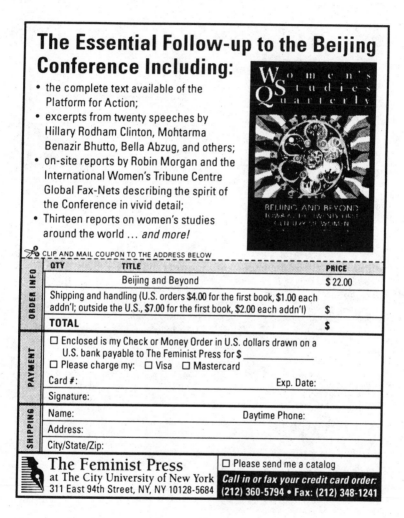

New and Rediscovered American Classics from The Feminist Press

Fettered for Life
Lillie Devereux Blake
Afterword by Grace Farrell

First published in 1874 and long out of print, FETTERED FOR LIFE is a remarkable early feminist novel, and an important missing link in the American women's literary tradition. Written a generation before *The Awakening* and *The Yellow Wall-Paper*, FETTERED FOR LIFE is the story of Laura Blake, a young painter who comes to New York to seek an independent life. She quickly becomes aware of the limitations that surround her because of her gender in a story that unfolds with page-turning melodrama. FETTERED FOR LIFE is a vivid portrait of life in nineteenth-century New York that advances a surprisingly contemporary review of relations between the sexes.

432 pages / 1-55861-155-X / $18.95 paperback

Among the White Moon Faces
An Asian American Memoir of Homelands
Shirley Geok-lin Lim

An unusually frank account of a Malaysian girlhood and the making of an Asian-American writer and teacher. The prize-winning poet and writer describes with telling energy her relationship to the homeland she left behind, the new homeland she inhabits, and the homeland she carries within herself.

248 pages / 9 b&w photos
1-55861-144-4 / $22.95 hardcover

The New Lesbian Studies
Into the Twenty-First Century
Edited by Bonnie Zimmerman and Toni A. H. McNaron

With forty essays, THE NEW LESBIAN STUDIES compiles the best scholarship and theory in considering the history, present, and future of the field. By celebrating the differences among lesbian scholars and attending to the ways in which the field has been shaped by shifting politics and the emergence of queer studies, this collection challenges the limits of lesbian studies while affirming its value.

320 pages / bibliography, index
1-55861-136-3 / $17.95 paperback

Back in Print!

Weeds
Edith Summers Kelly
With a New Afterword by
Charlotte Margolis Goodman

First published in 1923, WEEDS is a classic of American naturalism with a profoundly feminist turn—pioneer in a tradition of rural, working-class women's writing that includes *The Dollmaker, Yonnondio*, and *A Thousand Acres*. Set amidst the harsh life of rural Kentucky tenant farmers, WEEDS is the moving story of a hard-working, spirited young woman who must painfully submit to the limitations imposed by her time, her class, and her gender.

368 pages / 1-55861-154-1 / $15.95 paperback

New Edition of the Feminist Classic!

The Yellow Wall-Paper
Revised Edition
Charlotte Perkins Gilman
Afterword and Textual Notes
by Elaine Hedges

Since 1973, when The Feminist Press found and published Gilman's long-lost THE YELLOW WALL-PAPER, this narrative of confinement and madness has become essential to the canon of North American literature. This new edition is a complete and accurate rendition of the first published text of THE YELLOW WALL-PAPER—which appeared in *New England Magazine* in 1892—and contains new notes on the text.

64 pages / 1-55861-158-4 / $5.95 paperback

Making the Unknown Known

The Feminist Press
at The City University of New York
311 East 94th Street, New York, NY 10128-5684
Tel 212/360-5794 • Fax 212/348-1241

Please Enter My Subscription to the
Women's Studies Quarterly

	U.S. *1 year*	Outside U.S. *1 year*
Individual	[ ] $30.00	[ ] $40.00
Institution	[ ] $40.00	[ ] $50.00
	3 years	*3 years*
Individual	[ ] $ 70.00	[ ] $100.00
Institution	[ ] $100.00	[ ] $120.00

A charge has been added to foreign subscriptions for surface delivery.

Total enclosed $ _____ .

All orders must be prepaid with checks or money orders payable to The Feminist Press in U.S. dollars drawn on a U.S. bank.

Or charge your VISA/MasterCard *(circle one)*.

Acct # _____ Exp. date _____

Signature _____

Name _____

Institution _____

Address _____

_____

Phone (   ) _____

Mail to: *Women's Studies Quarterly,* The Feminist Press at The City University of New York, 311 East 94th Street, New York, NY 10128.
Tel. (212) 360-5790   Fax (212) 348-1241

NOTICE TO PROSPECTIVE CONTRIBUTORS

Women's Studies Quarterly publishes contributions that introduce new feminist scholarship and theory applied to teaching and the curriculum, original sources and resources of direct use in course and program development, and reflective essays and original creative work on various themes of concern to women's studies practitioners. The intersections of race and class with gender are of special concern, as are the perspectives of members of minority groups within the United States and those of the international community.

Contributions should run from nine to twenty manuscript pages, typed double-spaced throughout, including notes, and are expected to be written in language that is accessible to the nonspecialist. Submissions are reviewed by outside readers in the field. Please send three copies and consult *The Chicago Manual of Style* for manuscript form.

Because many of the issues are planned by guest editors and feature collections of material on specific themes, contributors are urged to consult announcements of upcoming issues in the *Quarterly* and communicate with the guest editors.